GREAT CLASSIC RECIPES OF THE WORLD

SANDY LESBERG

Great Classic Recipes of the World

A Collection of Recipes from the Great Dining Places
of the World

Galahad Books

NEW YORK

Great Classic Recipes of the World by Sandy Lesberg
© 1972 Peebles Press International
ISBN 0 88365 047 9

Library of Congress Cataloging Card No. 73 79811

DECORATIONS BY BETH HOLLICK

Printed and bound in Great Britain

This book is for my wife, Susan

FOREWORD

One of the basic pleasures, which has remained virtually unchanged during the years, is the enjoyment of good food and wine. Air travel has contributed in no small measure to a greater understanding of cosmopolitan gastronomy by people who, in the main, had only been exposed to their own national dishes. One might well claim that the classic French cuisine was all that might be desired and that there was therefore no need to look elsewhere for dining excellence. However, it only requires a quick glance through the pages of this book to appreciate the vast range of appetising and tempting fare available from all parts of the world.

Fortunately such culinary pleasures need not be restricted to customers of first-class restaurants in far-flung places of the globe. Many of the recipes are readily adaptable for one's own home, and indeed many similar dishes are regularly produced for passengers of the longhaul international airlines.

To those who appreciate good food and wine, the world has become smaller in the gastronomic sense, with more and more opportunities for sampling all types of international foods, from simple to exotic, and it is with great pleasure that I commend to you this book which features a truly cosmopolitan selection of first-class recipes.

A. C. CLIVAZ
General Manager Cabin Services

INTRODUCTION

I have long felt that the road toward understanding between peoples of different national and even ethical backgrounds could well begin with a mutual tasting of each other's food specialities.

This book contains 403 recipes from 42 countries, and was gathered together with the world-wide co-operation of BOAC.

Chicken Harlequin from Malawi is different from Chicken Pelicana from Barbados, which in turn is quite different from Chicken Jai Puri from Trinidad, which again is nothing like Chicken and Pineapple Boats from Fiji, nor, in fact, similar to Chicken Birjani from Bombay.

In fact you will be able to prepare chicken 50 different ways from as many national origins, all recommended by a leading restaurant or hotel chef, if you feel like working your way through the poultry section alone. There are also over 88 meat recipes gathered from New Zealand in the South Pacific to New York in North America, from Cyprus in the Mediterranean to Mauritius in the Indian Ocean. Some 400 recipes in all, covering every type of food category, and each one the specialty of a famous chef who, in most instances, is revealing the secrets of his culinary art for the first time. Those without specific reference to a restaurant or chef are from my own private collection.

GREAT CLASSIC RECIPES OF THE WORLD is an apt title. These *are* classic national recipes. I hope you agree that once prepared, served and consumed they are for the most part to be considered 'great', and they certainly do represent the major areas of the world. This is not, however, a basic primer in cooking. Certainly I have tried to ensure that each recipe is explicit in its requirements and detailed in its preparation instructions. In the main I have also tried to remain faithful to the words as handed me by the various chefs involved. And subject to your own culinary skill I suggest that you follow the form, as outlined, very carefully and specifically, at least until you have the hand of how the different spices, for instance, are sprinkled in Uganda as against how they are carefully placed in Caracas.

But a certain familiarity in the ways of a kitchen is presupposed before taking up this particular book. None of the recipes is terribly difficult, particularly if you follow the directions, and what better place than in the kitchen to extend yourself beyond past achievements.

The ease of international communication and international travel makes neighbors of us all. Hopefully this book will bring those 41 other countries a little bit closer to your home.

SANDY LESBERG

CONTENTS

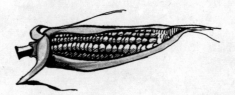

Kuala Lumpur Restaurant, Malaya Hotel, Kuala Lumpur, Malaysia
CHEF: CHAN KING FATT

Oyster Rolls

serves: 6

3 dried mushrooms
6 dried oysters
2 fresh scallops
6 crabs
1 dried plaice
   Fu pei (bean curd skin), about 36
     square inches
   Kai lan (greens)
4 ounces (125 grams) pork liver, diced
2½ ounces (80 grams) lean pork, diced
5 ounces (160 grams) fat pork, diced
4 water chestnuts, diced
1 spring onion, diced
3 teaspoons aji-no-moto (available in
   oriental food stores)
1 teaspoon salt
1 teaspoon dark soy sauce
1 teaspoon flour
2 teaspoons cornstarch
1 teaspoon sugar
½ teaspoon pepper
½ cup salad oil
   Caul fat (order from butcher), about
     36 square inches.

Cover mushrooms with cold water and soak for several hours or overnight. Clean, remove stalks, and parboil for 5 minutes. Drain and dice; set aside.

Soak oysters 1 hour in water to cover. Drain and wash well. Wash scallops. Steam on a rack over hot salted water, 45 minutes for the oysters, 1 hour for the scallops. Wash scallops again and squeeze dry. Dice oysters and scallops and set aside. Steam crabs for 15 minutes. Remove and save roe; use the rest of the crab for another dish.

Remove meat of plaice from bones. Fry plaice and fu pei in oil until plaice is golden. Set aside plaice; cut fu pei into 3-inch squares. Clean kai lan and slice into 3-inch pieces. Boil in salted water until tender. Drain. Wash and drain caul fat and cut into 3-inch squares. Mix meats, seafood, roe, water chestnut, mushrooms and onion together. Add aji-no-moto, salt, soy sauce, flour, cornstarch, sugar and pepper and mix well. Put a square of fu pei on a square of caul fat; place about 2 tablespoons filling on square and roll up neatly, tucking the ends in. Repeat until ingredients are used up. Steam the rolls on a rack over boiling water for about 30 minutes. Serve with kai lan and oyster sauce.

Hoppin John Restaurant, Hamilton, Bermuda
CHEF: FRITZ REITER

Pâté aux Morels

1 pound (500 grams) veal
13 ounces (400 grams) ham
10 ounces (330 grams) fat bacon
2 tablespoons brandy
2 tablespoons Madeira
5½ ounces (175 grams) pistachios
5½ ounces morels
6 tablespoons heavy cream
4 eggs
6½ ounces (200 grams) goose-liver pâté
**2 teaspoons pâté spices (or poultry
    seasoning)**
4 cups clear aspic (chicken, pork, or veal)

Pâté pastry

3 pounds (1500 grams) flour
1½ tablespoons salt
12 ounces (375 grams) lard
**1 pound (500 grams) thinly sliced
    fatback (fat salt pork)**
1 egg yolk

Cut veal, ham, and bacon in cubes.
Marinate in brandy and Madeira
for 24 hours, stirring several times.
Drain meats and dry thoroughly.
(Reserve the marinade.) Sauté meats
lightly by placing bacon in pan
first and using its fat for veal and
ham. Drain and set aside to cool.
Put meats through a very fine blade
of a meat grinder; add pistachios
and morels, cream and eggs. Mix
thoroughly. Finally mix in
marinade, pâté, and pâté spices.

Sift flour and salt together; cut in
cold lard until mixture resembles
coarse meal. Stir in water, a
tablespoon at a time, until dough
holds its shape. Roll out ¼ inch
thick and place in a pâté pan or
fancy 3-quart mold. Line with
slices of fatback.

Conclusion: Fill pastry with pâté
mixture. Cover top with slices of
fatback and cover with pastry. Brush
edges with beaten egg yolk and
crimp pastry to seal completely.
Cut a steam vent in the middle of
the top. Brush pastry with remaining
egg yolk beaten with 1 teaspoon
water. Bake in a 375° F. oven for
1½ hours. Pâté is done when meat
juices run clear. Let baked pâté
cool completely. Pour melted,
cooled aspic through vent in
pastry to fill completely. Chill until
completely set, preferably overnight.

serves: 20

*wine:
Château
Margaux*

Waialae Room, Kahala Hilton, Honolulu
CHEF: MARTIN WYSS

Kahala Hilton Pineapple Rumaki

Wrap a slice of bacon around large pineapple chunks. Sprinkle with curry powder and deep fry in vegetable oil.

Sashimi

Cut raw swordfish or tuna in thin slices and serve on shredded cabbage. Dip in a mixture of 1 teaspoon English mustard and ¾ cup soy sauce.

Papaya and Proscuitto

Cut papaya in small chunks, about 1 inch long and ½ inch thick. Wrap half a slice of proscuitto around papaya.

Hotel Inter-Continental Manila, Rizal, Philippines

Ceviche Acapulqueño

serves: 4

2 pounds (1 kilogram) lapu lapu (or flounder)
2 cups lime juice
2 medium tomatoes, peeled, chopped and seeded
2 onions, finely chopped
3 cans pimentos, chopped fine
½ cup olive oil
2 tablespoons white vinegar
½ cup chopped parsley
½ teaspoon oregano
1 green pepper, chopped
1 red pepper, chopped
Salt
2 avocados
Lettuce leaves
Lemon wedges
Tomato slices
Parsley sprigs

Cut fish in ½-inch cubes. Marinate in lime juice for 6 hours, stirring occasionally.
Drain fish and mix in all other ingredients except the avocados. Taste and add salt and lime juice marinade to taste. Refrigerate for 1 hour.
When ready to serve, carefully remove meat from avocado halves—in slices, if possible. Fill shells with ceviche and garnish with avocado slices. Serve on square wooden platter with lettuce, lemon, tomato slices and parsley.

Altavista Restaurant, Manila

Fried Lumpia
(Fried Egg Roll)

2 cloves garlic
3 tablespoons cooking oil
½ cup onions, chopped
¼ pound (125 grams) pork, sliced in
    thin strips
20 small shrimps, shelled
1½ cups togue (mongo sprouts)
3 cups shredded cabbage
2 cups string beans, cut in long thin
    strips
4 2″ × 2″ × ½″ pieces bean curd (tokwa)
    cut in strips
1 teaspoon salt
   Pepper
1½ cups water or soup stock
20 pieces lumpia wrapper

Lumpia wrapper

2 cups flour
1 cup cold water

serves: 4

Sauté garlic in cooking oil until light brown. Add onions, pork, and shrimps. Simmer for few minutes. Add water or soup stock and continue cooking over medium heat until pork is tender. Then mix in rest of vegetables. Season to taste with salt and pepper. Cook until all vegetables are done. Cool in a colander, allowing liquid to drain out. When cool, wrap in lumpia wrapper. Fry lumpia in deep fat. Serve with vinegar seasoned with salt and crushed garlic. May be served with jelly plum sauce.

Caution: Intense heat is to be avoided. Work with medium heat. Grease the carajay very slightly in the beginning, and avoid greasing it too often. When the wrapper is removed, scrape out any remaining dough in the carajay with a knife and wipe it with a clean cloth. Neatly trim the edges of the wrapper.

Mix the water and flour well. Work continuously with the hands in up-and-down motion until the dough can be picked up at once. Grease very slightly in a clean carajay (skillet). Drop in a small ball of dough, pressing it into a round sheet lightly and evenly over the deep part of the carajay; lift and pick up very thin crust that sticks as it dries.

Brasserie, New York City

Onion Tart

Pie dough

serves: 20

1 cup butter
2 cups shortening
4 cups flour
2 teaspoons salt
¾ cup cold water

Cut butter and shortening (lard is best) into flour and salt sifted together. Add water, a little at a time, just to make pastry hold together. Chill. Roll out thin to line 49-inch or 58-inch pie pans.

Filling

12 eggs
6 cups milk
Salt
Pepper
½ teaspoon nutmeg
4 large onions, coarsely chopped
¼ cup butter
4 cups diced Swiss cheese

Beat eggs and milk together just to mix. Add salt and pepper to taste and nutmeg. Sauté onions in butter until soft but not browned. Drain very thoroughly.
Arrange onions, then cheese, on pie crusts. Fill pans with custard mixture. Bake about 45 minutes (until custard is set) in a 325° F. oven. Serve hot.

Turkey

Cheese Boerek

makes:
16 pastries

1 pound (500 grams) pastry dough
¼ cup melted butter
2 tablespoons butter
½ pound (250 grams) cream or cottage cheese
1 egg
¼ cup milk
¼ cup chopped parsley

To make the boerek, Turkish pastry dough is the most suitable, although strudel pastry or puff pastry may be substituted. Cut pastry into individual serving pieces and brush with melted butter.
For the filling, cream butter well, beat cheese with fork and combine. Blend in egg, milk and parsley. Place some of the filling on each piece of pastry and roll or fold. Handle as little as possible. Put on greased baking dish, brush once more with melted butter, and bake in a 350° F. oven until crisp and golden, about 25 minutes.
(Other fillings may be made from cold meats, spinach, or onions, blended with egg, milk and butter.)

Venezuela

Carne Molida Venezolana
(Cocktail Meatballs)

1½ pounds (750 grams) beef
⅓ cup bread crumbs soaked in milk
1 tablespoon chopped parsley
2 slightly beaten eggs
2 tablespoons grated cheese
2 teaspoons salt
Dash pepper
½ teaspoon nutmeg, or to taste
1½ onions, chopped fine
½ cup vegetable oil
2 tomatoes, peeled and chopped
Oregano
Sweet basil
Garlic salt
Bay leaf
½ cup beef stock
Flour

Clean and mince beef. Squeeze bread crumbs as dry as possible. Mix together meat, bread crumbs, parsley, eggs, cheese, salt, pepper and nutmeg. Sauté half an onion, chopped fine, in 4 tablespoons oil and add to meat mixture. Sauté remaining chopped onions in the rest of oil; add tomatoes, remaining herbs and stock. Season with salt and pepper and cook slowly over low heat for about 4 minutes. Shape meat mixture into small balls, dredge with flour, and put into same pot in which sauce has been made. Cover pot and cook slowly for about 20 minutes. Serve on dish with sauce around the meatballs.

serves: 8

Tequeños
(Cheese-filled Pastry)

4 cups flour
½ teaspoon salt
2 egg yolks
1 teaspoon sugar
1 heaping tablespoon butter
1 cup water
1 pound (500 grams) soft cheese
Vegetable oil for deep frying

Combine all ingredients except cheese and oil. Add a little water, enough to make a soft dough. Put to one side. Cut cheese into strips about 2½″×½″ and cut dough into 4 pieces. Roll each piece of dough as thin as possible and then cut into ½-inch strips. Wind them around cheese strips so that cheese is completely covered. Deep fry in vegetable oil and serve immediately. Makes about 5 dozen canapés.

serves: 20

Greece

Keftaidakia
(Cocktail Meatballs)

serves: 10

1 pound (500 grams) minced steak
1 onion, finely grated
2 cloves garlic, crushed
   Salt
   Pepper
   Oregano
   Mint
2 slices white bread (trimmed)
½ cup dry white wine
1 egg
   Flour
   Olive oil and butter for frying

Mix together meat, onion, garlic, salt, pepper, oregano, and mint to taste. Moisten bread in wine and add to meat mixture together with egg. Knead mixture and form into balls approximately 1 inch across. Coat with flour and fry in olive oil and butter. Cook until thoroughly browned; serve hot.

Taramosalata
(Fish Roe Dip)

serves: 4

4 ounces (125 grams) tarama (carp roe)
1 small onion, finely chopped
1½ cups olive oil
4 slices white bread (trimmed)
   Juice of 2 lemons

Mash tarama and grated onion; add a little olive oil and mix thoroughly to a smooth paste. Moisten bread and squeeze out excess liquid. Beat mixture and add small pieces of bread, olive oil and lemon juice alternately. Continue beating until taramosalata is cream-colored. Serve as dip.

The Philippines

Tapa
(Marinated Beef or Pork Hors d'oeuvres)

serves:
4 or 6

1 pound (500 grams) top or bottom round
   roast of beef or loin of pork
2 cups raw sugar
1 cup kosher salt

Cut meat in ½-inch cubes. Mix sugar and salt well in a plastic bag. Add cubed meat and shake until meat is thoroughly covered with salt-sugar mixture. Place meat in a clean plastic bag and refrigerate overnight.
Bake, broil, barbecue or fry cubes when ready to serve. Beef will take only a few minutes to cook; pork should be cooked until well done. Spareribs may be substituted.

Coral Lanai, Halekulani Hotel, Honolulu

King Kamehameha Chilled Cream of Avocado Soup

2 large ripe avocados
1 medium onion, chopped
1 quart half-and-half coffee cream
Tabasco sauce
Salt
White pepper
Accent

Cut avocados in half and scoop meat into blender. Add chopped onions and cream. Blend until well mixed and smooth. Season to taste with salt, pepper, Tabasco sauce and Accent. Blend again until seasonings are well mixed. Strain soup and chill in the refrigerator. Serve soup chilled.

serves: 4 to 6

The Four Seasons, New York City

Cold Cream of Avocado Soup

1 large avocado
1 pint chicken stock
Chili powder to taste
1 teaspoon ground coriander
1 cup heavy cream
Red caviar (or salt)

Peel and cut avocado into small pieces. Whirl in the blender with the chicken stock, chili powder, and coriander. Heat in the top of a double boiler for 10 minutes. Allow to cool. Add cream and chill thoroughly in the refrigerator. Serve with 1 teaspoon caviar floating in each dish (or salt to taste).

serves: 6

Turkey

"Turquoise" Soup

3 cucumbers
2 teaspoons salt
1 clove garlic
1 tablespoon vinegar
1 teaspoon dill
2 cups yogurt
2 tablespoons olive oil
1 tablespoon chopped fresh mint or
**   ½ teaspoon dried mint leaves**

Peel cucumbers and cut them in quarters lengthwise, then cut these quarters into slices about ⅛-inch thick. Place in a bowl and sprinkle with salt. Rub another bowl with garlic. Pour vinegar in it and swish it around to pick up flavor. Add dill and yogurt and stir until mixture is of uniform consistency and fairly thick. Add a little cold water if it
(Continued at foot of facing page

serves: 6

"Sun and", Nassau, Bahamas
CHEF: PETE GARDNER

Bouillabaisse

serves: 8

8 whole raw crawfish
4 medium onions, chopped
3 stalks celery, chopped
3 carrots, finely sliced
1 teaspoon Italian seasoning*
1 teaspoon fish seasoning*
1 teaspoon garlic salt
   Pepper
2 # 2 cans tomatoes
4 bottles dry white wine
1 cup olive oil
3 cloves garlic
3 teaspoons chopped parsley
2 threads saffron
2 tablespoons pernod
8 mussels, cooked or canned
12 cooked shelled shrimp
8 extra cooked crawfish tails (optional)
½ pound (250 grams) red snapper,
   filleted and cooked
16 slices toasted French bread

Boil crawfish with their heads on with onions, celery, carrots, Italian seasoning and fish seasoning, garlic salt and black pepper to taste in enough water to cover crawfish to a depth of 1 inch. Cook for 40 minutes. Remove the crawfish, break the heads off and cut the tails in two. Put aside.

To the liquid which is left, add tomatoes, wine, olive oil, 2 cloves garlic, parsley and saffron. Boil very hard for 15 minutes (to break up the olive oil) and then over medium heat to reduce the liquid by one-third. Add pernod and remove from heat.

To serve, cook mussels, shrimp, crawfish tails and red snapper in the sauce just until hot through. (If raw seafood is used, cook until mussel shells open.) Put 2 of the crawfish heads in the center of each serving dish. Place a slice of toasted French bread rubbed with pressed clove of garlic on either side of heads and spoon bouillabaisse over them. Make sure each person has some of each variety of fish.

*French and Spice Island market these prepared spices.

"Turquoise" Soup (continued)

becomes too thick. Drain cucumber slices, pour this sauce over them and stir. Serve chilled in individual dishes with olive oil and mint.

Brasserie, New York City

Onion Soup

12 medium onions, sliced
 1 clove garlic, mashed
½ cup clarified butter
 2 quarts bouillon or water
   Worcestershire sauce
¼ teaspoon dried thyme
 1 bay leaf
   Salt
   Pepper
 6 slices French bread, toasted
½ pound (250 grams) Gruyère cheese,
   sliced or shredded

Sauté onions and garlic in butter until very brown. Add bouillon or water and a dash of Worcestershire and cook for 15 minutes. Add thyme and bay leaf, salt and pepper and pour into individual ovenproof cups or crocks. Add toasted French bread to cover surface of each casserole, sprinkle with cheese, and brown quickly under the broiler. Serve very hot.

serves: 6

Peacock Room, Ashoka Hotel, New Delhi
CHEF: ROSHAN LAL

Mulligatawny Soup

½ pound (250 grams) chicken pieces
 6 cups water
 1 medium onion, minced
 1 tablespoon minced fresh ginger
 2 tablespoons clarified butter
 3 tablespoons besan,* lightly roasted
 1 tablespoon curry powder (or to taste)
 1 tablespoon finely grated coconut
 1 tablespoon cashew nuts, finely ground
   Salt
   Pepper
 6 tablespoons cooked rice
   Lemon slices for garnish

Make stock with chicken pieces and 6 cups water. When stock is ready, remove chicken and shred meat; reserve to serve in soup.
Using a deep pot, fry onions and ginger in clarified butter until brown. Remove from butter and put into stock. Now into the butter put besan, curry powder, coconut, ground cashew nuts, salt and pepper. Fry until brown. Pour into chicken stock and cook over moderate heat for 5 minutes. Strain soup through very fine sieve or a muslin bag.
Serve hot with a spoonful of cooked rice and shredded chicken in each cup. Garnish with lemon slices.
*Besan is flour prepared from chana dal, a split Bengal pulse. If unavailable, flour made from finely ground yellow split peas may be used.

serves: 6

Repulse Bay Hotel, Hong Kong
CHEF: ROLF SCHNEIDER

Gazpacho

serves:
6 to 8

2 tablespoons chopped canned pimento
2 tablespoons chopped fresh green pepper
3 tablespoons chopped, peeled cucumber
2 tablespoons minced carrots
¼ cup tomatoes, peeled, seeded, and chopped
2 tablespoons chopped parsley
2 tablespoons tomato paste
4 cups chicken stock
5 to 8 drops Tabasco sauce
½ teaspoon Worcestershire sauce
1 teaspoon lemon juice
2 tablespoons salad oil
Salt
Pepper
Croutons

Mix all the vegetables. Add tomato paste, salad oil, Tabasco, Worcestershire, and lemon juice and mix well. Add the chicken stock and season to taste. Chill for several hours before serving with croutons.

Turkey

Turkish Wedding Soup

serves: 4

1 onion
1 medium carrot
4 cups water
1 pound (500 grams) lamb
2 pounds (1 kilogram) mutton bones
1 tablespoon salt
1 cup flour
12 tablespoons butter
Juice of 1 lemon
3 egg yolks, beaten
1 tablespoon paprika
Cayenne

Peel onion and scrape carrot. Place in the water with meat, bones and salt. Cover pan and cook over medium heat for about 3 hours or until meat is tender. Strain off stock. Chop meat and return it to stock.
Mix flour and half the butter in a large pan over low heat, stirring constantly for a few minutes until mixture is slightly browned.
Slowly add meat stock, stirring constantly, and simmer.
Combine lemon juice and egg yolks. Add 2 or 3 tablespoons of the hot stock. When this is well blended, stir it into soup. Melt remaining half of butter and add paprika and cayenne. Use this to garnish soup before serving.

Jamaica

Shrimp Soup

1 pound (500 grams) white fish
6 cups water
½ pound (250 grams) shrimp
1 teaspoon butter
  Pepper
  Salt
  Thyme
  Lime-peel and skellion
2 cloves
4 strips salt pork
  Squeeze of lime or lemon juice

serves: 6

Make fish stock by boiling fish in water until reduced to 4 cups. Separate flesh of shrimps, pound heads, tails and skins finely; remove fish and add ground shrimp heads and shrimp to stock. Add butter, seasoning and cloves; boil 10 minutes. Remove shrimp, cut in small pieces and place in soup tureen. Boil the rest of ingredients ½ hour more. Thicken with flour and pour over shrimp; add squeeze of lime or lemon juice.

Hong Kong

Tong Kwa Chung

(Meat Soup in Steamed Winter Melon)

¼ cup dried grass mushrooms
1 winter melon approximately 12″ × 8″
  Bone from Chinese ham
1 3-pound (1.5-kilogram) chicken
½ pound (250 grams) duck breasts, diced
¼ cup Chinese ham meat, diced
½ cup bamboo shoots, diced
1 slice fresh ginger
1 tablespoon Chinese wine or sake
2 spring onions, chopped
½ cup fresh leen jee (lotus seeds)
¼ cup abalone, diced
½ cup fresh grass mushrooms
  Salt
  Monosodium glutamate

serves: 4

Soak mushrooms in water to cover overnight and parboil 15 minutes. Drain and set aside.
Cut off top of melon about quarter way down. Scoop out seeds and pulp. Notch edge for effect. Parboil melon shell for 15 minutes and stand on a rack in a roasting pan. Cut ham bone into large pieces. Remove whole chicken breast and dice meat. Use carcass in soup.
Combine all ingredients except fresh leen jee, abalone and fresh grass mushrooms in melon shell. Steam for 5 hours or until flesh of melon is transparent and tender. Ten minutes before serving add leen jee, abalone and grass mushrooms. Add salt and monosodium glutamate to taste. Remove chicken carcass and ham bone from melon. Serve steaming hot.

The Captain's Galley, Hotel Inter-Continental, Auckland, New Zealand

Paua Soup

serves:
4 to 6

24 paua (abalone)
8 cups milk
1½ cups fish stock
Butter for frying
6 tablespoons butter
Paprika
Freshly ground pepper
Celery salt
½ cup cream
Fresh dill or parsley, chopped

Mince paua. Scald milk in a large saucepan. Add fish stock and bring to a gentle simmer. Meanwhile lightly fry minced paua in butter and drain. Add paua, butter, a pinch of paprika and pepper to the milk and stock. Stir until butter melts. Add celery salt. Stir in cream and reheat gently. Garnish with chopped fresh dill or parsley.

Fish stock

2 fish heads
1 onion, chopped
2 cups water
1 bay leaf
Salt
Pepper

Simmer fish heads in a large covered saucepan with chopped onion and seasonings. Reduce slowly until there are 1½ cups of stock after straining.

Chile

Congrio Soup

serves: 6

1 teaspoon paprika
3 tablespoons oil
2 onions, chopped
6 potatoes, quartered
1 green pepper, in thin slices
2 large carrots, sliced
6 cups water (or milk)
1 clove garlic, crushed
Salt
Pepper
6 cutlets congrio or other firm white fish
1 hard-cooked egg
Parsley
1 tomato, chopped (optional)
1 cup white wine (optional)

Mix paprika and oil in frying pan and fry onion until transparent. Transfer to earthen pot or casserole and place over medium heat. Add vegetables, water (or milk), and seasonings. Lower heat when liquid boils. When potatoes are half cooked, place fish cutlets on top and heat through. Remove cutlets carefully to heated soup dishes. Cover with vegetable broth; garnish with sliced egg and chopped parsley. Chopped tomato and a cup of white wine may be added if desired.

The Four Seasons, New York City

Cold Sour Cherry Soup

3 cups cold water
1 cup sugar
1 cinnamon stick
4 cups pitted sour cherries or drained
     canned sour cherries
1 tablespoon arrowroot
¼ cup heavy cream, chilled
¾ cup dry red wine, chilled

In 2-quart saucepan, combine the water, sugar and cinnamon stick. Bring to a boil and add the cherries. Partially cover and simmer over low heat for 35 to 40 minutes if the cherries are fresh or 10 minutes if they are canned. Remove the cinnamon stick.

Mix the arrowroot and 2 tablespoons of cold water into a paste, then beat into the cherry mixture. Stirring constantly, bring the soup almost to a boil. Reduce the heat and simmer about 2 minutes, or until clear and slightly thickened. Pour into a shallow glass or stainless steel bowl and refrigerate. Before serving—preferably in soup bowls that have been pre-chilled—stir in the cream and wine.

serves: 6

The Tower Suite, New York City

Chilled Minted Pea Soup

1 head romaine lettuce
1 large onion
3 slices lean bacon
2 quarts chicken stock
4 cups fresh or frozen green peas
2 sprigs fresh mint
1 teaspoon sugar
  Salt
  Pepper
¾ cup light cream
⅓ cup heavy cream
2 egg yolks
1 tablespoon arrowroot
2 tablespoons green crème de menthe
1 cup chopped cooked spinach
  Mint for garnish

Chop lettuce, onions and bacon coarsely. Place in soup kettle and bring to a boil with chicken broth. Add peas, mint, sugar, salt and pepper and the heavy and light cream.

Cook for 1 hour. If necessary, use egg yolks and arrowroot to thicken soup.

After cooking add crème de menthe and finely chopped spinach. Strain, chill and serve. Garnish with sprigs of fresh mint.

serves: 6

Le Chalet, Erawan Hotel, Bangkok
CHEF: ROLAND LAURENCEAU

Lobster Soup "Le Chalet"

serves: 4

wine:
Pouilly-
Fuissé

3 tablespoons olive oil
1 cup butter
1 cup chopped carrots
1 cup chopped turnips
1 cup chopped leeks
4 cups fish stock
  Pinch saffron
  Pinch nutmeg
2 cloves garlic
½ teaspoon thyme
1 teaspoon oregano
  Salt
  Pepper
4 river lobster tails
4 tablespoons pernod
1 medium onion, chopped
2 egg yolks
¼ cup cream

Heat olive oil and half the butter in a flameproof casserole. Add finely chopped vegetables and sauté gently for 5 minutes. Add fish stock, saffron, nutmeg, garlic, thyme, and oregano. Bring to a boil and cook until vegetables are tender. Season with salt and pepper.

Halve the lobster tails lengthwise and remove the long intestinal vein. Sauté gently in the remaining butter and flame with pernod. Sauté onion in a little butter. Pour in the previously prepared vegetable-stock mixture and boil for a few minutes. Remove lobster-sauce mixture from heat. Beat the egg yolks. Stir several spoonsful of the hot sauce into the egg yolks, then pour the egg mixture back into the casserole. Add cream gradually, stirring constantly. Heat gently but do not allow to boil after egg yolks and cream are added. Serve hot over toast or in pastry shells.

Turkey

Yogurt Beef Soup

serves: 8

3 cups yogurt
1 teaspoon salt
4 pints beef stock
6 tablespoons butter
¾ cup flour
1 tablespoon dried mint leaves

Place yogurt and salt in a mixing bowl. Add stock very slowly, stirring constantly until it is quite smooth. Melt butter in saucepan over a low flame. Add flour slowly. Stir constantly. Add yogurt and stock mixture slowly, still stirring, until it boils. To serve, pour into soup dishes and garnish with mint leaves.

Restaurant Napoleon, Paris
CHEF: GUY BAUMANN

Sole Pompadour

4 fillets of sole, about 1 pound (500 grams) each
Salt
Pepper
¾ cup white wine
¾ cup fish stock
1 bouquet garni (see Index)
12 shrimp, cooked and shelled (leave tails on)
16 mussels, steamed and shelled
12 mushroom caps, sautéed in butter
¼ cup butter
¼ cup flour
2 egg yolks, beaten
6 tablespoons cream
4 parsley sprigs

Poach fillets gently in white wine, fish stock and bouquet garni for about 10 minutes. Carefully place them on a warmed serving platter and arrange shrimp, mussels and mushrooms around fish. Keep warm. Make a roux with butter and flour; add boiling cooking liquid from poaching fish, reduced to 2½ cups. Thicken with 2 egg yolks and the cream. Do not boil after eggs and cream are added. To serve, pour over fish and decorate platter with parsley sprigs.

serves: 4

wine: Chablis

Repulse Bay Hotel, Hong Kong
CHEF: ROLF SCHNEIDER

Prawn Shashlick à l'Indienne

1 lemon
1 orange
2 red chilis, finely chopped
2 tablespoons curry powder
¼ cup brandy
½ teaspoon Worcestershire sauce
Salt
Pepper
3 dozen prawns, boiled and peeled
3 green peppers, cut in 1-inch squares
4 small tomatoes, quartered
1 large onion cut into 1-inch dice
½ cup melted butter

Grate rind of lemon and orange, then squeeze and strain juice. Mix together chilis, grated rind, juice, curry powder, brandy, Worcestershire sauce, salt, and pepper. Marinate the prepared prawns in this mixture for 1 hour.
Arrange in order on skewer a piece of green pepper, a quarter of a tomato, a piece of onion, and a prawn. Repeat until the skewer is full. Cook on a hot grill. Brush with melted butter and turn as necessary to brown all sides. Serve with melted butter and curried rice.

serves: 4

wine: White Burgundy

Gaddi's, Hong Kong
CHEF: ARMIN SONDEREGGER

Prawns au Sherry

serves: 4

wine: Blanc de Blanc or Fendand Montibeux

1¼ pounds (625 grams) fresh prawns, shelled
Salt
Pepper
Curry powder
¼ pound (125 grams) butter
3 cloves garlic, chopped
1 tablespoon parsley, chopped
4 tablespoons dry sherry

Sprinkle the prawns with salt and pepper on both sides. Add a dash of curry powder on one side. Melt the butter in a frying pan over a high flame; when slightly brown add the garlic and parsley. Stir and mix well and when very hot add the prawns. Fry quickly for approximately 2 minutes. Pour in the sherry, baste a few times and remove from the flame. Serve with steamed rice.

Fountain Café, Colombo, Ceylon

Prawn Fried Rice

serves: 8

1½ pounds (750 grams) Samba rice
3 teaspoons salt
½ cup oil or fat
1½ pounds (750 grams) prawns, boiled
6 tablespoons soybean sauce
¼ cup shredded carrots
¼ cup chopped leeks
¼ cup chopped celery
¼ cup tomato sauce

Cook rice with 1½ teaspoons salt until fluffy.
Heat oil and add shelled and deveined prawns. Mix in soybean sauce and set aside. Heat remaining oil. Add shredded vegetables and fry for 1 or 2 minutes. Add cooked rice and prepare prawns. Add tomato sauce and salt to taste; mix well before serving.
Note: Soy sauces available in many parts of the world are saltier than that used in Ceylon. Taste and adjust amount to sauce available.

Beach Luxury Hotel, Karachi

Prawn Pattia

serves: 4

2 large chopped onions
5 tablespoons fat
1 teaspoon curry powder
6 cloves garlic
1 teaspoon cumin seeds
1 teaspoon red chili powder
1 tablespoon vinegar
8 tablespoons sugar
Juice from ½ pound (250 grams) tomatoes
1 pound prawns

Fry the onions in fat until tender. Add curry powder; sauté a minute or two. Add the other ingredients except the prawns and cook for 20 minutes. Add prawns and simmer for another 10 minutes. Serve with rice.

The Four Seasons, New York City

Shrimp Kiev

18 cleaned jumbo shrimp
1 teaspoon salt
½ teaspoon pepper
3 tablespoons lobster butter
Flour
4 eggs, beaten
4 cups bread crumbs
Fat for frying

Split shrimp from the inside about three-quarters through to the back. Place, split side down, between two sheets of dampened wax paper. Pound very gently until flattened, taking care not to split the shrimp.

serves: 6

Conclusion: Place ½ teaspoon lobster butter inside each shrimp and fold the shrimp halves together. Dip shrimp into flour, eggs, and then bread crumbs. Fry in 450° F. fat until golden brown, or about 1 minute. Drain on paper towels and serve.

Lobster butter

1 cup lobster shells with legs and coral
(or lobster meat) or shells and meat of
other shellfish
¼ pound (125 grams) butter
2 tablespoons boiling water
Salt
White pepper

Dry shells and legs in a 375° F. oven for 8 minutes. Whirl in a blender to crush completely. (If you use shellfish meat, put it through the blender.) Melt the butter in the top of a double boiler. Add shells and coral (or meat) and cook over hot water for 10 minutes. Strain through a cheese-cloth. Add the 2 tablespoons of boiling water to the shells and let stand 5 minutes. Strain the water into the previously strained butter. Season to taste. Pour into a dish or crock and refrigerate for at least 2 to 3 hours. The butter will harden so that it can easily be removed from the liquid underneath. This butter may be frozen. (Shellfish meat will not give as much delicate color as the shells. A tablespoonful of tomato paste may be used to color the butter and add a slight additional flavor.)

The Four Seasons, New York City

Crisped Shrimp with Mustard Fruit

serves: 4

**16 large raw shrimp, shelled and deveined
  (about 1 pound or 500 grams)
2 tablespoons butter
2 tablespoons all purpose flour
1½ teaspoons prepared mustard
½ teaspoon salt
  Coarse ground pepper
1¼ cups milk
1 jar (8 ounces) mustard fruit,
  drained and finely chopped
  Flour for dredging**

In a large saucepan, combine 1 quart water and 1 tablespoon salt; bring to boil. Add shrimp; simmer 3 to 5 minutes, or until just tender. Drain well.

In small saucepan, melt butter; remove from heat. Stir in 2 tablespoons flour, mustard, ½ teaspoon salt and pepper to taste; gradually add milk, stir and bring to boiling point. Reduce heat and simmer 3 minutes. Remove from heat; stir in half the mustard fruit. Keep warm. Split shrimp down back; stuff with remaining mustard fruit, then roll the stuffed shrimp in flour.

Batter

**1½ cups flour
1½ teaspoons baking powder
½ teaspoon salt
1¼ cups milk
  Oil for deep frying**

Sift flour, baking powder and salt into a mixing bowl; add milk, stirring until smooth.

Meanwhile, in an electric skillet or heavy saucepan heat oil (1½ to 2 inches deep) to 380°F. on deep-frying thermometer.

Dip shrimp into batter. Fry, a few at a time, until golden brown, 3 to 5 minutes. Drain. Keep warm while frying remaining shrimp.

Arrange shrimp on warm plate and cover with mustard fruit sauce.

Hotel Inter-Continental, Karachi

Sea Shrimp Flambé

serves: 4

**5 dozen, about 3 pounds (1.5 kilograms)
  raw shrimp
  Juice of 2 lemons
6 tablespoons butter
1 whole onion
½ pound (250 grams) mushrooms
4 tomatoes, peeled, seeded and chopped
¼ cup brandy
6 tablespoons heavy cream
1 tablespoon pernod
2 tablespoons parsley, chopped**

Peel the raw shrimp and marinate them with lemon juice. Heat a frying pan and put the butter in; add the marinated shrimp and onions. Sauté a moment and flame with the brandy. Now add the heavy cream and the pernod along with the parsley. Sauté for 5 minutes until the sauce thickens a little. Serve with white rice.

Le Chaland Hotel, Plaine Magnien, Mauritius

Shrimp in Red Palm Heart

5 dozen shrimp
¼ pound (125 grams) butter
2 teaspoons salt
½ teaspoon thyme
2 tablespoons chopped parsley
1 pound (500 grams) tomatoes, peeled and
    seeded
2 tablespoons cooking oil
2 tablespoons cognac
1 palm heart

Remove the shrimp from their shells. Crush the shells and allow to boil in a pint of water for 15 minutes. Strain juice. Fry the shrimp in butter adding salt, thyme and parsley.
Crush the tomatoes into a paste, cook slightly in oil adding some parsley and thyme. Add the fried shrimp and the shell juice and allow to cook for five minutes. Add cognac and remove from heat. Allow the palm heart to boil for 45 minutes then cut it into slices about ¼-inch thick. Place the slices in a serving dish and pour the shrimp and sauce over them. Serve hot.

serves: 5

Fort Charles Grill, Barbados Hilton, St. Michael, Barbados

Curried Shrimp in Half Pineapple

1 medium onion, sliced
4 tablespoons butter
1 banana, diced
1 apple, diced
    Madras curry powder to taste
½ cup mango chutney
½ cup flour
4 cups fish stock
2½ pounds (1.25 kilograms) raw shrimp
1 tablespoon salt
    Pepper
    Juice of ½ lime
1 teaspoon Worcestershire sauce
2 tablespoons brandy
3 pineapples

Sauté the sliced onion in half the butter together with the diced banana and apple. Add curry powder, mango chutney and flour. Keep on a low fire and stir frequently; cook until flour browns lightly. Add the fish stock and stir well until smooth. Simmer for at least 2 hours. Season the peeled shrimp with salt, pepper, lime juice and Worcestershire sauce; sauté in butter and brandy. Strain the simmered sauce onto the shrimp and cook for another 10 minutes. Serve in halves of scooped-out pineapples and garnish with toasted shredded coconut. Serve rice pilaf (see Index) separately.

serves: 6

wine:
Chablis

Onion Soup

LE PARIS BREST, NEW YORK CITY

Oysters Tarantino

TARANTINO'S,
SAN FRANCISCO
(Chef: Donald E. Lynam)

Lobster Ball Sauté

MAN WAH RESTAURANT
MANDARIN HOTEL,
HONG KONG

La Bonne Chute, Mauritius
CHEF: PAPAYE

Skewers of Shrimp in Sauce "Ti-Malice"

serves: 4

2 pounds (1 kilogram) large fresh shrimp
1 large onion
1 tablespoon oil
1 tablespoon flour
1 hot green chili (or to taste)
½ cup orange juice
  Salt
  Pepper
2 tablespoons chopped parsley
½ cup self-rising flour
½ cup water
  Oil for frying

Remove the shrimp from their shells and arrange them on skewers with a minimum of 3 per skewer. Crush the shells and extract the juice.

Cut the onion into chunks and cook lightly in oil. Add flour and allow to cook slightly, stirring constantly. Add the shell juice, mixing carefully; allow to cook for 15 minutes. Complete the sauce by adding the crushed green chili and orange juice. Add salt, pepper and finely cut parsley. Keep warm. Dip the shrimp skewers into a batter of self-rising flour and water, then fry lightly in oil. Serve the shrimp skewers hot with rice pilaf. Serve sauce separately.

Canlis', Honolulu

Canlis' Shrimp

serves: 4 as entrée, or 6 as appetizer

2 tablespoons olive oil
2 pounds (1 kilogram) shrimp, shelled
  (except tails)
2 tablespoons butter
1 small whole garlic clove, crushed
¼ teaspoon salt
¼ teaspoon fresh ground black pepper
  Juice of 2 lemons
¼ cup dry vermouth

Heat olive oil in a large skillet. When simmering, add shrimp and allow to cook until golden brown. Reduce heat and add butter, garlic, salt, and pepper. When you think you might have too much salt—add more. This is one dish where one cannot oversalt.

When well blended, raise fire to very hot. Add lemon juice and dry vermouth and cook for about 1 minute, constantly stirring or shaking. The dish can be served as an appetizer or entrée.

Charley O's, New York City

Soused Shrimp

2 carrots, sliced
1 onion, quartered
2 lemons, cut in halves
3 celery leaves
5 bay leaves
  Salt
5 pounds (2.5 kilograms) raw shrimp

Put carrots, onion, lemon, celery leaves, bay leaves, and a pinch of salt in a saucepan of cold water. Bring the water to a boil and add the shrimp. Remove from heat as soon as the water comes to a boil again. Immediately drain the water from the saucepan and allow the pan to stand under cold running water until the shrimp are cooled, or at least 10 minutes.
Remove the shrimp and peel off shells. Be sure to remove the thin black stripe running from the head to the tail. Wash shrimp at least twice in cold water after peeling. They are now ready to marinate.

serves: 12

Marinade

 2 pounds (1 kilogram) onions, finely sliced
 8 lemons, finely sliced
12 bay leaves
 1 bunch fresh tarragon, finely chopped
 1 pint olive oil
 1 ounce Accent
 2 ounces tarragon vinegar
   Dash Worcestershire sauce
   Dash Tabasco sauce
   Salt
   Pepper

Combine all the ingredients in a large bowl. This should take at least 10 minutes, to insure that all the ingredients are thoroughly mixed together. Now add the cleaned shrimp, a few at a time, to the marinade. Continue to stir the marinade until all the shrimp are in the bowl.
Allow to stand in the refrigerator for a minimum of 12 hours.
Serve chilled.

Tavern on the Green, New York City

Shrimp Scampi

4 tablespoons butter
6 fresh butterflied jumbo shrimp
  Salt to taste
1 clove garlic
2 tablespoons dry vermouth
  Juice of ¼ lemon
  Chopped parsley

Heat the butter in a large frying pan until it starts to bubble.
Add the shrimp and sauté them until they are pink. Add the salt, garlic, vermouth and lemon juice and sauté for 2 to 3 minutes more. Place shrimp in oval casserole dish and garnish with chopped parsley.

serves: 2

Mirabelle Restaurant, London
CHEF: JEAN DREES

Sole Mirabelle

serves: 4

wine:
*Corton
Charlemagne*

**1 pound (500 grams) Dublin Bay prawns
  (or large shrimp)**
2 filleted whiting
2 egg whites
  Salt
  Pepper
2 cups cream
4 1-pound (500-gram) soles
4 shallots, chopped
¾ cup butter
¾ cup dry white wine
⅓ cup cognac

Put prawns and whiting through a fine mincer. Place in a large mixing bowl and add the egg whites, salt and pepper and mix well. Add half the cream and mix again for 2 minutes.

Bone the soles and stuff with prawn mixture. Close with skewers or tie up. Place the stuffed soles on the chopped shallots in a buttered deep roasting pan. Add salt and pepper; pour the wine and cognac over fish and bake in a 450° F. oven for 20 minutes. Remove the soles and place them on a serving dish; keep warm.

Strain the stock from the roasting pan into a saucepan. Bring to a boil. Add the rest of the cream and allow to reduce for about 5 minutes. Add the butter, pour over the soles and serve.

Michael's Caprice, Auckland, New Zealand

New Zealand Seafood Ragout

serves: 6

1 medium onion
4 tablespoons butter
½ pound (250 grams) boneless fish
½ pound (250 grams) prawns
1 medium lobster tail
½ pound (250 grams) scallops
  Salt
  Pepper
  Pinch saffron
½ cup flour
1 cup dry white wine
½ cup fresh cream
  Chopped parsley

Chop the onion finely and fry in half the butter until slightly browned. Add fish and toss gently; add prawns, lobsters and scallops and fry for 8 to 10 minutes. Sprinkle with salt and pepper; add pinch of saffron. Remove fish to a casserole and place in warming oven. Add remainder of butter and flour to cooking pan and cook gently so that the flour does not brown. Add white wine, finish by adding cream. Adjust seasonings to taste. Pour sauce over fish in casserole and brown lightly under the broiler and serve hot.

Bistro Bourgogne, Esso Motor Hotel, Amsterdam
CHEF: S. TOLSMA

Mussels "Mayflower"

½ **cup dry white wine**
1 **tablespoon chopped celery**
½ **teaspoon sage**
6 **white peppercorns, crushed**
1 **teaspoon salt**
4½ **pounds (2.5 kilograms) fresh mussels**
½ **cup butter**
1 **tablespoon chopped chives**
1 **tablespoon chopped parsley**
1 **tablespoon celery salt**
1 **clove garlic, crushed**
½ **cup cream**
2 **egg yolks**
1 **teaspoon salt**
½ **teaspoon curry powder**

In a medium saucepan, bring to a boil the white wine, celery, sage, peppercorns and salt. Add the mussels, cover and shake pan during cooking to loosen mussels from their shells—about 10 minutes. Remove from pan and remove mussels from shells. Set aside.

Cream butter with chives, parsley, celery salt and garlic. Grease an oven proof serving dish with it. Place mussels in the dish.

Beat cream, egg yolks, salt and curry powder until it is of medium thickness. Spread over the mussels. Place in a 425° F. oven for 2 or 3 minutes—or until the cream sauce begins to brown slightly.

serves: 4

wine:
Fleur
d'Alsace
"Hugel"
1970

Captain's Table Restaurant, Flagler Hotel, Nassau, Bahamas
CHEF: RALPH STROEH

Broiled Crawfish
(Languste)

4 **crawfish**
1 **lemon, sliced**
1 **teaspoon white pepper**
1 **small whole onion**
1 **bay leaf**
2 **teaspoons salt**
1 **teaspoon paprika**
8 **tablespoons butter**
2 **tablespoons capers**

Clean crawfish and cook 10 minutes in boiling water to cover with lemon, pepper, onion, bay leaf and salt. Drain crawfish and when cool enough to handle cut in half lengthwise. Sprinkle with paprika and dot with butter. Broil just until crawfish is fully done, about 5 minutes. Add capers to pan during the last 2 minutes the crawfish broils. Spoon butter drippings and capers over crawfish and serve at once.

serves: 2-4

Hotel Imperial, Copenhagen
CHEF: HOLGER ANDERSEN

Langoustines Flambés Amoureuses

serves: 4

wine:
White
Bordeaux

12 shallots
3 tablespoons oil
3 tablespoons butter
1 carrot, grated
1 teaspoon paprika
Pinch oregano
1 tablespoon fennel seeds
1 teaspoon dill seeds
1 teaspoon white pepper
40 middle-size langoustine tails
12 calamaris
12 scallops
12 mushrooms
Fresh tarragon
Juice of 1 lemon
2 teaspoons pernod
2 teaspoons cognac
Saffron
¾ cup crème fraîche*
Salt
Parsley
3 tomatoes, peeled and seeded

Sauté shallots in oil and butter with a grated carrot. Add paprika, a pinch of oregano, fennel seed, dill seed and white pepper.
Add the raw langoustine tails and calamaris and simmer with shallots and spices until the langoustine shells start turning red. Then add scallops, mushrooms, chopped tarragon, and lemon juice. Heat through and flame with cognac and pernod. Dust with saffron and mix in crème fraîche. Taste for seasonings; add salt if necessary. Decorate with chopped parsley and strips of tomato. Served with rice.

*Mix 2 parts heavy cream and 1 part sour cream. Let stand at room temperature for 6 hours, then store in the refrigerator.

Jamaica

Creamed Lobster

serves: 4

1 1-pound (500 gram) tin lobster meat
2 eggs
2 tablespoons cream
1 tablespoon grated cheese
1 tablespoon finely chopped shrimp
1 tablespoon mustard
Salt
Pepper
Cayenne pepper
2 teaspoons vinegar
4 crab shells

Drain liquid from lobster and reserve. Flake lobster. Boil eggs for 3 minutes; remove shells and mix eggs with cream and lobster liquid. Add cheese, shrimp, mustard, salt, pepper, cayenne pepper and vinegar. Stir in lobster and mix well. Pile into scrubbed crab shells or au gratin dishes. Bake for 30 minutes at 325° F.

Hotel Parmelia, Perth, Australia
CHEF: D. R. WILLIAMS

Rock Lobster Parmelia

1 large onion
3 tablespoons butter
¼ cup flour
¼ cup Chablis
1 cup hot milk
  Salt
  Pepper
2 pounds (1 kilogram) rock lobster meat
3 large tomatoes, peeled, seeded, and
    cooked until liquid has evaporated
½ cup cream
4 cups creamed mashed potatoes
2 tablespoons chopped parsley

serves: 4

Finely dice the onion, place in shallow pan, and cook carefully in butter; do not allow to brown. Add flour and cook 5 minutes. Add the Chablis, stirring continuously. Gradually add hot milk until a smooth sauce is achieved; strain and season to taste with salt and pepper. Cut rock lobster tails into 1-inch pieces. Add the strained sauce, and the tomatoes and simmer 20 minutes. Finish by blending in fresh cream.

Arrange lobster and sauce on a serving platter. Pipe creamed mashed potatoes around edge of platter, adding head and tail of rock lobster at opposite ends and legs, fanned apart, down the sides. Sprinkle with parsley.

Man Wah Restaurant, Mandarin Hotel, Hong Kong

Lobster Ball Sauté with Soybean and Green Pepper

1 3-pound (1.5-kilogram) lobster
  Flour for dredging
½ teaspoon black pepper
5 cups peanut oil
1 medium green pepper, sliced
¼ cup soybean purée
2 cloves garlic, crushed
1 teaspoon sugar
2 tablespoons Chinese wine
1 teaspoon poultry seasoning
1 teaspoon cornstarch
½ cup chicken stock

serves: 2

Boil lobster until shell turns red. Remove meat from shell, reserving shell, and chop meat into 1-inch pieces. Dredge in flour and black pepper and deep fry in peanut oil with slices of green pepper for a few seconds. Drain. Heat 2 tablespoons oil in a frying pan; add soybean purée, garlic, green pepper, and lobster pieces and sauté 2 minutes. Add sugar, Chinese wine, seasonings, cornstarch, and chicken stock. When sauce has thickened, remove lobster meat and green pepper; arrange in lobster shell on a serving platter. Spoon sauce over meat. Serve with rice.

Buena Vista, Nassau, Bahamas
CHEF: J. P. FAURE

Lobster Buena Vista

serves: 4

wine:
Chablis
Montee
Tonnere

4 medium lobster tails, boiled
3 tablespoons butter
1 clove garlic, sliced
1 onion, finely chopped
2 teaspoons chopped parsley
1 teaspoon English mustard
Few drops Tabasco sauce
1 teaspoon Lea & Perrins sauce
2 cups white sauce
Salt
Pepper
½ cup white bread crumbs

Cut lobster tails in halves; remove and dice meat. Retain and wash thoroughly 4 of the half shells. Melt butter in a saucepan and add garlic and onion. When onion is slightly browned, add lobster meat and simmer for a few minutes. Add parsley, mustard, Tabasco and Lea & Perrins sauce and continue to simmer for another few minutes. Finally, mix in the white sauce, bring to a boil and remove from the fire. Salt and pepper to taste, fill the 4 half shells with the mixture, sprinkle with bread crumbs and brown under the broiler.

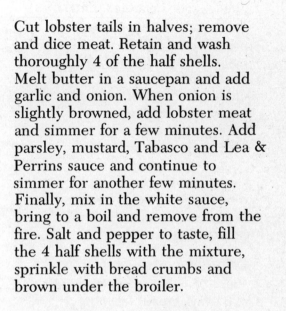

White sauce
6 tablespoons butter
6 tablespoons flour
2 cups milk
2 teaspoons salt
White pepper to taste

In the top half of a double boiler, melt butter over hot water. Add flour and blend thoroughly. Cook 10 minutes, stirring often. Add milk and cook until sauce thickens, stirring constantly. Season with salt and pepper.

The Four Seasons, New York City

Lobster Aromatic

6 tablespoons clarified butter
2 tablespoons chopped shallots
4½ cups sliced lobster meat
¼ cup pernod, warmed
1½ teaspoons salt
¼ teaspoon English mustard
¼ teaspoon paprika
¼ teaspoon cayenne
¼ teaspoon curry powder
  Juice of ¼ lemon
1 tablespoon minced chives
1 tablespoon minced parsley
1½ cups lobster sauce
½ cup whipped cream

Lobster sauce (sauce Cardinal)

1 cup Béchamel sauce (see Index)
⅓ cup heavy cream
10 tablespoons lobster butter (see Index)
½ teaspoon Tabasco sauce

serves: 6

Heat butter in pan. Add shallots and sauté until soft, but do not brown. Add lobster, mix well, and allow to heat through. Flame with the pernod, which will brown the shallots slightly.

Mix salt with mustard and spices. Add to lobster mixture and mix well. Add lemon juice, chives, parsley, and lobster sauce and mix well. Reduce the mixture by boiling gently for 3 to 5 minutes, stirring constantly. Remove from heat and add whipped cream, mixing well. Serve at once.

Mix Béchamel with cream. Cook for 5 or 6 minutes over medium heat, stirring constantly. Add the lobster butter and Tabasco, mix well and strain.

Fountain Café, Colombo, Ceylon

Lobster à la Fountain

2 1-pound (500-gram) lobsters, boiled
¼ cup butter or cooking oil
¼ cup onion, chopped
¼ cup white sauce
  Salt
  Pepper
½ cup grated mild cheese
  Parsley sprigs

serves: 4

Remove lobster claws and legs. Cut carefully in half. Remove all meat; wash shells, drain, and reserve. Cut the lobster meat into cubes.

Heat the cooking fat in a thick-bottomed pan, add the onion, lobster meat, and white sauce and season to taste. Turn two or three times, but do not overheat or the meat will toughen. Remove pan from the fire, add half the grated cheese, and mix well.

Place the lobster mixture in the cleaned lobster shells and fill neatly. Sprinkle with the rest of the grated cheese and brown under the broiler. Serve on a silver dish. Decorate with parsley.

Hotel Imperial, Copenhagen
CHEF: HOLGER ANDERSEN

Special Lobster Curry Imperial

serves: 2

wine:
White
Bourgogne

1 large lobster
Paprika
Salt
10 shallots, chopped
10 mushrooms, sliced
1 tablespoon mild curry powder
4 tablespoons clarified butter
¼ cup crème fraîche (see Index)
1 slice pineapple
1 teaspoon chopped pickled hot red
pepper
Grated coconut
Chopped parsley

Cook whole lobster for 20 minutes in boiling water with 1 teaspoon paprika and salt added per quart. Drain and cool; split shell and cut meat in 1-inch cubes. Reserve shell. Sauté shallots, mushrooms and curry in clarified butter for 5 minutes. Add crème fraîche and simmer for another 10 minutes. Add pineapple slice, cut into small pieces, red pepper and lobster meat and heat through. Spoon mixture into halved lobster shells and sprinkle with grated coconut and chopped parsley. Serve with rice pilaf (see Index).

Publick House, Sturbridge, Massachusetts

Publick House Individual Lobster Pie

serves: 6

4 tablespoons melted butter
4 tablespoons flour
1 pint milk, scalded
1 pint light cream, scalded
1 pound (500 grams) lobster meat
½ teaspoon paprika
¼ cup butter
½ cup sherry wine
Pinch cayenne pepper
1 teaspoon salt
4 egg yolks

Lobster pie topping
¾ cup grated fresh bread crumbs
¾ teaspoon paprika
3 tablespoons crushed potato chips
1 tablespoon Parmesan cheese
5 tablespoons melted butter

Combine 4 tablespoons melted butter with flour in saucepan. Cook over slow fire (do not brown). Add milk and cream and cook 15 minutes, stirring often. Strain sauce. Sauté lobster meat, paprika and butter. Add ¼ cup sherry and cook for another 3 minutes. Add the cayenne pepper and salt and the sauce. Blend 4 tablespoons of the sauce into the egg yolks, then stir back into the whole mixture. Stir until it bubbles and thickens. Take off the fire and stir in the remaining sherry. Spoon the lobster mixture into casseroles making sure to distribute the lobster meat evenly. Sprinkle with topping and brown in 400°F. oven.

Gaddi's, Hong Kong
CHEF: ARMIN SONDEREGGER

Lobster "Playpen"

4 mangoes
2 chopped shallots
2 tablespoons butter
4 whole lobsters, boiled and diced
  Salt
  Pepper
1 tablespoon brandy
2 tablespoons white wine
  Curry cream sauce
4 tablespoons cream
  Tabasco sauce
  Fresh lemon juice

Cut each mango in half. Scoop the flesh from the mangoes with a tablespoon and set aside. Reserve the shells. Sauté the shallots in butter in a frying pan. Add the diced lobster meat and sauté together for about 1 minute; season with salt and pepper. Pour on the brandy and ignite, shaking the pan gently until the flames die down. Add the white wine and then strain the curry cream sauce into the pan. Add the fresh cream and bring the mixture to a boil. Finally, add the scooped-out pieces of mango and simmer gently for approximately 2 minutes. Season with Tabasco and lemon juice. Serve with buttered rice.

serves: 4

wine:
Chablis or
Pouilly-
Fuissé

Curry cream sauce
 6 tablespoons butter
 3 tablespoons flour
 3 cups fish stock
 1 tablespoon curry powder
 3 tablespoons mango chutney
 2 tablespoons pineapple juice
 2 tablespoons tomato catsup
 1 tablespoon Worcestershire sauce
½ tablespoon Maggi sauce

Melt the butter in a pan over a low flame. Add the flour and stir until the mixture blends completely. Pour in the fish stock and cook gently for approximately 15 minutes, adding more stock if necessary. Add the rest of the ingredients and keep simmering the sauce gently.

Jimmy's Kitchen, Hong Kong
CHEF: HO PO YUEN

Crabmeat Canneloni

serves: 1

wine:
Berncasteler
Estate wine,
Green Label,
1966

¼ **pound (125 grams) crabmeat**
¼ **spring onion, chopped coarsely**
¼ **teaspoon dry mustard**
2 or 3 drops Worcestershire sauce
Salt
White pepper
2 teaspoons butter
1 8-inch thin pancake
¼ **cup Mornay sauce (see Index)**
2 tablespoons Parmesan cheese

Mix together the crabmeat, spring onion, mustard, and Worcestershire; season the mixture with salt and pepper. Brown the butter in a heavy frying pan and sauté the crabmeat mixture. Place crabmeat along the center of the pancake. Fold over the edges to form a rectangle approximately 8 inches long and 2 inches wide. Turn the stuffed pancake over so that the overlapping edges are on the bottom, and place on a flame-proof dish or plate. Cover with the Mornay sauce and sprinkle the Parmesan cheese on top. Place under a hot broiler until golden. Serve immediately with potato croquettes and a green salad.

Royal Hawaiian Hotel, Honolulu
CHEF: ALEXANDER SCHLEMMER

Baked Coquille of Crabmeat Royal Hawaiian

serves: 4

5 tablespoons Hollandaise sauce
(see Index)
2 tablespoons chopped chives
1 egg yolk
1 pound (500 grams) lump crabmeat
4 cleaned scallop shells or au gratin dishes
Salt
Pepper
4 strips pimento
4 strips anchovies

Mix ¼ cup Hollandaise, chives, and egg yolk and add to crabmeat. Season and mix carefully to avoid breaking lumps and shape to conform to scallop shells or au gratin dishes. Place in scallop shells, top with 1 tablespoon Hollandaise, pimento and anchovies. Bake in moderate oven (350° F.) for 15 to 20 minutes.

Carriage House, Miami, Florida
CHEF: HEINZ WARICH

Crabmeat Balloons

Cooking oil
5 eggs
2 cups milk
2 cups flour
Salt
Pepper
Pinch nutmeg
Rice or barley pilaf

Cover bottom of a sauce dish 3 inches in diameter and approximately 2 inches high with 2/3 inches cooking oil.
Beat eggs, add milk and blend in flour and seasonings. Add batter to sauce dish until oil floats to rim. Bake approximately 40 minutes at 350°F. Set in cool place to dry about 10 minutes. Fill one-third full of rice or barley pilaf.

serves:
6 to 8

½ pound (250 grams) bacon, thinly sliced
½ pound (250 grams) ham, sliced
½ medium onion, sliced
4 whole pimentos, sliced
3 stalks celery, sliced
¼ cup clarified butter
½ cup chopped parsley
15 cooked mushrooms, sliced
3 cups tomato juice
6 ounces (180 grams) king crabmeat, thoroughly drained
2 tablespoons light rum

Sauté first 5 ingredients in butter until celery is tender. Add parsley, mushrooms and tomato juice and simmer for 5 minutes. Set mixture aside. Sauté crabmeat in butter. Add rum and 2 tablespoons of meat-vegetable mixture and heat again. Pour into baked shell and serve immediately.

Speke Hotel, Kampala, Uganda
CHEF: ABDUL R. KHATIB

Baby Spider Crab

½ cup butter
½ cup flour
1 cup milk
¼ cup tomato sauce
½ pound (250 grams) boiled crabmeat
16 small crab shells
½ cup grated cheese

Heat butter in frying pan. Stir in flour and cook without browning for 15 minutes. Add milk and cook, stirring constantly, until thick. Put the mixture in a saucepan with tomato sauce and beat until the sauce is smooth and pink in color. Arrange the crabmeat in shells and top with sauce.
Spread the grated cheese on top of the sauce and bake at 400°F. for 15 minutes. Serve hot with rice.

serves: 4

wine:
White Burgundy, Chablis or "Meursault"

"Sun and", Nassau, Bahamas
CHEF: PETE GARDNER

Curried Coconut Crab

serves: 14

2 #2 cans tomatoes
3 medium onions, diced
3 strips bacon, diced
¼ cup olive oil
   Meat from 12 land crabs, flaked
½ teaspoon thyme
½ teaspoon marjoram
2 tablespoons chopped parsley
   Curry powder to taste
5 tablespoons mixed cooked peas and
   rice
7 whole coconuts
1 cup fresh grated coconut meat

Sauté tomatoes, onions and bacon in olive oil. Add the meat from the land crabs and stew for approximately 20 minutes, or until crabmeat is cooked; then add thyme, marjoram, parsley and curry powder. Stew for a further 10 minutes and add peas and rice. Cook for another 5 minutes, drain liquid off, fill half coconut shells with mixture, sprinkle with flaked coconut and put under the broiler to brown coconut. Serve at once.

The Forum of the XII Caesars, New York City

Fiddler Crab Lump à la Nero

serves: 2

10 ounces (300 grams) lump crabmeat
2½ pieces pimento
1 teaspoon chopped chives
3 tablespoons butter
3 tablespoons dry sherry
1 tablespoon brandy
2 teaspoons Escoffier Sauce Robert
2 teaspoons A-1 Sauce
4 tablespoons chili sauce
4 tablespoons catsup
½ teaspoon English mustard
3 tablespoons cream
   Juice of ½ lemon

Place the lump crabmeat in a silver chafing pan. In the center of the pan place the pimento. Garnish the top of the pimento with the chopped chives. Place pan on fire and add the butter. When the butter is melted, add the dry sherry and let cook until sherry is reduced by half. Flame with brandy. Mix together the Escoffier Sauce, A-1 Sauce, chili sauce, catsup, and mustard, and add. Then add cream and simmer 2 minutes. Just before serving add the lemon juice.
Serve over wild rice.

Hotel Russell, Dublin
CHEF: P. ROLLAND

St. Jacques à l'Irlandaise

Flour for dredging
20 scallops
4 tablespoons butter
2 cups cream
2 minced shallots
1 tablespoon chopped parsley
½ cup Irish Mist
Salt
Pepper
4 scallop shells, scrubbed and dried
4 egg yolks

Flour scallops and sauté for 3 minutes in a saucepan with half the butter. Add cream, shallots, parsley and the Irish Mist. Season with salt and pepper. Allow ingredients to cook for a further 3 minutes. Take scallops from saucepan and place them in 4 empty scallop shells. Reduce sauce to half; add rest of the butter and the egg yolks. Once eggs are in sauce be careful not to overheat. Whisk together and pour the sauce over the scallops. Place under the broiler and glaze; serve immediately.

serves: 4

The Sir Walter Raleigh Room, Vancouver, British Columbia

Oysters Onassis

1 12-inch metal pie plate
1 8-inch shallow casserole dish
Sufficient rock salt to bed casserole dish firmly in pie plate
¼ cup chopped Spanish onion
1 tablespoon butter (salted)
6 medium-sized oysters
6 mushroom caps
3 or 4 slices pimento
1 cup saffron rice
4 lemon wedges

Heat pie plate-casserole assembly and rock salt to piping hot.
Sauté chopped onion in butter until soft. Add oysters, mushrooms, and pimento. Simmer 2 to 3 minutes (do not over-cook). Serve over saffron rice in hot casserole assembly with lemon wedges as garnish.

serves: 1

wine:
Rhine or
Moselle

Saffron rice

1 cup steamed rice
¼ cup onion, chopped
1 tablespoon butter
¼ teaspoon saffron
Salt
Pepper

Sauté onion in butter. Add saffron and cook 2 minutes. Mix well with rice and season with salt and pepper to taste.

The Four Seasons, New York City

Cheese and Oyster Soufflé

serves: 4

3 tablespoons butter
3 tablespoons flour
1 cup scalded milk
½ cup sharp, grated cheddar cheese
6 raw oysters
1 teaspoon salt
4 eggs, separated
1 additional egg white

Melt the butter and blend in the flour. Remove the pan from the heat (or cook over hot water in a double boiler). Gradually stir in the milk, blending it in smoothly. Return to the stove and continue cooking and stirring until the mixture is thick and smooth. Cool sauce lightly, add grated cheese, raw oysters that have been cut in julienne strips and salt. Beat the egg yolks until light and lemon colored and pour the cream mixture into them. Set aside. Beat the egg whites until they are stiff but still moist. Fold half of the egg whites into the cream sauce fairly well. Then fold the second half in very lightly. Pour the mixture into a greased soufflé dish or straight-sided casserole and bake, uncovered, in a 375° F. oven until the soufflé has puffed up and browned, about 35 minutes. Serve at once or it will fall.

Fiji Mocambo Hotel, Nadi Airport, Fiji
CHEF: JACORO

Kovu Vonu

(Baked Turtle)

serves: 4

wine:
Burgundy

1 pound (500 grams) onions
8 ounces (250 grams) hot chilis
3 tablespoons salt
1 tablespoon pepper
6 pounds (3 kilograms) fresh turtle meat

Dice onions, chop chilis finely, and dice turtle meat. Season with salt and pepper and mix well. Divide into 4 portions. Wrap each portion in a square of aluminum foil or in a banana or sugar-cane leaf if available. Bake in a 350° F. oven for 2 hours.
Note: Pork or beef can be substituted for turtle meat.

Normandie Grill, Oriental Hotel, Bangkok
CHEF: MICHEL GRANGE

Moules Farcies

20 mussels
½ cup white wine
2 tablespoons chopped shallots
Bouquet garni
1 teaspoon salt
6 peppercorns
Savory butter
½ cup fine bread crumbs
Lemon wedges

Choose only mussels that are tightly closed. Scrub shells thoroughly with a stiff brush and rinse in several changes of cool water.
In a deep pot combine wine, shallots, bouquet garni, salt, and peppercorns. Add mussels and steam only until shells open, 5 to 10 minutes. Discard any mussels that do not open. Discard "lid" part of shell and arrange the bottom shells containing the mussels on an ovenproof serving dish. Top each mussel with 2 teaspoons savory butter and sprinkle with fine bread crumbs. Place under broiler just long enough to brown crumbs. Serve with lemon wedges.

serves: 1

wine:
Muscadet

Savory butter

1 cup butter
2 cloves garlic, minced
3 tablespoons finely chopped shallots
2 anchovy fillets, chopped
2 tablespoons lemon juice
2 tablespoons very finely grated dry coconut
¼ cup dry white wine
2 tablespoons cognac

Let butter soften somewhat. Work all the other ingredients into butter. Chill if butter begins to melt—it should be soft but not liquid. Use as called for in recipe or with any seafood. Store in the refrigerator.

BOAC Cabin Service

Trout Carmelite

4 whole small trout
1 avocado
½ cup button mushrooms
1 cup white wine
Salt
Pepper
½ cup butter
2 egg yolks
½ cup cream

Clean the trout and remove the bones, cutting into the fish from the back, but leaving the head and tail intact. Stuff with a mixture of diced avocado and chopped mushrooms using only the best parts and leaving the remaining debris for the sauce. Poach in white wine *(Continued at foot of facing page*

serves: 4

Tarantino's, San Francisco, California
CHEF: DONALD E. LYNAM

Oysters Tarantino

serves: 1

wine:
Pinot
Chardonnay

½ cup cream sauce (see Index)
2 tablespoons raw spinach, finely chopped
1 green onion, finely chopped
4 teaspoons grated Parmesan cheese
2 tablespoons dry white wine
   Salt
   Pepper
2 egg yolks
   Rock salt
6 oysters and their half-shells
3 tablespoons melted butter
1 lemon, quartered

Place cream sauce in pan; add spinach, green onion, 1 teaspoon grated cheese, white wine, and salt and pepper to taste. Bring to a rolling boil, stirring constantly. Remove from heat. Beat egg yolks and beat a few tablespoons of hot sauce into them, then add to the sauce. Heat, stirring constantly. Put 6 mounds of rock salt in a pie tin and place the oyster shells in the mounds, making sure they will not tip over. Place the oysters in the shells, heap sauce on each oyster, sprinkle the rest of the grated cheese on top, and brush with melted butter. Bake in a 450° F. oven until golden brown.
Serve hot with lemon quarters.

Turkey

Baked Fish

serves: 4

2 pounds (1 kilogram) bass
½ cup olive oil
2 medium onions, sliced
¼ cup tomato paste
1½ cups water
3 cloves garlic, crushed
   Paprika
   Salt
   Juice of ½ lemon
3 stalks chopped celery
4 small carrots, diced
½ teaspoon parsley, chopped
   Lemon slices

Clean fish well, fillet it and cut into small slices, about 1 inch thick. Put ⅛ cup olive oil in a pan and fry onions until they are brown. Add tomato paste, water, garlic, paprika, salt, lemon juice, the rest of the olive oil, celery and carrots. Cover pan and cook for 25 minutes. Put fish slices in a deep baking dish and cover with sauce. Place in a 400° F. oven and bake for 25 minutes. Garnish with parsley and lemon slices.

Trout Carmelite (continued)

adding the remainder of the avocado and salt and pepper. Remove the trout, skin carefully and place in a buttered baking dish. Reduce the stock by half, stir in the butter and beaten egg yolks, and finish with cream. Coat the trout with the sauce and glaze under the broiler.

The White House Restaurant, London
CHEF: PETER GOSTICK

Sole de Douvres Tout-Paris

(Poached Dover Sole with Wine & Lobster Sauces)

4 1 pound fresh Dover soles
4 scallops of lobster tails
4 medium button mushrooms
⅓ pint vin blanc sauce
  Potatoes duchesse
4 fleurons
4 slices of black truffle
1½ pints of fish stock
½ pint Nantua sauce

Poach the skinned soles in the fish stock and when cooked clean off the side fins. Make a border of duchesse potatoes on a large oval dish and brown the potatoes slightly under the grill. Butter the dish, place the four soles in a row and put the cooked button mushrooms and cooked lobster tails on each sole. Coat one half of each sole with the Nantua Sauce, the other half with Vin Blanc Sauce. Garnish each sole with the truffles and fleurons.

serves: 4

wine:
Meursault—
Charmes

Nantua Sauce

¼ pint fish stock
¼ pint dry white wine
1 measure cooking brandy
¼ pint double cream
  Lobster butter
  Raw lobster coral
2 ounces flour
4 ounces butter

Reduce by a good third the fish stock with the dry white wine. Add the brandy and cream. Mix in the lobster butter and pass sauce through fine muslin.

Vin Blanc Sauce

¼ pint fish stock
¼ bottle dry white wine
1 pint fish velouté (white sauce made
  with fish stock)
4 ounces butter
¼ pint double cream
  Lemon juice
  Cayenne pepper

Reduce by a third the fish stock and dry white wine. Add the fish velouté, double cream, lemon juice and a touch of cayenne pepper.

The Empress, London
CHEF: GINO SCANDOLO

Filets de Sole Dugléré Froid

serves: 6

wine:
Sancerre,
Château de
Sancerre
1969, or
Beaune,
Clos des
Mouches
J. Drouhin
1966

3 large soles
½ clove garlic
¼ cup finely chopped shallots
½ cup fish stock
½ cup white wine
¼ cup tomato concasse
¾ cup light cream
2 tablespoons beurre manié
1 tablespoon fresh tarragon, chopped
1 egg yolk
3 tablespoons butter
Salt
Pepper
Juice of ½ lemon
Tabasco sauce
Chopped parsley

Fillet the soles and place them in a shallow buttered poaching pan. Season, rub with the garlic, and sprinkle with shallots. Add fish stock, wine, and tomato concasse. Cover with buttered paper and poach for approximately 6 minutes, until cooked but still firm. Drain the fillets and chill; reduce the liquor by a quarter. Add the cream and whisk in the beurre manié and fresh tarragon. Mix the egg yolk and the butter together and add to the sauce away from heat. Check the seasonings and allow to cool.
Place the cold fillets in a serving dish and sprinkle with lemon juice. Check the consistency of the cold sauce and finish with a suspicion of Tabasco. Decorate with chopped parsley.

Jamaica

Red Herring à la Dauphine

serves: 2

4 red herrings
2 cups milk
2 cups water
3 tablespoons butter
2 egg yolks
Fines herbes
Bread crumbs
Toast
Cayenne pepper

Remove heads, tails and backbone of herrings. Soak 1 hour or longer in warm milk and water. Drain, wipe dry. Melt butter and mix in yolks of eggs and fines herbes. Dip fish into mixture; spread thickly with fine bread crumbs. Fry over medium heat until clear brown. Serve on hot buttered toast. Sprinkle with cayenne pepper.

The Empress, London
CHEF: GINO SCANDOLO

Mousse of Avocado and Smoked Salmon

2 envelopes unflavoured gelatin
½ cup Béchamel sauce (see Index)
1 cup very heavy cream
6 ounces (185 grams) trimmings of smoked salmon
Juice of ½ lemon
Salt
Pepper
Cayenne
1 avocado, peeled and diced
Worcestershire sauce
Parsley sprigs

Soak gelatin in ½ cup water to soften. Divide the Béchamel equally between two saucepans and heat gently. Whip the cream lightly and put it in the refrigerator.
Take the trimmings of smoked salmon and gently simmer in the Béchamel until the salmon is soft; add half the gelatin and pass through a fine sieve. Place this purée in a basin, season with half the lemon juice, salt, pepper, and cayenne. When cold fold into this mixture half the whipped cream and put it into a mold in the refrigerator for about half an hour. Meanwhile take the rest of the Béchamel, also warmed, and add to it the avocado. Add the rest of the gelatin and heat until it dissolves; add the rest of the lemon juice and pass through a sieve. When cold, add the rest of the whipped cream, taking care it does not curdle.
Add salt and pepper and a dash of Worcestershire.
Fill the mold with this mixture (on top of the smoked-salmon mixture) and chill for about 1½ hours.
Unmold and garnish with parsley.

serves: 6

*wine:
Gewurz-
traminer
Grand Cru
Hugel 1967
or 1969*

The Savoy, London
CHEF: SILVINO S. TROMPETTO

Haddock Monte Carlo

2 smoked haddock
4 chopped peeled tomatoes
½ cup very heavy cream
Freshly ground pepper

Remove skin and bone from haddock; place the tomatoes and haddock in a buttered ovenproof dish sprinkled with pepper. Add cream. Cook in a 325° F. oven for 10 to 12 minutes and serve hot.

serves: 2

Malmaison Restaurant, Central Hotel, Glasgow
CHEF: JEAN MAURICE COTTET

La Casserolette de Filets de Sole des Maîtres Queux

Duxelles

serves: 4

wine:
Chablis

½ pound mushrooms, sliced
1 medium onion, finely chopped
1 clove garlic, minced
4 tablespoons butter

Cook sliced mushrooms, finely chopped onion, and minced garlic in butter on low heat until all liquid evaporates. Set aside and keep warm.

Filling

2 pounds (1 kilogram) fillets of sole
2 cups fish stock
½ cup dry white wine
2 cups very heavy cream
2 egg yolks
4 tablespoons whipped cream
  Salt
  Pepper
2 cooked lobster claws
4 large mushroom caps
2 tablespoons butter
½ pound (250 grams) puff-pastry dough
4 sprigs parsley
4 slices truffles

Poach sole in fish stock and white wine for 8 minutes. Remove and keep warm. Reduce stock to ¼ cup; add cream and reduce again until sauce thickens. Remove from heat; stir in egg yolks and fold in whipped cream. Season sauce with salt and pepper and keep warm. Dice lobster claws. Sauté mushroom caps in butter.

Shape 4 large individual pastry cases and 4 separate handles; bake on a pastry sheet until golden. Fill pastry cases with duxelles, fish, and lobster. Top with mushroom caps and cover with sauce. Place under broiler just long enough to brown the sauce lightly. Put handles in place to form baskets. Garnish with parsley sprigs and truffle slices.

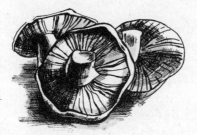

Bristol Hotel, Beirut, Lebanon
CHEF: NAGIB SFEIR

Brown Sayyadie

5½ pounds (2.5 kilograms) bass or
     similar fish
2½ teaspoons salt
1⅛ pound olive oil
 ½ pound (250 grams) onions, sliced
3¼ cups boiling water
    Juice of 2 lemons
 1 pound (500 grams) rice, cleaned
     and soaked in warm water
 ½ teaspoon ground cumin

Split small fish or fillet larger ones. Sprinkle with some of the salt and put in refrigerator for 2 hours. Heat oil in a large skillet; add onions and fry them until they become very dark (but not burned), turning them constantly. Add the onions to the boiling water and allow to cook until very soft. Pour into a strainer (reserve liquid). Mash onions through the strainer back into the water in a pot large enough to hold the fish. Add fish and rest of salt. Allow to boil about 40 minutes. Remove fish from broth. Also take out 1½ cups of broth. Reduce by one-third and add lemon juice. Reduce again by one-third and use hot as sauce over rice and fish. Add rice to the rest of the broth. Boil briskly at first, then reduce heat to moderate until rice is cooked. Serve the rice on a platter and the fish on another dish. Sprinkle cumin on rice.

serves: 4

*wine:
Hock*

Monarch Room, Royal Hawaiian Hotel, Honolulu
CHEF: ALEXANDER SCHLEMMER

Poached Salmon Mona Lisa

 2 pounds (1 kilogram) salmon
 ¼ cup butter
 ¼ cup cooked, chopped oysters
1½ teaspoons salt
 1 small onion, chopped fine
 1 cup Béchamel sauce (see Index)
 1 cup white wine
    Dash Worcestershire sauce
 ½ teaspoon white pepper

Cut the salmon into 4 pieces; remove the bones and skin and poach until fish flakes. Drain well and set aside; sauté for 2 minutes, then add white wine. Reduce wine for 5 minutes. Add Béchamel, Worcestershire, white pepper and cover poached salmon with sauce. Serve hot.

serves: 4

Bistro Bourgogne, Esso Motor Hotel, Amsterdam
CHEF: S. TOLSMA

Fillet of Halibut "Lafayette"

serves: 4

wine:
Pouilly-
Fuissé 1968

2 tablespoons butter
1¾ pound (875 grams) halibut, filleted
½ small leek, thinly sliced
1 teaspoon salt
1 bay leaf
1 sprig parsley, chopped
4 slices lemon, peeled
⅓ cup dry white wine
2 medium sweet red peppers, chopped
2 medium sweet green peppers, chopped
½ cup fresh mushrooms, sliced
4 fleurons (puff-pastry medallions)
4 whole sprigs parsley
1 lemon, quartered

Grease a copper pan with the butter. Sauté filleted halibut lightly with leek, salt, bay leaf, parsley, lemon slices, white wine, red and green peppers and mushrooms. When fillets are lightly browned, cover the pan with foil and cook slowly until fish flakes easily, about 10 minutes.

Fennel sauce

¼ cup white wine
2 tablespoons fennel vinegar
1 teaspoon salt
1 teaspoon freshly ground white pepper
1 bay leaf
1 tablespoon chopped onion
1 tablespoon fresh or dried fennel, or
    to taste
6 egg yolks
½ cup butter
    Chopped fennel for garnish.

Cook white wine, vinegar, salt, pepper, bay leaf, onion and fennel together until the mixture is quite thick and creamy. Sieve the mixture into a mixing bowl and beat in egg yolks thoroughly. Melt the butter and add it slowly to the sauce.
To serve, place fillets and vegetables on warm dinner plates. Decorate each plate with fleurons, a sprig of parsley, a lemon quarter and a sprinkling of chopped fennel. Pass sauce separately.

Promenade Café, New York City

Baked Salmon with Cucumbers and Frozen Horseradish

6 salmon steaks
  Juice of 2 lemons
¼ cup white vinegar
¼ cup white wine
1 teaspoon cracked pepper
1 tablespoon salt
½ bundle fresh dill
6 pats butter
  Turmeric
2 cucumbers, peeled, seeded and diced
  Dash Tabasco sauce
1 teaspoon lemon juice
  Salt
  Pepper
1 tablespoon butter
  Fresh dill for garnish

Cover a flat, deep dish with half of the dill; arrange salmon steaks on it. Cover the salmon with the remaining dill. Combine juice of 2 lemons, vinegar, wine, cracked pepper and salt and pour over fish. Cover dish and marinate overnight in refrigerator.

serves: 6

Conclusion. Place salmon in a well-buttered baking pan and sprinkle lightly with turmeric. Place 1 pat of butter on each salmon steak and bake in preheated oven at 375° F. for approximately 10 to 15 minutes or until tender. Be sure not to over-cook the salmon.

While salmon is in the oven, sauté cucumbers with salt, Tabasco and 1 teaspoon lemon juice in 1 table-spoon melted butter. Spread cucumbers over salmon just prior to serving and garnish with sprig of fresh dill. Pass horseradish sauce separately.

Frozen horseradish (to be prepared in advance)
  Juice of 1 lemon
½ cup white wine
  Pinch salt
  Pinch pepper
  Pinch sugar
1 cup heavy cream, whipped
½ cup fresh horseradish, grated

Combine lemon juice, wine, salt, pepper and sugar in saucepan and let simmer until reduced by two-thirds. Remove from heat and combine with whipped cream and fresh horse-radish making sure not to overstir. Place in serving container and freeze overnight.

Player's Grill, Johannesburg
CHEF: MICKY JOSEPH

Sole Cleopatra

serves: 1

Salt
Pepper
½ cup lemon juice
1 sole, filleted
Flour for dredging
4 tablespoons butter
1 tablespoon brown sauce
1 tablespoon chopped parsley
1 dozen tiny shrimp
6 button mushrooms
1 lemon, sliced
1 tomato, sliced

Mix salt, pepper and ⅓ cup lemon juice; place sole fillets in marinade and let stand in refrigerator for 2 hours. Drain and dry sole, dust with flour and fry in butter in a shallow pan. Set aside and keep warm. Prepare sauce of remaining lemon juice, brown sauce and chopped parsley. Sauté shrimp and mushrooms in butter. Spread shrimp and mushrooms over sole, then pour on sauce. Garnish with lemon and tomato slices.

The Lali Room, Suva TraveLodge, Suva, Fiji
CHEF: ERIC SHAANING

Kokoda

serves: 6

wine:
Chablis

3 pounds (1.5 kilograms) raw walu, rock cod or other white fish, skinned and boned
Juice of 5 large lemons
2 green peppers
2 large tomatoes
Milk of 2 coconuts
1 teaspoon Tabasco sauce
2 teaspoons salt
1 teaspoon pepper
1 small head lettuce
2 tablespoons parsley, chopped
2 lemons cut in wedges

Cut the fish into ½-inch chunks and cover with the lemon juice. Cover and place in the refrigerator for at least 12 hours to allow the fish to marinate. Chop the green pepper and tomato (skinned and seeded). Remove the milk from the coconuts, grate the coconut meat and squeeze out in clean cheese-cloth; add this "cream" to the coconut milk. Add to the marinated fish the tomato, green pepper, the coconut milks, Tabasco sauce, salt and pepper. Return mixture, covered, to the refrigerator for another hour. Serve very cold on a bed of lettuce; sprinkle with chopped parsley and garnish with lemon wedges.

Hong Kong

Tso Lau Ue Pin
(Fried Fish with Chinese Vinegar)

**1 pound (500 grams) smoked haddock or
  cod, cut in 2-inch slices**
  Salt to taste
  Dash monosodium glutamate
1 egg white
2 tablespoons cornstarch
1 teaspoon Chinese wine
  Oil for frying

Wash and dry fish fillets. Season
with salt and monosodium glutamate.
Mix egg white with starch and wine.
Dip fillets in batter and deep fry in
hot oil for 2 minutes.

serves: 2

Sauce

 1 tablespoon lard
 ¼ teaspoon Chinese vinegar
 1 tablespoon stock
  Dash monosodium glutamate
  Salt to taste
  Sugar
 2 tablespoons wine sauce
 ½ teaspoon starch and cold water
 2 tablespoons chicken fat
 ½ teaspoon chopped spring onion
 ½ teaspoon ginger oil

Heat lard in frying pan. Add
vinegar, stock, monosodium
glutamate, salt, sugar, wine sauce
and starch mixed with cold water,
stirring constantly until sauce is
thick. Then add chicken fat, spring
onion and ginger oil, and mix well.
Place fish on plate and pour on
sauce. Serve hot.

Chile

Codfish Biscay

2 pounds (1 kilogram) cod
1 cup olive oil
1 clove garlic
2 onions, thinly sliced
3 tomatoes, peeled
½ pimento, sliced
1 tablespoon chopped parsley
  Bay leaf
  Tabasco sauce
  Pepper
½ cup white wine
2 pounds potatoes

Soak cod in warm water 12 hours,
changing water several times. Drain,
cut into 2-inch pieces and then into
strips. Heat oil in deep pan and fry
garlic gently; remove. Fry onion
slowly. Chop tomatoes; retain
juice. Put tomato and juice in pan,
with pimento, parsley, bay leaf,
Tabasco sauce and pepper. Mix;
cook for ½ minute. Stir in strips of
cod and wine. Simmer for 20
minutes, or until fish is tender.
Serve on a large hot platter
surrounded with boiled potatoes.

serves: 6-8

The Savoy, London
CHEF: SILVINO S. TROMPETTO

La Mousseline de Sole Fecampoise

serves:
8 as hors
d'oeuvres
4 as fish
course

1 pound (500 grams) fillet of sole
1 tablespoon salt
2 egg whites
4 cups very heavy cream

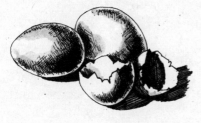

Mince the fillet of sole fine and pass it through a very fine sieve. Place in a saucepan and set pan in larger pan of crushed ice. Add salt and mix thoroughly until fish purée is firm. Add the egg whites one at a time, stirring slowly and continuously for about 3 minutes after each addition. Add cream slowly, stirring in until all the cream is used. When the mixture has hardened, scoop it out with a large spoon and poach, covered completely, in just simmering water or fish stock. Cook very slowly for 10 to 15 minutes. Remove quenelles from poaching liquid with a slotted spoon and drain thoroughly. Serve with Newburg sauce (i.e. a rich sauce flavored with lobster and sherry).

Top of the Town, Hotel Inter-Continental, Auckland, New Zealand

Trout Hamurana

serves: 4

1 rainbow trout
Fish stock (see Index)
1½ pints aspic jelly
20 peeled prawns
Truffles
¾ pint mayonnaise
2 hard-boiled eggs
4 tomatoes
16 asparagus tips
8 artichoke bottoms

Poach the trout in a well seasoned fish stock and allow to cool in the stock. Drain. Arrange the trout on a dish. Remove the skin from the middle section and glaze with aspic jelly. Garnish with prawns, truffles and piped mayonnaise.
As a garnish use the eggs, sliced and decorated with slices of tomato and truffles and cooked asparagus tips, held in place on the artichoke bottoms with aspic.

Le Coq d'Or, London
CHEF: JEAN C. BRESNIER

Les Quenelles de Brochet Nantua

¾ cup fine stale bread crumbs
1½ cups milk
4 pound (2 kilograms) pike (or other firm
    white fish)
  Salt
  Pepper
2 eggs, separated
¼ pound butter
6 cups fish stock or chicken broth
1 truffle, sliced
2 crayfish tails, cooked and sliced

serves: 4-6

Place bread crumbs and milk in a heavy saucepan. Cook over medium heat (do not scorch) stirring often with a wooden spoon. When mixture holds its shape, remove from heat and cool.

Chop pike through the finest mill. Add salt and pepper and mix well using an electric mixer. Add 2 egg whites one at a time; while still mixing add the bread-crumb mixture gradually. Still mixing, gradually add butter, then the 2 egg yolks.

Let the mixture stand for an hour in the refrigerator. Mold between two spoons making egg shapes and poach in light fish stock for 7 or 8 minutes.

Serve with light cream sauce (see Index) and garnish with sliced truffles and crayfish tails.

Le Morne Brabant Hotel, Mauritius

Fish Vindaye

2 pounds (1 kilogram) white fish fillets
  Salt
  Pepper
  Flour for dredging
  Oil for frying
2 teaspoons turmeric
2 teaspoons dry mustard
1 tablespoon chili powder
4 medium onions, sliced
½ cup olive oil
2 tablespoons vinegar

serves: 4

Season fillets with salt and pepper. Dredge in flour and sauté until very lightly browned in hot cooking oil. In the same skillet, fry spices, which have been mixed together and ground finely in a mortar with a pestle or with oil in a blender, and onion. Stir frequently for about 10 minutes. Taste for salt. Add vinegar (taste; add more if necessary). Return fillets to sauce and cook about 10 minutes. Do not overcook; fish should hold its shape.

French Restaurant, Midland Hotel, Manchester, England
CHEF: GILBERT LEFEVRE

Braised Salmon Trout with Lettuce Leaves

serves: 5-6

wine:
Batand-
Montrachet
1969

1 2-pound (1-kilogram) salmon trout
5 chopped shallots
  Salt
  Pepper
½ pound (250 grams) fish forcemeat,
    whiting or silver hake
18 green lettuce leaves
1 cup dry white wine
1 cup rich fish stock
½ pound (250 grams) butter
½ pound potatoes (250 grams), cooked,
    mashed, and seasoned
3 egg yolks
½ cup whipped cream
6 mushrooms
6 slices truffles
1 tablespoon meat glaze
6 pastry fleurons

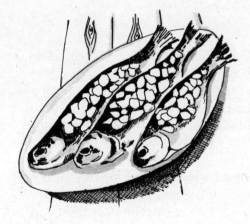

Scale a fresh salmon trout, cut the fins off and with a sharp knife open the fish along the backbone and clean the inside. Wash well and dry carefully.

Put the chopped shallots, salt and pepper into a buttered ovenware dish slightly larger than the fish. Place the fish on its belly in the dish on the bed of shallots; cover the fish with the fish forcemeat and cover the whole dish with 6 blanched lettuce leaves. (Keep the remainder for a purée.) Add the white wine, the fish stock and 2 ounces of butter. Bring slowly to a boil, then cover with a sheet of buttered cooking parchment and cook in a 350° F. oven until fish flakes easily. Baste often. When the fish is cooked, transfer it to a serving dish decorated beforehand with a mixture of two-thirds mashed potatoes, one-third cooked lettuce purée mixed and bound with egg yolks. Keep hot.

Strain the braising liquid into a small pan and reduce it by one third. Skim the top and add the remainder of the butter, gently whisking well for consistency. Add the whipped cream, correct the seasoning to taste. Ornament the fish with mushrooms, coat it with the sauce and glaze quickly under the broiler. On each mushroom put a slice of black truffle glazed with meat glaze and arrange the pastry fleurons around the fish.

Speke Hotel, Kampala, Uganda
CHEF: ABDUL R. KHATIB

Muhogo Na Samaki Wa Kupaka

(Cassava with Coconut Grilled Fish)

Cassava

2 pounds (1 kilogram) cassava
2 onions, large, sliced
   Liquid from two coconuts (two cups)
   Salt to taste

Boil cassava in a large open sauce-pan for 15 minutes; drain. Add onions and coconut juice. Let mixture boil for 15 minutes more, until the juice becomes thick. Taste for salt and serve.

serves: 4

wine:
White
Bordeaux
"Sauternes"

Fish

½ pound (250 grams) onions, diced
1 pound (500 grams) tomatoes, peeled and
   seeded
2 teaspoons curry powder
   Liquid from 2 coconuts
2 pounds (1 kilogram) whole grilled
   tilapia (or other firm white fish)

Cook onions, tomatoes and curry powder together for 15 minutes. Add coconut juice and boil until juice thickens. Put fish on serving plates. Pour the sauce over the fish and cooked cassava.

Biggs Restaurant, Chicago
CHEF: BRIAN KUZMAN

Poached Fish Cubaine

4 filets sole, turbot or flounder
1 shallot, minced
1 carrot, chopped
½ cup celery, chopped
1 bay leaf
4 peppercorns
   Salt
1 can condensed cream of mushroom soup
¼ pound cooked shrimp, shelled and
   deveined
¼ pound crab meat, flaked
⅓ cup heavy cream, whipped

Place filets in a shallow pan. Add shallot, carrot, celery, bay leaf, and peppercorns, and sprinkle with salt. Add just enough water to cover fish. Simmer until fish turns white and flakes easily. Carefully put filets on a platter and keep them warm. Heat soup and add shrimp and crab meat. Fold whipped cream into sauce and reheat just until sauce bubbles. Spoon sauce over fish. Serve garnished with parsley.

serves: 4

Ruwenzori Room, Apolo Hotel, Kampala, Uganda
CHEF: F. PEREIRA

Engege Apolo

serves: 2

wine:
Chablis

1 pound (500 grams) whole tilapia lake fish
Salt
Pepper
1 teaspoon curry powder
Olive oil for frying
1 onion
2 large ripe tomatoes
2 sweet green peppers
1 small lime
Chopped parsley

Clean the tilapia, season it with salt, pepper and curry powder and fry in oil on both sides until golden. Slice the onion, 1 tomato and 1 green pepper and fry in the same oil. Squeeze the juice of half the lime into this mixture and pour it on the tilapia. Cover with foil and bake for 10 minutes at 375° F. Serve on a flat silver dish decorated with the other tomato and sliced green pepper, chopped parsley and lime wedges.

Kahala Hilton, Honolulu
CHEF: MARTIN WYSS

Opakapaka Caprice

serves: 4

4 6-ounce (180-gram) fillets opakapaka
(red snapper)
Salt
White pepper
¼ pound (125 grams) butter
1 shallot, finely chopped
6 fresh mushrooms, sliced
Lemon juice
⅓ cup white wine
1 tablespoon flour
½ cup half-and-half (milk and cream)
½ cup whipped cream
1 egg yolk
2 bananas
4 teaspoons chopped parsley

Season opakapaka with salt and pepper. Sauté in half the butter. In a separate saucepan, sauté shallot in the rest of the butter. Add sliced mushrooms, salt, pepper, a few drops of lemon juice, and white wine. Cook rapidly until wine has almost evaporated. Mix 4 tablespoons of soft butter with 2 tablespoons of flour and blend with the mushrooms.
Reduce heat to low. Add half-and-half and simmer for a few minutes. Remove from the fire. Blend in whipped cream and egg yolk. Pour sauce into 4 shirred-egg or similar dishes. Place fish on sauce and top each serving with half a peeled banana cut lengthwise and lightly sautéed. Glaze in oven and sprinkle with chopped parsley.

Century Plaza Hotel, Los Angeles
CHEF: WALTER ROTH

Darne de Saumon Commodore Armstrong

6 6-ounce (185-gram) salmon fillets
  Salt
  Pepper
  Seasoned salt
12 shrimp, shelled and deveined
6 oysters, shucked
3 teaspoons chopped shallots
3 cups extra dry champagne
3 teaspoons lemon juice
3 cups fish—white wine sauce
6 tablespoons cream
½ tablespoon brandy
6 teaspoons lobster butter (see Index)
6 puff pastry medallions, baked
6 truffle slices

Season fillets with salt, pepper and seasoned salt and place in a large buttered saucepan. Add shrimp, oysters and shallots. Pour champagne over fish and cook slowly 6 to 8 minutes, until fish is done.

Transfer fish to a serving platter and keep warm. Arrange the shrimp and oysters over the salmon. Mix lemon juice and fish-white wine sauce in saucepan and bring to a boil. Cook the sauce 3 to 4 minutes, then add cream, brandy and lobster butter. Cook again for 2 minutes and season to taste. Pour sauce over the salmon fillets and garnish with pastry medallions and truffle slices. Serve immediately.

serves: 6

wine: Pinot Chardonnay, Wente Brothers (1968)

Waterlot Inn, Southampton, Bermuda
CHEF: PETER SCHMID

Bermuda Ocean Delight

1 4-pound (2-kilogram) rock fish
2 medium bread rolls
1 medium onion, chopped
¼ cup carrots, chopped
¼ cup celery, chopped
1 sprig parsley
2 eggs
  Pinch salt
  Pinch pepper
  Pinch thyme
  Pinch fennel
¾ cup butter, half melted, half clarified
2 tablespoons rum

Wipe fish with damp cloth. Clean, split, and remove all bones possible. (The best method is to cut the fish from head to tail along the upper back edge.) Set aside. Soak bread rolls in water; when soft squeeze out water. Fry onion and remove from heat; add carrots, celery, parsley, bread, eggs, and spices. Beat all well together. Stuff the fish and stitch up. Place in pan with a little melted butter and brush fish well with melted butter. Bake for 1 hour at 350° F., basting with the butter occasionally. Serve immediately with clarified butter with the rum added.

serves: 4

wine: Meursault "Les Chevalières D'Or" 1967

Mussels "Mayflower"　　　BISTRO BOURGOGNE, ESSO MOTOR HOTEL, AMSTERDAM
(Chef: S. Tolsma)

*Langoustines Flambés
Amoureuses*

HOTEL IMPERIAL,
COPENHAGEN
(Chef: Holger Andersen)

Lobster Curry

La Boucan Specialty Restaurant, Trinidad Hilton Hotel, Port of Spain, Trinidad
CHEF: HANS ZACH

Stuffed Red Snapper

serves: 2

wine:
Chablis 1966

1 tablespoon chopped onions
1 tablespoon chopped chives
1 tablespoon chopped celery
1 tablespoon chopped ham
1 clove garlic
1 peeled chopped tomato
2 slices soaked toasted bread
12 mangrove oysters (or mussels)
1 tablespoon chip chip (or baby clams)
1 egg yolk
  Salt
  Pepper
  Tabasco sauce
1 1-pound (500-gram) red snapper
3 cleaned shrimp
1 tablespoon butter
½ cup fish stock
½ cup dry white wine
4 lime wedges
1 tablespoon chopped parsley

Sauté the onions, chives, celery, ham and garlic. Add the tomato and soaked toasted bread (pressed dry) and the oysters, chip chip and egg yolk. Season to taste with salt, pepper and a dash of Tabasco sauce.
Remove head and tail from fish. Clean from head end; do not slit belly or back. Wash well and stuff with onion-seafood mixture. Garnish with the shrimp. Place in a buttered baking dish, add fish stock and white wine until one-fourth of the fish is covered. Bake in the oven at 350°F. for 25 minutes. Place the fish on a platter and garnish with lime wedges and parsley. Serve with white sauce.

Café Henry Burger, Hull, Quebec
CHEF: WERNER LEDERMANN

Fruits de Mer à la Newburg

serves: 4

wine:
Meursault,
Chablis, etc.

3 tablespoons butter
4 fresh boiled lobsters
1 cup fresh sliced mushrooms
1 pound (500 grams) cooked shelled
  shrimp
2 pounds (1 kilogram) fresh steamed
  mussels, shucked
½ teaspoon paprika
  Dash of cayenne, nutmeg, ginger
1½ tablespoons flour
¼ cup shooting sherry
1 tablespoon port
2½ cups cream
½ teaspoon dry mustard
2 egg yolks
6 thin slices truffles
3 cups cooked rice

Melt butter in a heavy saucepan. Add the meat of the lobsters, cut in 1-inch pieces, the sliced mushrooms, shrimp, and mussels. Sprinkle with paprika and cayenne and simmer for 2 minutes, stirring gently all the time. Add flour and mix in well, being careful not to break seafood pieces; add sherry and port. Then blend in 2 cups cream, mustard, spices, and salt. Beat egg yolks with ½ cup cream; add to the seafood mixture just before serving. Remove from heat and pour into a chafing dish. Top with truffle slices and serve with fluffy rice.

.–C

Pilot House Hotel, Nassau, Bahamas

Baked Bahamian Grouper Nassau Style

1 6-pound (3-kilogram) grouper with head
    and tail
Salt
Pepper
Juice of 1 lemon
¼ cup cooking oil
1 onion, sliced
½ sweet pepper, sliced
6 stewed tomatoes
½ teaspoon thyme

Rub the cleaned fish with salt, pepper and lemon juice and lay on a baking dish greased with oil. Chop onion and sweet pepper and fry in hot oil. Add the tomatoes and thyme. Cook gently for 15 to 20 minutes, then pour the mixture over the fish. Bake in a 350° F. oven for 25 minutes. Serve with plain white rice or Bahamian peas and rice.

serves: 6

wine:
dry white
wine

Bahamian peas and rice
1 medium onion, chopped
1 tomato, peeled, seeded and chopped
3 tablespoons bacon fat
1 #2 can pigeon peas
4 cups water
1½ cups raw rice
Salt
Pepper
1 teaspoon thyme

Sauté onion and tomato in fat until onion is soft. Add pigeon peas and water. Bring to a boil and add rice, salt to taste, pepper, and thyme. Cook slowly, covered, until rice is done and the mixture is almost dry.

Three Star Beach Hotel, Port Elizabeth, South Africa

Fillet of Sole Capri

1 center-cut fillet of sole, about 8 ounces
    (250 grams)
Salt
White pepper
3 tablespoons butter
¼ cup dry white wine
1 teaspoon paprika
¼ cup grated mild cheese
½ cup sliced fresh mushrooms
½ cup whole cooked small shrimp
Celery sticks
Parsley sprigs

Dry fillet thoroughly and sprinkle with salt and pepper. Melt butter and pour 1 tablespoon into a baking dish large enough to hold the fillet without crowding. Place fillet in dish and baste with butter. Place in a 350° F. oven for about 5 minutes or until sole is opaque but not quite tender. Baste often until butter is used up. Mix wine, paprika, and cheese and pour over fish. Cook another 5 minutes. Spread mushrooms and *(Continued at foot of facing page*

serves: 2

wine:
chilled rosé

Maison Prunier, London
CHEF: JEAN LECORRE

Grillade au Fenouil

(John Dory)

serves: 4

2 1½-pound (750-gram) John Dory or turbot
2 bunches dried fennel
2 tablespoons brandy

wine:
Muscadet
1966

Quickly brown the fish on both sides under the broiler, then put it in a 250° F. oven for 20 minutes. When cooked, lay the fish on a rack which will fit over a heatproof dish. Lay dried fennel on the dish underneath the rack and pour brandy over it; ignite. As it burns, turn the fish so that both sides receive some of the fragrant flavoring of the burning herb and brandy.

Sauce Fenouil

2 tablespoons peppercorns
1 tablespoon star aniseed
1 tablespoon fresh fennel
¾ cup dry white wine
1 tablespoon vinegar
1 cup cream
6 tablespoons butter
Salt

In a saucepan place peppercorns, star aniseed and fennel, all roughly crushed, wine and vinegar. Cook until reduced to 2 tablespoons. Add cream and when mixture boils again, put in butter. Cook and stir vigorously for 1 minute, then remove from heat. Strain into a sauceboat and serve separately.

Fillet of Sole Capri (continued)

shrimp over fillet and baste well with pan juices. Continue cooking, basting often, until sole flakes easily, about 5 or 10 minutes more. Do not overcook. To serve, carefully remove fillet and garnishes to a hot platter. Pour pan juices over fish and decorate with celery sticks and sprigs of parsley.

Restaurant des Ambassadeurs, George Hotel, Edinburgh, Scotland
CHEF: G. PRANDSTATTER

Cullen Skink

2 small onions, sliced
2 small carrots, sliced
1 bay leaf
1½ pounds (750 grams) finnan haddock
½ pound (250 grams) butter
½ cup flour
5 cups hot milk
Salt to taste
White pepper, freshly ground
1 cup cream
¼ cup chopped parsley

Gently cook the onions, carrots, bay leaf, and 1 pound of skinned finnan haddock in ½ cup butter in a thick-bottomed pan. Do not allow to brown. Mix in the flour and cook over gentle heat to a sandy texture without browning. Remove from heat and cool. Gradually mix in the hot milk and add seasoning. Stir while bringing barely to a boil and simmer gently for 1 hour. Poach the remaining finnan haddock and flake it carefully. Strain the soup through a very fine sieve and put it in a clean saucepan. Reboil, correct the seasoning, add the cream, remaining butter, flaked finnan haddock, and chopped parsley. Serve very hot.

serves: 8

wine:
Florio
Marsala

Sulo Restaurant and Cocktail Lounge, Rizal, Philippines

Inasal Na Isda

(Fish Chunks on Skewers)

1½-pound (750-gram) Spanish mackerel,
    cut into chunks
4 pieces calamansi (native limes)
    or ½ lemon
Salt
Pepper
2 onions
2 green peppers
1 eggplant
4 medium tomatoes
1 cup butter
10 slices bacon

Season fish chunks with calamansi or lemon juice; salt and pepper to taste. Set aside and let stand for 30 minutes. Sauté all vegetables, cut in wedges, in hot butter separately. Transfer to serving container. Wrap fish chunks in bacon slices and arrange on skewers, about five chunks each. Cook over charcoal broiler or griddle until done. Garnish with the sautéed vegetables.

serves: 4

wine:
Petit Chablis,
Dircks &
Fils

Hotel Southern Cross, Melbourne, Australia
CHEF: H. KAHN

Fillet of South Australian Whiting Capricornia

Sauce

serves: 6

Juice of 2 lemons
1 cup chablis
5 egg yolks
Salt
Pepper
½ pound (250 grams) melted butter

In the top of a double boiler, over hot, not boiling water, mix lemon juice, wine, egg yolks, salt and pepper and beat until mixture sticks to whisk. Take care not to overcook. Remove from over hot water and beat a few more minutes; then add butter, blending in small amounts at a time. Keep this delicate sauce in a warm place; do not beat any more.

Garnish

¾ pound (375 grams) apples
¾ pound (375 grams) pineapple
¼ pound (125 grams) butter
2 tablespoons lemon juice

Cut apples and pineapple into julienne strips. Cook for 1 minute in ¼ pound butter with 2 tablespoons lemon juice added; set aside.

Fish

12 4-ounce (125-gram) fillets whiting
Juice of 3 lemons
Salt
Pepper
1½ cups flour
2 tablespoons paprika
½ cup melted butter
6 ounces macadamia nuts, toasted
Lemon wedges
12 sprigs parsley

Remove all bones from fish and marinate for at least 30 minutes in lemon juice, salt and pepper. Dust with flour and paprika mixed, then brush with butter. Place in a baking pan ready for broiling or fry in a large pan. Cook only until fish flakes.
Place fish fillets on an oval server. On top of each fillet put a portion of the fruit and sprinkle with toasted and crushed macadamia nuts. Decorate with lemon wedges and parsley. Serve the sauce separately.

The Coachman Restaurant, Wellington, New Zealand
CHEF: DES BRITTEN

New Zealand Sole Stuffed with Bluff Oysters, Shrimp and Nelson Scallops

4 1-pound (500-gram) whole soles
16 oysters
8 tablespoons shrimp
16 scallops
Salt
½ cup clarified butter
1 teaspoon rosemary (optional)
Mornay sauce
2 tablespoons grated cheese
4 tablespoons chopped parsley

Skin soles with a sharp, pointed knife and make a slit down the center bone. Slide the knife under the flesh on each side to make two pockets. Place 2 oysters in each pocket. In the gap down the center, lay 2 tablespoons shrimp. Top the shrimp with 4 scallops sliced in half. Season the soles lightly with salt and brush generously all over with clarified butter. If you like the flavor, a light sprinkling of rosemary will give an interesting taste. Place the soles under a hot broiler until they are cooked through. When the underside of the sole has lost its transparency, remove immediately from heat. Pour off any excess clarified butter and pour on some mornay sauce. Top with the grated cheese and put back under the broiler for a few minutes, just until lightly browned. Sprinkle with chopped parsley and serve.

serves: 4

wine:
White
Burgundy

Mornay sauce
2 tablespoons butter
4 tablespoons flour
½ teaspoon salt
Freshly ground white pepper
1½ cups boiling milk
Pinch freshly grated nutmeg
Pinch cayenne pepper
¼ cup grated cheese

Melt the butter over medium heat. Stir in the flour, salt, and pepper. Cook together for 2 minutes. Remove the white roux from the heat and when the mixture has stopped bubbling, pour in all the hot milk and beat with a wire whisk until it is thoroughly blended

(Continued at foot of facing page

Restaurant Ab Sofus, Göteborg, Sweden
CHEF: FRIEDRICH SCHWAKE

Salmon Soufflé

serves: 4

wine:
White
Burgundy

6 egg yolks
3 cups light cream
½ cup flour
2 pounds (1 kilogram) fresh salmon
    without skin and bones
2 ounces (60 grams) smoked salmon
    without skin and bones
10 egg whites
    Salt
    Freshly ground white pepper
1 tablespoon dry white wine
3 teaspoons arrowroot
    Butter for greasing soufflé dishes

Combine egg yolks, 1 cup cream and 1½ tablespoons flour. Bring to a boil, beating constantly. Put aside to cool.

Run the fresh and smoked salmon through a fine mincer 3 times. Put the minced fish in a pan and over ice. Carefully stir in 3 unbeaten egg whites and 2 cups cream. Add salt and pepper to taste. Mix with the cool egg-yolk mixture and pass through a fine strainer.

Take 8 tablespoons of the sieved mixture and add to it the wine and arrowroot. Beat 7 egg whites until very stiff and glossy and mix in carefully. Generously butter and flour 4 soufflé dishes 6 inches in diameter. Fill the dishes to the top with the soufflé mixture and bake at 350° F. for 10 minutes. Increase the heat to 400° F. and bake another 20 minutes. Cover the soufflés with foil the last 15 minutes. Serve at once with a fine white wine sauce.

Mornay sauce (continued)

and smooth. Simmer over low heat for 1 minute, stirring all the time. Remove from the heat and add fresh nutmeg and grated cayenne pepper. Stir in the grated cheese. Check seasonings carefully by tasting. Skim the surface with butter if the sauce is not to be used immediately. This will prevent a skin forming.

Waterlot Inn, Southampton, Bermuda
CHEF: PETER SCHMID

Crêpes Scandinavia

1 egg
¼ cup flour
1 cup milk
  Few drops oil
  Pinch salt
  Pinch sugar
  Butter for frying

Filling

1 medium onion, chopped
4 ounces (125 grams) smoked salmon,
  chopped
2 hard-boiled eggs, chopped
  Fresh ground dill
  Chopped parsley
  Fish sauce

Fish sauce

2 tablespoons butter
3 tablespoons flour
2 tablespoons white wine
1 cup fish stock

Hollandaise sauce

½ cup butter
 2 egg yolks
 1 tablespoon white wine
  Few drops lemon juice
  Few drops Worcestershire sauce
  Salt to taste
  Chopped parsley

Beat all ingredients together until smooth. Grease a small hot pan with a few drops of melted butter; tilt pan to one side and pour ⅛ of the mixture gently until bottom of pan is covered. When mixture is slightly colored and firm, quickly turn and then remove. Repeat for a total of 8 crêpes.

Fry onion until brown; add salmon and eggs. Add spices and fish sauce and mix well. Let boil once. Put this mixture into crêpes and roll. Place on silver serving platter and leave in 450° F. oven for 3 minutes.

Make a roux with butter and flour; add wine and 1 cup fish stock made by boiling fish bones, 1 bay leaf, 3 cloves, and a slice of onion in water for 30 minutes, then remove bones. Boil sauce for 30 minutes more. Add no salt.

Clarify butter. Mix egg yolks, white wine, lemon juice, and Worcestershire. Beat this mixture over hot water until it starts to thicken. Remove from heat but keep beating until mixture cools slightly. Slowly beat warm clarified butter into the mixture and add a little salt if required.
Conclusion: Cover crêpes with a little of this sauce and grill briefly until golden brown and glazed. Sprinkle with chopped parsley and serve.

serves: 4

wine:
Bernkastler
Green Label
Deinhard
1968
(medium-dry white wine)

Maison Prunier, London
CHEF: JEAN LECORRE

Terrine Dieppoise

serves: 6

wine:
Chablis
1969

2 pounds (1 kilogram) mussels
2 pounds (1 kilogram) turbot
2 pounds (1 kilogram) sole
1 pound (500 grams) red mullet
½ pound (250 grams) shrimp
2 leeks
1½ pounds (750 grams) onions, shredded
1 bunch celery
1 bottle dry white wine
1 sprig thyme
1 bay leaf
6 parsley stalks
1½ teaspoons salt
Pinch cayenne
3 slices bread
5 ounces (150 grams) butter
2 cups cream

Cook the mussels just until the shells open in a large pot with 1 inch of water on the bottom. Do not overcook. Remove mussels and set aside. Reserve cooking liquid. Make a fish stock by using the fish heads cut into pieces and adding the cooking water from the mussels. Add the leeks, onions, celery, white wine, thyme, bay leaf and parsley stalks. Cook for 30 minutes.

Place the pieces of fish and the shrimp in a saucepan. Season with salt and cayenne, add the fish stock and cook very slowly for 15 minutes.

Cut the bread with a heart-shaped cookie cutter and sauté in 2 tablespoons butter over medium heat until crisp. Set aside.

Place the pieces of fish in a shallow dish with the mussels, shelled, and the shrimp on top of the fish. Reduce the fish stock for a few minutes to give more flavor. Add cream and the rest of the butter and pass through a fine sieve. Pour the sauce evenly over seafood, sprinkle with croûtons and serve at once.

The Empress, London
CHEF: GINO SCANDOLO

Matelote d'Anguille Château du Verdom

5 pounds (2.5 kilograms) eels
½ pound (250 grams) butter
  Mirepoix of vegetables
  Bouquet garni
  Salt
  Pepper
¾ cup flour
⅓ cup cognac
1⅓ cup Burgundy wine
2 cups fish stock
⅔ cup brown sauce
  Juice of 1 lemon
½ pound (250 grams) button onions
2 teaspoons sugar
½ pound button mushrooms
10 ounces (300 grams) fresh soft fish roe
12 prawns
¼ cup chopped parsley
12 slices French bread (cut in croûtons)
2 whole cloves garlic

Skin and wash the eels and cut into portions 2 inches thick. Fry in the butter with mirepoix and bouquet garni; season. When the eel and vegetables are brown, sprinkle with flour and cook for 2 minutes, then flame with the cognac. Add the Burgundy and reduce the liquid for 2 minutes. Add the fish stock, cover the pan, and cook for a further 15 minutes. Remove eel pieces from pan, add the brown sauce, and reduce the sauce. Pass the sauce through a fine sieve, adjust the seasoning, and add the lemon juice. Add 4 tablespoons butter to the sauce piece by piece, beating in thoroughly.

Parboil the button onions; drain. Finish by sautéing in a little butter and sugar to glaze until golden brown. Fry the button mushrooms in butter. Poach the soft roe in a little water.

Place this garnish in a shallow casserole; add the eel and the prawns. Reheat the sauce and add the chopped parsley just before serving. Pour over the dish. Toast the croûtons, rub them with garlic, and serve separately.

serves: 6

*wine:
Gewurz-
traminer
Grand Crû
Hugel 1967
or 1969*

The Nine Muses, Hollywood, California
CHEF: HARLEY WHITE

Frog Legs à la Nine Muses

serves: 4

wine:
Chablis or
Rhine wine

12 pairs small frog legs
¼ cup lemon juice
¼ cup light cream
   Salt
   White pepper
½ cup butter
2 teaspoons minced shallots or garlic
1 tablespoon minced onion
1 cup dry white wine
½ cup Marsala
3 large or 4 small oysters, minced
½ cup sliced sautéed mushrooms
   (optional)
   Dash cayenne
½ cup grated Gruyère or jack cheese
1 lemon, sliced

Soak frog legs in very cold water for 3 hours. Drain on cloth. Dip in mixture of lemon juice and cream. Sprinkle sparingly with salt and white pepper.

Melt butter in medium skillet. Stir in shallots and onion. Add frog legs. Sauté very slowly for 3 minutes on each side. Add white wine and ¼ cup Marsala. Poach gently, turning once, for 15 minutes, or until tender (flesh should be white and opaque). Remove frog legs to ovenproof platter or casserole. Strain pan juices into small saucepan. Add minced oysters, mushrooms, and remaining ¼ cup Marsala. Simmer 10 to 15 minutes or just until alcohol is cooked out. Season with cayenne and salt to taste.

Pour this sauce over frog legs. Sprinkle with grated cheese. Place in hot oven or broiler for 3 to 5 minutes, until cheese is bubbly and lightly browned. Serve immediately. Garnish with lemon wedges and fried parsley.

Fried parsley
2 bunches parsley
   Oil for deep frying

Wash parsley and separate into sprigs. Dry thoroughly, then drop into very hot cooking oil. Fry 3 to 5 minutes. Remove from oil when parsley is a deep green. Drain on absorbent paper.

The Four Seasons, New York City

Chicken in Champagne with Truffles

3 chicken breasts
¼ cup melted butter
  Salt
  Pepper

Have the chicken breasts skinned, halved, and boned, leaving the upper part of the wing on and removing the wing tip. Place chicken in a shallow baking dish and brush with melted butter. Season lightly. Cover dish. Bake in a 375° F. oven 8 to 12 minutes, or until chicken springs back when pressed with the finger. Remove to serving platter. Reserve pan drippings. Keep warm in a low oven.

serves: 6

Sauce

½ cup chopped shallots
¼ cup butter
1½ cups champagne
½ teaspoon salt
½ teaspoon sugar (optional)
1 tablespoon flour
2 white truffles, sliced
½ cup heavy cream

Cook shallots in butter until soft, but not brown, or about 15 minutes. Add the champagne, salt, and sugar. Bring to a boil and allow to boil for 10 minutes. Blend flour with a few drops of water and quickly stir into sauce; stir constantly until thickened. Scrape pan drippings from the chicken into the sauce and add the truffles. Lower heat and stir in the cream. Heat gently, but do not boil. Serve over chicken breasts.

The Pelican, Bridgetown, Barbados

Chicken Pelicana

1 4-pound (2-kilogram) chicken
2 stalks celery
  Pepper
  Salt
1 medium onion, chopped
1 medium sweet pepper
1 tablespoon butter
  Fresh thyme
1 can of mushroom soup
  Paprika
  Parsley

Boil chicken with celery, salt and pepper. When cooked, cut meat into cubes. Chop onion and sweet pepper and sauté in butter; add minced thyme and stir in cubed chicken. Finally add mushroom soup and pour into an ovenproof serving dish. Sprinkle paprika on top and bake for about 15 minutes at 300° F. Remove from oven and decorate with parsley.

serves: 6

Le Relais, Café Royal, London
CHEF: G. MOUILLERON

Poularde Tante Louise

serves: 4

wine:
Fleurie

1¼ cups very heavy cream
1 teaspoon chopped parsley
1 teaspoon chopped tarragon
1 teaspoon chopped chervil
2 tablespoons chopped fresh spinach
2 tablespoons chopped fresh sorrel
  Salt
  Pepper
  Allspice
1½ pounds (750 grams) finely ground
    fresh pork, medium lean
1 4-pound (2-kilogram) tender chicken
1 piece of pig's caul fat about 15
    inches square
1 bottle white wine
4 cups chicken stock
1 large carrot
1 large onion
1 sprig savory

Mix ¼ cup very heavy cream, 1 tablespoon mixed chopped herbs, salt, pepper, and allspice with the ground pork to make a stuffing. Fill the chicken with this stuffing and wrap the caul fat around it. Poach the chicken in a stock made of the white wine, chicken stock, onion, carrot, and savory sprig. It will take about an hour to cook. Strain about ½ cup of the stock into a saucepan, reduce by half, and add the rest of the chopped herbs. Boil for a minute or so, then add the rest of the cream. Boil until it thickens and taste for seasoning. Carve the chicken before pouring the sauce over it.
Rice pilaf (see Index) goes well with this dish.

Gaylord Restaurant, Port of Spain, Trinidad
CHEF: TILAK RAJ

Chicken Jai Puri

serves: 6

wine:
rosé,
or
Rhine
wine

1 cup cooking oil
3 large onions, finely chopped
¼ pound (125 grams) fresh ginger, chopped
8 cloves garlic
1 teaspoon paprika
1 teaspoon turmeric
1 teaspoon cinnamon
1 teaspoon ground coriander
½ pound (250 grams) tomatoes
  Salt
2 4-pound (2-kilogram) chickens,
    skinned and cut in 8 pieces each
1 cup yogurt
2 egg whites
4 hard-boiled eggs

Heat cooking oil. Brown onion; add chopped ginger, garlic, other spices, tomatoes and salt. Cook for 15 minutes. Add chicken which has been marinated in yogurt. Cook chicken in spices for 15 to 20 minutes, until tender. Add 2 cups of water, along with the egg whites. Stir to blend, then add the chopped hard-boiled eggs. Before taking off the fire add butter. Serve with boiled rice or rice pilaf (see Index).

Mount Soche Hotel, Blantyre, Malawi
CHEF: HERBERT FUESSEL

Chicken Harlequin

2 whole chicken breasts, split,
   skinned and boned
½ cup fine bread crumbs
2 tablespoons chopped blanched almonds
¼ cup clarified butter
8 sweet cherries
¼ cup dry sherry
   Curry sauce

Curry sauce

2 tablespoons clarified butter
2 teaspoons mild curry powder
1 small onion, finely chopped
2 tablespoons chopped green pepper
⅛ teaspoon dry mustard
½ clove garlic
2 teaspoons lemon juice
2 teaspoons currant jelly
¾ cup coconut milk (or ½ cup milk)
1 tablespoon tomato purée
   Salt
   Chicken stock, if necessary

Dry breasts well; roll in bread crumbs and almonds. Sauté in clarified butter until deep golden brown on both sides—chicken will be done when brown. Serve at once garnished with cherries which have been marinated in sherry. Pass curry sauce.

serves: 4

Heat butter in a heavy saucepan and sauté slowly curry powder, onion, green pepper, dry mustard and garlic for 10 minutes. Stir frequently and do not allow to burn. Stir in lemon juice, jelly, coconut milk or milk, tomato purée and salt to taste and simmer uncovered for 1 hour. (Make the day before if desired.) To serve, check seasonings and reheat sauce if it has been stored in refrigerator. If sauce is too thick, add chicken stock to dilute. Pass sauce hot.

Fiji Mocambo Hotel, Nadi Airport, Fiji
CHEF: BILL BECHU

Pinaviu Toa

(Chicken and Pineapple Boats)

2 pineapples
4 teaspoons cornstarch
6 cups pineapple juice
2 fresh tomatoes, diced
¼ cup tomato sauce
4 drops Tabasco sauce
   Salt
¼ cup lemon juice
½ cup mayonnaise
1½ pounds (750 grams) cooked chicken
¼ cup grated coconut

Halve pineapples and scoop out meat; set aside. Reserve shells. Dissolve cornstarch in pineapple juice; bring to a boil and cook until thickened. Add tomatoes, tomato sauce, Tabasco, salt, and lemon juice. Simmer for 5 minutes, cool, and add mayonnaise to form a smooth dressing. Dice chicken and pineapple; blend well with dressing. Serve chilled in pineapple boats with shredded coconut.

serves: 4

wine:
Calvet

Hotel Southern Cross, Melbourne, Australia
CHEF: H. KAHN

Seasoned Legs of Capon Mildura (Victoria)

serves: 6

12 capon legs
Salt
Pepper
¾ pound (375 grams) liver pâté
¾ pound (375 grams) fresh pork sausage
¾ pound (375 grams) cooked ham,
  finely cubed
1½ cups fresh bread crumbs
4 eggs
2 tablespoons chopped parsley
2 tablespoons chopped chives
1½ cups flour
2 tablespoons paprika
¾ cup melted butter
1 cup dry white wine
2 cups chicken gravy
6 cling peach halves
6 red cherries
6 sprigs parsley

Bone the capon legs carefully, taking care not to break the skin. Season with salt and pepper and set aside. Blend pâté, sausage, ham, bread crumbs, eggs, parsley and chives thoroughly. Fill the legs and close openings by folding the longer piece of skin over, making a triangle of the leg. Roll in a mixture of flour and paprika and place in a roasting pan. Brush with butter and roast for 40 minutes at 375° F. When golden brown, add wine and simmer until wine is reduced by half. Add chicken gravy and simmer for another 10 minutes.

Transfer legs to another dish and press gravy through a strainer over them. Return to the oven for another 5 minutes.

In the meantime grill peach halves and place cherries in the center of each. Serve with rice pilaf. Place rice in the middle of an oval platter, arrange capon legs around it and decorate with peaches and parsley sprigs.

Speke Hotel, Kampala, Uganda
CHEF: ABDUL R. KHATIB

Pollo Capuqueño

serves: 4

wine:
Rosenda
(Spanish
rosé)

2-pound (1-kilogram) whole chicken
1 cup milk
½ cup ground almonds
½ cup shredded coconut
½ cup crushed pineapple
3 tablespoons pernod

Poach the chicken in milk and white wine until tender. Mix almonds, coconut and pineapple and spread on top of the chicken. Pour pernod over the chicken and flame. Serve at once.

Le Paris Brest, New York City

Poitrine de Volaille Farcie

(Stuffed Breast of Chicken)

**1 3-pound (1.5-kilogram) chicken, cut
 in quarters
 Stuffing
2 tablespoons butter, melted**

Bone breasts of chicken, thighs and
legs. Place cooked stuffing on breast
and cover with boned leg. Tie firmly
together with butcher's net or
coarse cheesecloth.
Place in pan with butter in a preheated 350° F. oven for 25
minutes. Turn and baste after 15
minutes. Serve with wild rice.

serves: 2

Stuffing

**¼ pound (125 grams) ground veal
¾ pound (375 grams) ground chicken liver
1 egg
¼ cup Chablis
2 finely chopped shallots
 Salt, pepper**

Mix all ingredients together. Place
in deep pan; set pan into another
pan of hot water. Bake in a preheated 350° F. oven for 45 minutes.
Cool thoroughly before using.

Taj Mahal Hotel, Bombay
CHEF: M. A. MASCARENHAS

Chicken Biryani

**4 tablespoons butter
1 large onion, chopped
1 teaspoon ginger
1 clove garlic
½ teaspoon cumin seeds
½ teaspoon coriander seeds
⅓ teaspoon chili powder
5 or 6 coriander leaves, chopped
5 or 6 mint leaves, chopped
1 3-pound (1.5-kilogram) chicken, cut into
 8 pieces
2 teaspoons tomato purée
¼ cup yogurt
4 small potatoes, halved
2 tablespoons cooking oil
1⅓ cups raw rice
1½ teaspoons salt
½ teaspoon cardamon seeds
1 whole clove
1 pinch saffron**

Melt butter and fry onions until
light brown. Grind ginger, garlic,
cumin seeds, coriander seeds, chili
powder, coriander leaves, and mint
leaves into a paste in an electric
blender or with a mortar and pestle.
Fry 7 to 10 minutes on low heat.
Add chicken and cook another 5 to
7 minutes. Add tomato purée and
yogurt and let simmer until chicken
is tender, about 30 minutes. Fry
potatoes in hot oil and add to the
chicken mixture.
Boil rice in salted water with a few
cardamon seeds and the clove until
three-quarters cooked. In a flame-
proof pan put a layer of chicken
with gravy, then a layer of rice;
repeat. Dissolve saffron in a little
water and sprinkle on top of the
rice. Cover the pan tightly and
cook slowly until the rice is
completely cooked.

serves: 4

Taj Mahal Hotel, Bombay
CHEF: M. A. MASCARENHAS

Tandoori Chicken

serves: 4

1 3-pound (1.5-kilogram) chicken, cut in 8 pieces
2 teaspoons salt
¼ cup vinegar
1 teaspoon fresh ginger
3 cloves garlic
3 green chilis
½ teaspoon coriander seeds
1 teaspoon black pepper
½ teaspoon cumin seeds
½ teaspoon oil
2 or 3 drops orange food coloring
1 cup yogurt
2 lemons, sliced
8 green onions

Skin the chicken and make deep cuts in the meat with the point of a knife or an icepick. Sprinkle with salt and rub with vinegar. Allow to stand 15 minutes. Grind ginger, garlic, chilis, coriander seeds, pepper, cumin seeds, oil, and food coloring together finely in an electric blender or with a mortar and pestle. Beat in yogurt. Put chicken to marinate in this mixture for 2 to 3 hours. Cook over glowing charcoal and serve very hot with sliced lemons and green onions.

Strand Hotel, Rangoon, Burma

Chicken Khaukswe

serves: 10

1 3½-pound (1.5-kilogram) chicken
1 teaspoon saffron
3 teaspoons salt
10 onions
4 cloves garlic
2 slices fresh ginger (or 2 teaspoons dry ginger)
4 green chilis, seeded, or chili powder to taste
½ cup oil
1 tablespoon cornstarch
3 cups coconut milk
3½ pounds (1.5-kilogram) egg noodles, cooked according to package instructions
4 hard-boiled eggs, chopped
¾ cup green onions, chopped
3 limes cut in wedges
Chili powder

Cut chicken into small pieces about the size of olives. Rub with saffron and poach in 2 quarts water with salt until tender. Cut meat from bones. Crack bones and add to stock. Continue to simmer stock. In an electric blender or with mortar and pestle grind 9 onions, garlic, ginger, and chilis together. Rub over chicken. Heat oil in a 2-quart saucepan until smoking. Slice 1 onion and brown in oil. Add chicken and brown. Strain stock, add and simmer. Make paste of cornstarch and 1 cup water. Add to stock and cook 10 to 15 minutes. Pour coconut milk in and boil a few minutes longer. Add more salt if necessary. Serve hot, ladled over cooked noodles. Present at the table side dishes of the eggs, green onions, lime wedges, and chili powder.

The Savoy, London
CHEF: SILVINO S. TROMPETTO

Le Poulet Sauté Cannoise

1 5½-pound (2.8-kilogram) chicken
2 cups chicken stock (made from the
    remains of the chicken)
  Salt
  Pepper
½ cup olive oil
1 large onion, finely chopped
3 cloves garlic
2 eggplants, diced
1 medium vegetable marrow, diced
8 peeled tomatoes or 1 large can
    tomatoes, diced
1 bay leaf
1 sprig fennel, chopped
1 pimento, diced
¾ cup dry white wine

Cut chicken into 8 meaty serving pieces. Discard backbone and wing tips. Cover with water; add giblets, salt and pepper. Simmer 1 hour. Strain and reserve.
Sauté chicken and onion until golden brown in the oil in a thick saucepan. Add garlic, eggplants, vegetable marrows, tomatoes, bay leaf, fennel and pimento. Sauté for another 5 to 10 minutes, then pour in wine and stock. Cook until chicken is tender. Season to taste with salt and pepper. Serve cold. This recipe may be served hot if butter is used instead of olive oil.

serves: 4

Moghul Room, Oberoi Inter-Continental Hotel, New Delhi
CHEF: HANS RAJ KAPOTRA

Chicken Shashlik

1 green pepper
1 tomato
1 onion
6 ounces (180 grams) chicken pieces
    about 1 inch square
  Salt
  Pepper
2 tablespoons clarified butter
½ cup boiled rice
1 sliced tomato
1 sliced cucumber
1 sliced lemon

Seed the green pepper and tomato and cut pepper, tomato and onion into pieces approximately same size as the chicken pieces. Skewer alternate pieces of chicken and vegetables and sprinkle lightly with salt and pepper to taste.
Roast for about 20 minutes at 275° F. basting frequently with clarified butter. Serve hot on bed of rice garnished with tomato, cucumber and lemon slices.

serves: 1

wine:
dry white
wine

Mirabelle Restaurant, London
CHEF: JEAN DREES

Suprême of Poulet Curzon

serves: 4

wine:
Puligny
Montrâchet

1 carrot
1 onion
1 bunch celery
8 tablespoons butter
4 chicken wings
  Salt
  Pepper
1 teaspoon fines herbes
¾ cup dry white wine
¼ cup whisky
2 cups cream

Chop the vegetables very fine and cook slowly until tender in 7 tablespoons butter. Place chicken wings on top of vegetables and season. Cook for 10 minutes; turn and add wine and whisky and allow to boil for 5 minutes. Add cream and let cook until sauce thickens. Season to taste.
Remove chicken wings and arrange on serving platter; keep warm.
Put the other tablespoon of butter in the sauce, pour it over the chicken and serve hot.

Man Wah Restaurant, Mandarin Hotel, Hong Kong

Grilled Suprême Lemon Chicken

serves: 4

1 2-pound (1-kilogram) chicken
1 tablespoon soy sauce
2 egg yolks
4 tablespoons cornstarch
½ teaspoon poultry seasoning
3 tablespoons peanut oil
1 tablespoon fresh lemon juice
½ cup chicken stock
½ teaspoon sugar

Remove all bones from the chicken, marinate meat in soy sauce, egg yolks, 1 tablespoon cornstarch, and poultry seasoning for 20 minutes. Drain the chicken meat and dredge pieces in 2 tablespoons cornstarch; sauté in heated oil until well done, browned and very tender. Chop into bite-size pieces, lay on platter the shape of a chicken. Mix lemon juice with stock, sugar, and 1 tablespoon cornstarch; heat in pan in which chicken was sautéed. When sauce has thickened, splash over the chicken.

Peacock Room, Ashoka Hotel, New Delhi
CHEF: ROSHAN LAL

Chicken Badam Pasanda

3 1½-pound (800-gram) chickens, cleaned
    and skinned
4 eggs
2 teaspoons ground ginger
2 cloves garlic, minced
2 teaspoons chili powder
    Salt
    Juice of 2 lemons
1½ cups clarified butter
2 pounds (1 kilogram) onions, chopped
¾ cup unsalted cashew nuts
2 teaspoons poppy seeds
½ teaspoon cardamon seeds
1 teaspoon cinnamon
½ cup sliced blanched almonds
1 teaspoon nutmeg
½ teaspoon black pepper
1 cup yogurt
2 cups finely chopped tomatoes
¾ cup cream

serves: 6

Quarter chickens. Beat together eggs, ginger, garlic, chili powder, a dash salt and lemon juice. Dip chicken pieces into this thin batter and fry lightly in clarified butter. Remove chicken from pan. Now fry onions until crisp and brown. Remove onions and grind together fried onions, cashew nuts, poppy seeds, cardamon seeds, cinnamon, half the almonds, nutmeg and salt to taste. Combine this mixture with the yogurt and cook in the chicken skillet for about 5 minutes. Add tomatoes and cook for 2 minutes. Add 6 cups water and simmer over low heat for about 20 minutes. Into the gravy so formed place the lightly fried chicken. Cover with cream and simmer for 10 minutes. Garnish with the remainder of the sliced almonds. Serve hot with Malai Kofta.

Malai Kofta

6 bananas, slightly green
½ pound (250 grams) fresh cream or
    cottage cheese
2 teaspoons ground cumin seeds
2 teaspoons ground coriander
    Salt
2 tablespoons fresh coriander, chopped
1½ cups clarified butter
½ cup chopped onion
1 teaspoon ground ginger
1 teaspoon poppy seeds
1 teaspoon chili powder
2 chopped hot green chilis
½ cup yogurt
3 bay leaves
¾ cup cream

Boil the bananas whole. Skin and mash them and combine with cheese to form a thick smooth dough. Add 1 teaspoon each of cumin seeds and ground coriander. Salt to taste. Form the dough into small balls. Make a hole in each ball with finger and put in some of the coriander leaves; pinch the top together. Deep fry cheese balls in clarified butter until golden brown. Remove fried balls from butter. Now fry onions until crisp and brown. Remove onions and grind together with ginger, poppy
(Continued at foot of facing page

Moghul Room, Oberoi Inter-Continental Hotel, New Delhi
CHEF: HANS RAJ KAPOTRA

Tandoori Chicken Moghul

serves: 6

2 cups yogurt
4 tablespoons ground ginger
2 cloves garlic, coarsely chopped
2 tablespoons ground cumin seeds
2 tablespoons ground coriander
1 tablespoon red chili powder
1 tablespoon white pepper
  Salt
2 or 3 drops red food coloring
3 2-pound (1 kilogram) chickens
1 cup clarified butter
3 lemons, sliced

Combine yogurt with ginger, garlic and spices. Add salt to taste and 2 or 3 drops food coloring. Marinade should be a thick smooth paste. Marinate the skinned chickens in this paste for at least 6 hours.
Roast in a 325° F. oven for about 1 hour, or skewer and roast in rotisserie for approximately 20 minutes at 275° F. Baste frequently with clarified butter. Serve hot with garnish of sliced lemons.

Ruwenzori Room, Apolo Hotel, Kampala, Uganda
CHEF: F. PEREIRA

Suprême de Volaille Ougandaise

serves: 2

wine:
Sylvaner

¼ pound (125 grams) butter
  Salt
  Pepper
2 whole chicken breasts
1 banana
1 medium eggplant, sliced
2 pineapple rings
  Watercress for garnish

Place the butter in a pan on a fairly hot flame. Season the chicken breasts and cook until golden brown on both sides, about 5 minutes. Then fry separately in butter the banana, eggplant and pineapple. Serve on a flat silver dish. Garnish with watercress. Serve melted brown butter from browning pans as sauce.

Malai Kofta (continued)

seeds, 1 teaspoon ground cumin seeds, 1 teaspoon ground coriander, chili powder and green chilis. Mix spice mixture with yogurt. Put into cooking pot. Add bay leaves and cook in clarified butter for about 2 minutes. Add 2 cups of water, lower heat and simmer for about 10 minutes. Put in fried balls, cover with cream and simmer for another 10 minutes. Serve hot.

Biggs Restaurant, Chicago
CHEF: BRIAN KUZMAN

Poitrine de Capon Vieux Carré à la Biggs

(Breast of Capon in Cream Sauce)

8 boneless whole breasts of capon
2 cups sherry
¼ teaspoon pepper
1 teaspoon salt
2 tablespoons dry mustard
½ cup butter

Place chicken breasts in a shallow pan. Combine sherry, pepper, salt, and mustard. Pour over chicken and let marinate 1 hour or longer. Drain and pat dry. Melt ½ cup butter in a skillet. Brown chicken breasts on all sides; simmer until chicken is tender.

serves: 8

Sauce

½ cup butter
½ cup shallots, finely chopped
¼ cup flour
¼ cup dry mustard
¼ cup paprika
2 tablespoons sherry
1 clove garlic, finely chopped
2 cans condensed chicken broth
2 egg yolks
1 cup heavy cream
2 cups cooked shrimp
2 cups sautéed mushrooms
Chopped parsley

Melt butter and sauté shallots in it until wilted but not brown. Stir in flour, mustard, paprika, sherry, and garlic. When well blended, gradually blend in chicken broth. Cook, stirring, until sauce bubbles and thickens. Beat egg yolks with cream and stir quickly into sauce. Do not boil. Place chicken breasts on a platter and spoon sauce evenly over them. Garnish with tiny cooked, shelled, and deveined shrimp and small sautéed mushroom caps. Sprinkle with parsley.

Miramar Theatre Restaurant, Hong Kong

Roast Spring Chicken

1 whole 3-pound (1.5-kilogram) chicken
Juice of 2 limes
2 tablespoons light soy sauce
2 tablespoons light syrup
3 tablespoons tapioca flour or cornstarch
3 cups cooking oil
3 tablespoons apricot jam
1 tablespoon vinegar

Parboil whole chicken 15 minutes. Drain and pat dry. Season inside and out with lime juice and outside with soy sauce and syrup mixed with tapioca flour or cornstarch. Hang chicken or place it upright on a rack for 4 to 5 hours; let it drip until thoroughly dry.
Heat cooking oil. Place chicken on a rack in a 3-inch-deep baking pan. Roast in a 400° F. oven, basting frequently with hot oil, until tender and very brown and crisp, about 45 minutes. Cut into pieces and serve while hot with sauce made of apricot jam and vinegar.

serves: 6

wine: Champagne

Restaurant Zakuro, Tokyo
CHEF: MAIE YOSHINORI

Shabu-Shabu

serves: 4

wine:
rosé

6 cups chicken broth
1 pound (500 grams) thinly sliced beef
   Sesame sauce
   Vinegar sauce
4 spring onions, finely cut
4 to 6 leaves Chinese cabbage, roughly cut
2 bunches bean-jelly sticks
8 1-inch cubes bean curd
½ pound (250 grams) vermicelli

Prepare a Shabu-Shabu pot (a thick-bottomed copper pot) with a small burner of some sort to put on the dinner table; provide a set of chopsticks for each person. Pour the chicken broth into the pot, set it on the burner, and bring it to a boil. It must continue boiling throughout the meal. Each person picks up slices of beef with chopsticks and dips them 2 or 3 times into boiling broth. The meat should not be overcooked, or it will harden and lose its flavor. It is at its most delicious when pale pink. When the meat is just right, it is dipped into one of the sauces and eaten immediately. When all the meat has been eaten add the vegetables to the broth. They are to be eaten as they are done. At last, put the vermicelli into the broth and season with salt and pepper. Serve this in soup bowls.

Sesame sauce

 2 teaspoons bruised sesame seeds
½ teaspoon soy sauce
 1 teaspoon wine vinegar
½ teaspoon pepper soybean paste
½ teaspoon anchovy paste
½ teaspoon monosodium glutamate
 1 teaspoon finely chopped spring onion

Mix all ingredients and shake before serving at room temperature.

Vinegar sauce

 1 cup soy sauce
½ cup wine vinegar
½ cup lemon juice

Mix just before serving.

Taj Mahal, Kuala Lumpur, Malaysia
CHEF: BILLY HAY

Chicken Tanduri

4 tablespoons yogurt
1 small onion
8 cloves garlic
1-inch piece ginger
1 teaspoon white cumin seeds
1 tablespoon red chili powder
   Salt to taste
1 2-pound (1-kilogram) chicken
   Juice of 1 lemon
2 tablespoons vinegar
2 tablespoons melted butter
   Onion rings (see Index)
   Green chutney (see Index)

Whip yogurt; grind onion, garlic, and ginger to a paste. Roast cumin seeds and grind; mix thoroughly garlic paste, cumin seeds, chili powder, and salt. Clean the chicken thoroughly, wash and dry with cloth. Make one or two cuts on the legs and breast. Mix yogurt, lemon juice, and vinegar and rub mixture all over the meaty parts of the chicken. Marinate in a cool place 3 to 4 hours. Roast over a charcoal fire, turning constantly to brown evenly, or bake in a 400° F. oven about 1 hour, until meat is tender. Pour 2 tablespoonfuls of melted butter over the chicken just before serving. Serve with onion rings and green chutney.

serves: 4

wine: Domtal white wine

Beach Luxury Hotel, Karachi

Chicken Farcha

1 4-pound (2-kilogram) fowl, cleaned and
   cut in serving pieces
   Green chutney
   Bread crumbs
3 eggs
   Clarified butter for frying

Cover chicken with green chutney and marinate for at least 6 hours. When ready to cook, roll chicken pieces in bread crumbs, brush with beaten eggs, and fry in hot clarified butter on very low heat until golden. Serve hot.

serves: 4

Green chutney

1 coconut, scraped
1 teaspoon jeera
1 big bunch coriander leaves
8 green chilis
   Juice of 1 lime
1 tablespoon sugar
1 teaspoon salt
1 small bunch mint leaves

Grind all ingredients together until very fine in a blender or with a mortar and pestle. Store in the refrigerator.

Beach Luxury Hotel, Karachi

Murgh Mussallam

serves: 4

1 3-pound (1.5-kilogram) chicken, cut in
    serving pieces
1 cup ground papaya (about 1 small or
    ½ medium papaya)
4 medium onions
1 clove garlic
1 teaspoon ground ginger
½ teaspoon cinnamon
2 tablespoons red pepper
1 teaspoon salt
10 whole cloves
½ teaspoon cumin seeds
¼ cup almonds
1 teaspoon allspice
2 tablespoons poppy seeds
½ teaspoon nutmeg
½ teaspoon mace
½ pound (250 grams) cottage cheese,
    sieved
1 pound clarified butter
  A few cardamon seeds
1 tablespoon flour

Clean chicken and prick all over with a fork. Grind papaya and spread over the chicken; leave in refrigerator 4 hours. Grind 2 onions and garlic, ginger, cinnamon, red pepper, salt, cloves, cumin seeds, almonds, allspice, poppy seeds, nutmeg, and mace. Mix with cottage cheese and put on the chicken; marinate 1 hour. Heat clarified butter in a frying pan; slice 2 onions and fry with cardamon. Dust chicken with flour and add to skillet. Cook on very low heat. Turn and cook until the chicken is tender. Serve with parathas.

Auberge de France, Lythe Hill Hotel, Haslemere, Surrey, England
CHEF: ASSELIN

Poulet à l'Estragon

serves: 3-4

1 2-pound (1-kilogram) chicken
3 cups chicken stock
1½ cups dry white wine
1 sprig fresh thyme or 1 teaspoon dried
    thyme
1 bay leaf
2 sprigs fresh tarragon or 2 teaspoons
    dried tarragon
12 whole small fresh mushrooms
3 tablespoons butter
1 tablespoon flour
½ cup heavy cream
  Salt
  Pepper

Cut the chicken into serving pieces. Use bony pieces and giblets to make stock. Poach chicken in stock, wine, thyme, bay leaf, tarragon and mushrooms. When chicken is tender, about 30 to 45 minutes (do not overcook), add butter blended with flour and cream. Cook slowly until the sauce is thick and smooth. Taste for salt and pepper and season to taste. Serve very hot.

Maile Restaurant, Kahala Hilton, Honolulu
CHEF: MARTIN WYSS

Chicken Baked in Pineapple

1½ pounds (750 grams) boiled chicken,
    boned and sliced
½ cup sliced mushrooms
3 tablespoons butter
¼ cup sherry
1 tablespoon flour
2 cups chicken broth
1½ cups heavy cream
  Salt
  Pepper
1 tablespoon slivered almonds
1 egg yolk
2 whole pineapples
  Puff pastry for garnish

Sauté diced chicken and mushrooms in 2 tablespoons butter. Add sherry and simmer until half of the sherry has evaporated. Blend the rest of the butter and the flour and mix with chicken broth. Simmer for 15 minutes, then add to chicken and mushrooms along with ½ cup of the cream. Mix well without mashing chicken and simmer for a few minutes. Season to taste with salt, pepper and lemon juice and add slivered almonds. Blend carefully with 1 egg yolk and 1 cup of heavy cream, whipped.

Cut pineapples in half lengthwise. Scoop out fruit. Heat pineapple shell in a 400° F. oven until hot. Then fill with the chicken mixture and glaze to a golden brown in oven. Garnish with baked puffed paste in the form of a chicken's head.

serves: 4

Beach Luxury Hotel, Karachi

Chicken Charga

½ teaspoon fresh ginger
4 cloves garlic
4 green chilis
½ medium onion
½ teaspoon red chili powder
3 to 4 coriander leaves
½ teaspoon white cumin seeds
½ teaspoon turmeric
1 teaspoon salt
2 whole cloves
½-inch piece of stick cinnamon
  Juice of 1 lemon
1 3-pound (1.5-kilogram) chicken
  Cooking oil

Grind together first 11 ingredients. Sprinkle and mix with the lemon juice to make a paste. Cut the chicken in four portions; slit the pieces slightly on the top with a knife. Marinate with the paste, covered, 4 to 5 hours.

Prepare a charcoal spit and grease 2 skewers with cooking oil.

Grill the pieces of chicken over the charcoal fire. Keep turning the skewers as the chicken becomes tender and slightly brown. Serve immediately with purri.

serves: 4

(See foot facing page

Café Martinique on Paradise Island, Nassau, Bahamas
CHEF: HENRI BUANNIC

Chicken Portolla

serves: 1

1 coconut
4 tablespoons butter
1 small onion
1 small green apple
1 small bay leaf
3 tablespoons flour
1 tablespoon curry powder
1 cup chicken stock
½ cup cream
Salt
Maggi seasoning
½ cup cooked light meat of chicken
1 red pepper
1 large mushroom
2 tablespoons coconut meat
½ cup cooked corn
Pie crust or stiff flour-and-water paste

Cut off top of coconut and drain out the liquid. Remove enough meat to make 2 tablespoons when shredded. Reserve shell.

Melt the butter in a shallow pan. Chop the onion and apple coarsely and add, with bay leaf, to the butter. Cook until soft but not brown. Add the flour and stir until blended. Add curry powder and blend. Add the chicken stock and cook, stirring constantly, until thickened. Strain and add cream. Season to taste with salt and Maggi.

Cut the chicken into bite-size pieces. Chop pepper and mushroom coarsely and add with shredded coconut meat and corn to the sauce and simmer for 10 minutes. Place the mixture in the coconut and replace the top, sealing the seam with a 1-inch strip of pastry or flour-and-water paste. Bake for 20 or 25 minutes at 350° F. Remove the coconut top and serve in the shell.

Purri
(Fried puffed bread)

¼ teaspoon salt
1 cup white flour
1 tablespoon cooking fat
Water
Fat for deep frying

Blend salt with flour and lightly blend cooking fat into it, adding just enough water to make a soft dough. Knead well until smooth and velvety. Put aside for 10 minutes. Divide dough into small balls, rolling out each ball separately. Fry one at a time in deep fat for half a minute on each side. Serve hot with curries.

Hotel Parmelia, Perth, Australia
CHEF: D. R. WILLIAMS

Chicken Swan Valley

2 2-pound (1-kilogram) chickens
1 teaspoon curry powder
½ cup butter
½ cup flour
½ cup cream
½ cup raisins
½ cup sultanas
½ cup slivered almonds
2 tablespoons brandy
½ cup rice
1 large onion
1 medium green pepper
1 medium tomato, peeled and seeded
Salt
Pepper
3 large carrots
2 tablespoons sugar

Boil chickens in 8 cups of water. *serves: 4*
When cooked remove from stock.
With a little water make the curry
powder into a paste and add to the
chicken stock; boil for another 15
minutes. Melt ¼ cup butter in a pan.
Add flour, stir, and cook well without coloring. Gradually add chicken
stock until a smooth sauce is ob-
tained. Strain, add salt to taste,
and finish off with cream.
Remove all skin and bone from the
chicken. Place chicken in clean pan,
cover with sauce, and simmer 20
minutes.
Sprinkle raisins, sultanas, and
almonds with brandy.
Cook rice to light and fluffy stage.
Finely dice 1 onion, green pepper,
and tomato; fry all lightly in 2
tablespoons butter and add the rice.
Season to taste, then add the raisins,
sultanas, and almonds.
Cut carrots into balls, cook in water
until tender; drain. Finish with 2
tablespoons butter and sugar.
Arrange chicken and gravy on
serving platter. Garnish with
glazed carrot balls and onion
rings.

Onion rings
1 large onion
Batter for frying

Slice the onion into rings, dip
into frying batter, and fry quickly
in deep fat. Drain on absorbent
paper and set aside.

Hotel Inter-Continental, Karachi

Chicken Tikka

serves: 4

2 3-pound (1.5-kilogram) chickens
2 cups yogurt
2 teaspoons pressed ginger
2 teaspoons pressed garlic
4 tablespoons lemon juice
4 tablespoons red chili powder
  Salt
  Pepper
4 tablespoons olive oil
  Tomato slices
  Onion rings
  Green chilis
  Mint leaves
  Lemon wedges
  Lettuce leaves

Skin the chicken and divide into 4 pieces (2 legs, 2 breasts). With a sharp knife make incisions in chicken pieces every ½ inch, right to the bone. Put the yogurt in a large bowl and mix in ginger, garlic, lemon juice, chili powder, salt and pepper. Place the chicken in this mixture and let it marinate for 2 hours. Check seasoning. Take out the chicken pieces and fix them on skewers, sprinkle with olive oil and broil over charcoal for 6 minutes on each side. Serve with sliced tomatoes, onion rings, fresh green chilis, fresh mint leaves and lemon on a bed of lettuce.

Madrid Restaurant, Rizal, Philippines

Gallina en Pepitoria con Soufle de Naranja
(Chicken in Pepitoria)

serves: 6

1 4-pound (2-kilogram) hen
  Oil for frying
2 cloves garlic
1 sliced onion
1 cup good white wine
1 tablespoon flour
2 cups hot stock
2 bay leaves
  Salt
  Pepper
1 sprig thyme
12 finely chopped almonds
½ teaspoon saffron
2 chopped hard-boiled eggs
½ cup fried bread crumbs
2 tablespoons chopped parsley

Disjoint the hen and fry in the oil but do not allow to brown excessively. Then add garlic and onion and cook lightly; pour white wine in and allow to reduce slightly. Stir in the flour, then about 2 cups of hot stock, which should be just enough to cover the meat, the bay leaf, salt and pepper to taste, and thyme. Now cover the pan and cook slowly. After half an hour add the almonds and saffron and continue the cooking until the hen is tender. When serving sprinkle with chopped egg, the crumbs and parsley.

Altavista Restaurant, Manila

Adobong Manok Sa Gata
(Chicken Adobo and Coconut Milk)

**1 roasting chicken, about 2½ pounds
    (1 kilogram) or more
½ cup vinegar
1 teaspoon salt
3 cloves garlic
6 peppercorns
2 coconuts, grated**

Soak the chicken pieces in a vinegar marinade seasoned with salt, garlic and peppercorns for 1 hour.
Prepare the coconut milk as follows: Grate the coconuts and extract pure coconut milk by pressing with a potato masher several times. Strain the pure coconut milk and set aside. Combine the coconut particles in the strainer with the pressed coconut, add about ¾ cup water and press again to get the second extraction of coconut milk.
Place the chicken and the marinade in a cooking vessel; boil and simmer until tender. When chicken is done, add coconut milk (second extraction) and boil for 5 minutes. Then add the first extraction coconut milk and simmer for another 5 minutes. Serve hot with steamed rice. If desired, serve cooked chicken in several whole coconuts (tops sawed off and used as lids). Cover and place in medium oven until ready to serve. The coconut container will keep the chicken hot for the duration of the meal.

serves: 4

Speedbird House, Karachi Airport

Vindaloo

**1 3-pound (1.5-kilogram) duck or chicken
¼ cup chopped onions
¾ cup cooking oil
4 cloves garlic
1 teaspoon ground ginger
1 teaspoon gira
½ teaspoon cardamon
1 teaspoon chili powder
½ teaspoon cloves
¼ cup vinegar
¾ cup water**

Cut raw duck or chicken into 6 pieces. Fry chopped onions until slightly golden. Separately fry the duck or chicken in oil until brown on all sides.
Mix the poultry and the onions and add garlic, ground ginger, gira, cardamon, chili powder, cloves, vinegar and water. Cook slowly for about 25 minutes or until the gravy is almost evaporated.

serves: 6

Shepheard's Hotel Restaurant, Cairo

Pullet Aly Baba

serves: 4

wine:
*Rubis
d'Egypte
(Rosé Wine)*

1 3-pound (1.5-kilogram) pullet, completely boned
½ cup carrots, chopped
½ cup French celery, chopped
⅓ cup onion, chopped
1 clove garlic
½ cup butter
1 pound (500 grams) chopped round veal
1 teaspoon mustard
2 tablespoons chopped walnut
½ teaspoon nutmeg
2 tablespoons Worcestershire sauce
3 ounces (100 grams) lamb kidney
Salt
Pepper
2 tablespoons raisins
4 whole tomatoes
8 very small carrots, whole
12 small white onions
8 small stalks celery

Bone pullet completely without breaking it (or ask the butcher to do it for you). Sauté chopped vegetables with butter for 10 minutes. Add this mixture to the chopped meat with all the other ingredients except whole vegetables and stir well for 10 minutes. Stuff pullet with it and wrap the bird in oiled glacé paper. Place in a roasting pan with whole vegetables and roast at 350° F. until chicken is done, about 1½ hours. Serve with potatoes Boulangère or oriental rice.

Sulo Restaurant and Cocktail Lounge, Rizal, Philippines

Manok Sa Piña

(Chicken with Pineapple)

serves: 6-8

wine:
*Pouilly-
Fuissé, Cruse*

2 frying chickens
3 medium fresh pineapples
1 teaspoon crushed garlic
2 onions, minced
2 cups tomato sauce
1 bay leaf
1 teaspoon salt
1 teaspoon peppercorn
2 green peppers, cut in strips
1 red pepper, cut in strips
1 teaspoon monosodium glutamate
1 cup shortening

Cut chicken into serving pieces. Set aside.
Make pineapple boats: scoop out the meat carefully and cut in chunks. Sauté garlic and onions in hot shortening. Add chicken and sauté until golden brown. Add tomato sauce, bay leaf, salt and pepper and cook for 15 to 20 minutes. Add pineapple chunks, green and red peppers and monosodium glutamate and continue cooking for 10 minutes more. Correct seasoning. Serve hot in pineapple boats.

Mount Lavinia Hyatt, Mount Lavinia, Ceylon

Chicken Curry

- 1 3-pound (1.5-kilogram) chicken
- 1 medium red onion
- 1 or 2 green chilis
- 2 tablespoons cadju
- 2 thin slices ginger
- 2 tablespoons rice
- 4 tablespoons roasted coconut
- 3 whole cloves
- ½ teaspoon cardamon seeds
- 1 tablespoon chili powder
- 1½ teaspoons cumin seeds
- ½ teaspoon fenugreek
- Salt
- 6 tablespoons oil
- 1 inch rampe
- 2 small tomatoes
- 1½ cups first and second extracts of coconut milk*
- 4 tablespoons fresh chopped coriander
- ½-inch cinnamon stick

serves: 4

Cut the chicken into 8 pieces. Chop onions and green chilis. Grind the cadju, ginger, rice, roasted coconut, cloves, and cardamon seeds into a fine paste.

Add all the powdered and ground ingredients and salt to the chicken and mix well. Marinate for 20 minutes.

Heat oil in a pan until very hot. Add the rampe and tomatoes and fry until light brown. Add the chicken and toss for 5 to 10 minutes; then add the coconut milk and other ingredients and bring to a boil. Simmer until chicken is completely tender.

*Grate the meat of a fresh ripe coconut. Pour 1½ cups boiling water over coconut and let stand 20 minutes. Squeeze through 2 layers of cheesecloth. Store milk in the refrigerator. Pour another ¾ cup boiling water over coconut. Soak 20 minutes and squeeze again. Store separately in refrigerator.

Hotel Inter-Continental Manila, Rizal, Philippines

Pollo Pibil

- ½ teaspoon salt
- 20 peppercorns
- 1 whole garlic, peeled
- ½ teaspoon oregano
- ¼ teaspoon cumin
- ½ teaspoon allspice
- 2 tablespoons anatto (achuete)
- ½ cup orange juice
- ¼ cup calamansi juice (or lime juice)
- 2 2-pound (1-kilogram) chickens cut in eighths
- 4 banana leaves (or 4 pieces of cooking parchment)

serves: 4

Mix all ingredients except the chickens in a blender until very fine. Add chicken and marinate for 24 hours.

Wrap 4 pieces chicken in banana leaf, cover chicken with marinade and then wrap with foil. Repeat until all chicken and marinade have been used. Cook for 2½ hours in a 325° F. oven.

Remove aluminium foil and serve in an earthenware pot. Pass rice separately.

Chicken and Pineapple

SULO RESTAURANT,
RIZAL, PHILIPPINES

Fish Chunks

*Burmese Duck
à la Nine Muses*

THE NINE MUSES,
HOLLYWOOD, CALIFORNIA
(Chef: Harley White)

Roast Spring Chicken

MIRAMAR THEATRE
RESTAURANT,
HONG KONG

Hotel Caribbee, Hastings, Christ Church, Barbados

Braised Chicken Breast Caribbee

serves: 4

wine:
Chablis

½ teaspoon salt
½ teaspoon poultry seasoning
4 boned chicken breasts
½ cup flour for dredging
⅓ cup oil or shortening
1 cup sliced mushrooms
1 small green pepper, diced
1 teaspoon onion powder
2 ripe tomatoes, peeled and diced
⅔ cup champagne or Chablis
2 small cantaloupes, halved
1 cup chicken stock
1 chicken bouillon cube
Maraschino cherries for garnish

Mix salt and poultry seasoning and sprinkle breasts with it; dredge with flour. Heat oil or shortening in heavy skillet and sauté chicken breasts until brown. Remove chicken and sauté mushrooms and green pepper for 5 minutes. Add onion powder, ham, tomatoes and chicken. Place skillet in preheated 350° F. oven for 20 minutes and baste often with champagne or wine. Place chicken breasts in cantaloupe halves. Add chicken stock and chicken bouillon cube to remaining ingredients in skillet to form sauce. Put cantaloupe with chicken back in hot oven for 15 minutes before serving. Spoon sauce from skillet over each portion. Decorate with maraschino cherries and serve hot.

India

Chicken Curry

serves: 4

2 onions, finely sliced
4 cloves garlic, sliced
2 cloves
2 cardamon seeds
1 2-inch stick cinnamon
4 tablespoons cooking fat
  Salt
1 tablespoon ground coriander
½ teaspoon ground turmeric
½ teaspoon ground ginger
½ teaspoon ground cumin
  Red pepper
1 frying chicken, cut into serving pieces
  Lemon juice

Fry onions, garlic, cloves, cardamon seeds and cinnamon in fat. When onions are golden, add other ingredients except chicken and lemon juice. Stir thoroughly and cook on low heat for about 5 minutes. Add chicken pieces and fry in curry mixture, stirring occasionally. After a few minutes, add enough water to form a thick sauce. Cover pan and simmer until chicken is tender. Before serving, squeeze lemon juice over curry.

W.—D

Hotel Imperial, Copenhagen
CHEF: HOLGER ANDERSEN

La Belle Poularde Vald'isere

1 3-pound (1.5-kilogram) chicken
1 cup good port
4 cups water
¼ cup white wine
3 onions, whole
3 carrots, sliced
3 leeks, sliced
4 teaspoons salt
   Sauce Raifort
   Chopped parsley

Clean and truss chicken. Make deep cuts in the meat of the breast and legs. Marinate 10 hours in port in the refrigerator, turning several times. Let bird come to room temperature and poach in water and wine with vegetables and salt for about 30 minutes, or until tender. To serve, remove chicken from stock and drain well. Remove skin and cut into serving pieces. Spoon Sauce Raifort over chicken and sprinkle with chopped parsley.

serves: 2-3

wine:
Bordeaux
Red

Sauce Raifort

1 tablespoon butter
⅓ cup flour
2 cups very heavy cream
   Salt
½ cup freshly grated horseradish, or to taste

Melt butter and blend in flour. Cook for 5 minutes but do not allow to brown. Heat cream but do not let it boil. Blend cream into roux and cook over hot water, stirring constantly, until thickened. Season with salt to taste and stir in horseradish. Allow to heat through.

Turkey

Turkish Chicken

1 stewing chicken
6 pints water
1 large onion
   Parsley
1 carrot
1 teaspoon salt
   Pepper
2 cups walnuts, shelled
1 tablespoon paprika
3 small slices white bread

In a large pot, place chicken, water, onion, parsley, carrot, salt and pepper. When the liquid has come to a boil, skim the surface, removing froth. Cover pan and cook for 2 hours.
Take chicken out of stock, put to one side and allow to cool. Remove skin and bones and cut meat into small pieces.
Put walnuts through a mincer twice and add paprika. Squeeze this

serves: 6

(Continued at foot of facing page

India

Kosher Curry

serves: 8

8 cloves
2 hot green peppers
1 1-inch stick ginger, crushed
1 teaspoon red chili powder
¼ teaspoon cinnamon
½ teaspoon coriander
½ teaspoon ground cumin seeds
1 tablespoon Madras curry powder
  Kosher margarine
2 large onions, chopped finely
4 breasts chicken, skinned
4 legs chicken, skinned
1¾ cups stock or water
3 tomatoes, chopped fine
1 tablespoon lemon juice
½ cup parsley, chopped fine
1½ cups non-dairy "cream"
  Salt
  Parsley for garnish

Mix cloves, green peppers, ginger, chili powder, cinnamon, coriander, cumin seeds and curry powder together in a bowl. Melt margarine in a heavy pan, add onions and sauté on medium heat until onions are golden. Add pieces of chicken and stir for 15 minutes. Care must be taken that chicken does not stick or burn. Pour ¼ cup lukewarm stock into pan and add the spices from the bowl. Continue stirring for a few more minutes on lower heat. Add tomatoes, lemon juice and parsley, stirring constantly. After a few minutes, add non-dairy "cream" and stir for another 5 minutes. Pour a further 1½ cups of stock into pan and simmer for about 30 minutes. Correct seasoning. Serve with onion rice or saffron rice and garnish with parsley.

Turkish Chicken (continued)

mixture through a double layer of cheesecloth. This should result in about 2 tablespoons oil for garnishing.
Soak bread in chicken stock. Squeeze it dry and mix it well with minced walnuts and paprika. Put this new mixture through mincer 3 times, add about a cup of chicken stock and work it into a paste. Combine half of this mixture with minced chicken, making sure that it is well blended. Spread remainder of paste over chicken mixture. Garnish with the red walnut oil and serve cold.

India

Chili Chicken

2 tablespoons dried white mushrooms
1 1½-pound (750-gram) chicken
  Salt
¼ teaspoon red pepper
¼ teaspoon black pepper
2 egg whites, beaten just until foamy
1 tablespoon flour or cornstarch
1 cup salad oil
1 large cucumber, peeled and seeded
1 spring onion, chopped
6 cloves garlic, chopped
1 tablespoon ground ginger
¼ cup chopped green pepper
6 hot green chilis

Soak mushrooms in water to cover overnight. Boil in same water for 15 to 20 minutes. Drain and set aside. Remove skin and bones from chicken. Use bones, giblets and wingtips to make stock. Wash and pat dry meaty parts of bird and cut into 12 pieces. Sprinkle with salt, red pepper and black pepper. Mix in egg whites and flour. Heat ½ cup salad oil and fry a few pieces of chicken at a time for 4 or 5 minutes until all of them are done. Remove from oil and put to one side.

Dice cucumber, sprinkle with salt and leave 15 to 20 minutes. Squeeze out water. Heat remaining oil and fry separately onion, garlic, ginger, mushrooms, green peppers, green chilis and cucumber, adding a pinch of salt to each. Add fried diced chicken and sauce. Cook for about 5 minutes. Serve hot with noodles and vegetables or boiled rice.

serves: 3

Sauce
1½ teaspoons cornstarch
  3 tablespoons water
  1 tablespoon vinegar
¼ cup chicken stock
  2 tablespoons rum or sherry
½ teaspoon salt
  1 tablespoon soy sauce
  1 tablespoon sugar
  1 teaspoon ve-tsin (Chinese flavoring)
  1 teaspoon white pepper

Mix cornstarch with water to make a smooth paste. Add other ingredients and blend well. Use as called for in recipe.

The Barrie Grill, Kensington Palace Hotel, London
CHEF: LARRY STOVE

Pantoufle Perigourdine

serves: 4
4 breasts of chicken (¼ pound)
½ pound (250 grams) butter
¼ pound (125 grams) foie gras
¾ cup madeira
1 cup rich brown sauce
1 small truffle
½ cup sherry

Take 4 breasts of chicken, flatten and fill with 1 oz. foie gras and 2 ozs. butter—then roll the chicken. Place the chicken in a sauté pan and fry in butter till cooked. Remove from the pan and add Madeira wine allowing sufficient time for the wine to reduce to half its volume. Add the brown sauce, bring to the boil and add a half-cup of sherry and a little butter. Season to taste. Strain the sauce and add one small truffle, finely chopped. Pour the sauce over the chicken and serve.

Player's Grill, Johannesburg
CHEF: MICKY JOSEPH

Stuffed Baby Chicken Alba

serves: 2
2 baby chickens (or Cornish hens)
4 tablespoons butter
1 onion, chopped
1 green pepper, chopped
2 cloves garlic, minced
1 stalk celery
2 teaspoons curry powder
4 tablespoons almonds, chopped
½ cup cooked rice
¼ cup sultanas (raisins)
Salt, pepper
Tabasco sauce

Sauce
1 cup cream
½ cup vinegar
2 teaspoons honey
1 teaspoon mustard
1 teaspoon sultanas
4 tablespoons brandy
6 drops Tabasco sauce
Pinch salt

Bone the chickens. Sauté in butter finely cut onion, green pepper, garlic, celery and curry powder. Add almonds, cooked rice and sultanas. Season to taste with salt, pepper and Tabasco sauce. Stuff the chickens with this mixture. Close with needle and thread and truss. Roast in a 325° F. oven, tightly covered, until tender, about 1½ hours.

Bring all the ingredients to boil. Pour over chicken and reduce by a third without lid.

Bristol Hotel, Beirut, Lebanon
CHEF: NAGBI SFEIR

Chicken Moughrabia

(Lebanese Couscous)

½ pound (250 grams) chickpeas
1 pound (500 grams) butter
2 4-pound (2-kilogram) chickens
1⅔ pounds (800 grams) rump of mutton
or beef with bones
3 teaspoons salt
Pepper
7 pints boiling water
3⅓ pounds (1500 grams) small onions,
peeled and whole
2 pounds (1 kilogram) couscous
(moughrabia)
1½ teaspoons paprika
1 teaspoon cayenne
½ teaspoon cinnamon

serves: 8-10

Soak chickpeas overnight in water to cover.

Heat butter in a skillet and brown chicken. Remove to a large pot. Brown meat and bones and add to pot with 1½ teaspoons salt, pepper to taste, and boiling water. Thoroughly drain soaked chickpeas and fry in the same butter; add to chicken and meat. Cook over high heat first, then reduce heat to low to simmer until moughrabia is done. Sauté onions in butter and set aside. Put the prepared moughrabia (couscous) in a pan and sprinkle with half the spices, ½ teaspoon salt, and melted butter from skillet. Stir to coat with butter. Pour moughrabia into a strainer. Place in a pot half full of water (the water should not touch the strainer). Cover the pot very tightly and place over high heat to boil hard for 15 minutes. Stir moughrabia from time to time with a flat ladle. Cover top of moughrabia pot with a wet cloth and reduce heat to medium. Re-wet the cloth as it gets dry; stir moughrabia each time the cloth is dampened. This operation requires 2 to 3 hours. About 45 minutes before time to serve, take out the moughrabia, pour it into a shallow pan, add rest of salt and pepper, and stir.

Fifteen minutes before removing meats, put onions into chicken-meat pot to simmer until tender.

Take chickens from pot and cut

(Continued at foot of facing page

Mama Leone's, New York City

Chicken Tetrazzini alla Leone

serves: 6

18 mushroom heads, sliced
6 tablespoons butter
3 pounds (1.5 kilograms) chicken, boned, cooked and cut into bite-size pieces
¾ cup dry sherry
Béchamel sauce
12 ounces (375 grams) spaghetti
12 tablespoons grated Parmesan cheese

Sauté the mushrooms in butter; mix in chicken, sherry, and Béchamel sauce. Set aside and keep warm. Cook and drain the spaghetti. Divide it into 6 portions in individual casserole dishes. Top pasta with mushroom-meat mixture. Sprinkle 2 tablespoons grated Parmesan cheese over each serving and bake until the tops turn golden brown.

Béchamel sauce (cream sauce)

3 tablespoons flour
3 tablespoons melted butter
1 cup cream
½ cup milk
Salt
Pepper

Blend flour and butter in the top of a double boiler and stir in the cream and milk. Cook until the mixture thickens. Add salt and pepper to taste. Cook for an additional 5 minutes.

Chicken Moughrabia (continued)

each into 4 pieces; keep warm. Slice the meat and keep it warm. Take the onions and chickpeas and some of the broth from pot. Put pan with the moughrabia over low heat and gradually add broth, stirring all the while. Now remove moughrabia to the dish on which it is to be served. Arrange the pieces of chicken and meat and onions on top of it. Pour enough broth over all to moisten. Serve the remaining broth in a separate dish.

Carriage House, Miami Beach, Florida
CHEF: HEINZ WARICK

Bernard's Festive Chicken Salad

4 cups chicken or other cooked meat
1 cup finely diced celery
1 cup sliced water chestnuts
2 cups seedless white grapes, fresh
    or canned
¼ cup toasted slivered almonds
    Salt
    White pepper
1½ cups mayonnaise
    Dash of white vinegar
2 tablespoons Escoffier Sauce
    Diable
    Lettuce cups

Mix the first 4 ingredients and season to taste with salt, white pepper, mayonnaise and wine vinegar; add Escoffier Sauce Diable. Serve in individual cold crisp lettuce cups and garnish with raw vegetables or hard-cooked egg slices.

serves: 8-10

The Lali Room, Suva TraveLodge, Suva, Fiji
CHEF: ERIC SHAANING

Toa Kamikamica

2 3½-pound (1.5-kilogram) chickens
4 whole pineapples
1 large onion
2 stalks celery
1 large green pepper
1 large carrot
2 cups water
¼ cup white vinegar
1 tablespoon sugar
½ tablespoon tomato purée
¼ tablespoon salt
¼ teaspoon pepper
1 teaspoon root or stem ginger
2 teaspoons cornstarch
2 tablespoons butter

Cut the raw chicken meat into ½-inch cubes. Slice the tops off the pineapples and put aside. Scoop out the meat, leaving the pineapple hollow and with a firm base (take a thin slice off the bottom so the pineapple will "sit" upright on the serving dish). Cut the onion, celery, pineapple meat and green peppers into ½-inch pieces; slice the carrot thin. Place in a saucepan with water, vinegar and sugar, and simmer for 30 minutes. Add tomato purée, salt, pepper and ginger. Mix cornstarch with a little water and add to the sauce to thicken.
Melt the butter in a frying pan; add the raw chicken and cook gently for 3 to 4 minutes without browning. Add the sauce to the chicken and
(Continued at foot of facing page

serves: 4

wine: Champagne

The Forum of the XII Caesars, New York City

Chicken Baked in Clay

serves: 6

2 2-pound (1-kilogram) chickens
½ cup butter, softened
1 tablespoon dried basil (optional)
1 tablespoon parsley, chopped
1 tablespoon cognac
1 lemon
2 recipes basic bakers' clay

Allow the chickens to come to room temperature. Mix softened butter with dried basil (optional), parsley and cognac in a small bowl. Spread the seasoned butter between the wing joints, over the breasts and in the body cavities. Slash 1 lemon in several places and place inside the chickens. Wrap each bird securely in foil.

Roll out each recipe of basic bakers' clay about ½ inch thick. Put a foil-wrapped bird in the center. Mold the clay around the chicken so that all areas are completely covered. Bake chickens in a roasting pan for 45 minutes in a hot oven (500° F.). Break the clay with a mallet, peel off the foil, and carve.

Basic bakers' clay

3 cups flour
2 cups salt
1 tablespoon poultry seasoning
  About 1¼ cup water

Mix flour with salt and poultry seasoning in a large bowl, blending all together nicely. Gradually add enough water to make a stiff paste. The dough must not be sticky. Lift from the bowl and knead 2 minutes. Roll out in a circle about ½ inch thick. Plop onto a square of plastic wrap for easier handling. Wrap clay around bird neatly, sealing edges with water.

Toa Kamikamica (continued)

simmer for another 4 minutes. Pour into the hollow pineapples and replace the pineapple tops. Serve immediately, allowing one filled pineapple per person. Serve with pilaf or saffron rice.

BOAC Cabin Service

Pheasant Strasbourgoise

1 young pheasant
3 slices fat unsmoked bacon
3 tablespoons butter
½ cup chicken stock
1 tablespoon brandy
2 tablespoons cream
1 teaspoon meat extract
  Salt
  Pepper
2 tablespoons pâté de foie gras

Bard the pheasant and brown it in butter in a casserole. Add stock and cook in a 350° F. oven until the pheasant is slightly underdone. Remove the pheasant and reduce the cooking liquor. Add brandy, cream and meat extract and pass through a fine strainer. Correct seasoning and finish the sauce with diced pâté de foie gras. Do not boil. Cut the pheasant into portions, place in a baking dish and coat with the sauce. Heat in the oven for 15 minutes and serve.

serves: 1

Hungary

Szeged Goulash of Fowl

4 onions
6 tablespoons lard
2 tablespoons paprika
  Caraway seeds
3 chickens
6 potatoes
3 carrots
2 tomatoes

serves: 8

Mince the onions and fry them golden brown in the lard. Add paprika, a little water, a few crushed caraway seeds, the chickens, each divided into 8 parts, and let the whole stew, slowly. When the meat is half done add the diced potatoes, the sliced carrots and tomatoes or tomato purée. Stew until chicken is tender, adding a little water now and then. The sliced carrots may be boiled in a separate saucepan and their liquor used instead of water.
Before serving boil some csipetke (see Index) in the gravy.

Foie Gras (Goose Liver) Porkolt

4 large onions
5 ounces (150 grams) goose lard
3 tablespoons paprika
1 clove of garlic finely chopped
1½ pounds (750 grams) goose liver

serves: 6

Fry some finely shredded onions a delicate brown in goose lard and season with paprika and a little garlic. Cut goose liver into rough squares and sauté for a few minutes in a saucepan. Mix with the onions
(Continued at foot of facing page

Forum of the XII Caesars, New York City

Orange and Foie Gras with Wild Rice

serves: 2

1 cup wild rice
2 tablespoons butter
1 medium orange, peeled and diced
2 tablespoons foie gras
4 tablespoons dry sherry
  Dash Tabasco sauce
  Salt
  Pepper

Cook rice in salted water and strain but do not let it cool.
Melt the butter in a skillet; add the diced orange. Cook for 2 minutes, then add rice. Sauté and mix in the foie gras, crushing it with a fork. When very well blended and still hot, add the sherry, Tabasco, and salt and pepper to taste. Serve with roast duck, Cornish hen, pheasant, or game.

Publick House, Sturbridge, Massachusetts

Turkey Turnovers

serves: 5

2 heaping teaspoons chopped onion
1 tablespoon butter
2 cups diced turkey
¾ cup suprême sauce
½ teaspoon salt
⅛ teaspoon pepper
2 teaspoons parsley
1 egg yolk
  Pie crust pastry (see Index)

Sauté chopped onion in butter. Combine with the other ingredients. Roll pastry out into 5 rounds, each 5 inches in diameter. Place mound of the turkey mixture in centers. Brush edges with egg yolk beaten with 1 tablespoon water. Fold over to make a half-moon shape. Seal edges. Brush with egg wash. Place on a cookie sheet and cook in 400° F. oven until golden brown, approximately 25 minutes. Serve with additional suprême sauce.

Suprême sauce

½ cup mushrooms, sliced
1½ cups medium white sauce (see Index)
⅓ cup cream
  Salt

Cook mushrooms gently in sauce for ½ hour. Blend in cream and salt just before serving.

Foie Gras Porkolt (continued)

and paprika and stew for 10 minutes. Add some tomato purée and a little salt. When done take out the liver, rub the gravy through a sieve, pour it over the liver and let it come to boil again. Serve with steamed rice.

Peking Restaurant, Hong Kong
CHEF: CHUNG KEE PEH

Peking Duck

1 4-pound (2-kilogram) duck
Salt
Pepper
1 cup honey
12 thin crêpes
12 spring onions, chopped (leave
    green portion on)
Bean sauce

Wash duck and pat dry. Sprinkle
inside and out with salt and pepper.
Truss duck and arrange on a spit
carefully so that bird is balanced.
Baste and rub all over with honey.
Roast bird over charcoal or in a
425° F. rotisserie. Baste often with
honey. The duck is done when juice
running from a pricked thigh is
clear instead of pink and the skin
is very dark and crisp.
To serve, remove skin and divide
into 4 portions. Carve duck and
keep warm. Serve skin first: guests
roll skin in crêpes with green onion
and bean sauce. Then serve sliced
duck as usual.

serves: 4

Maile Restaurant, Kahala Hilton, Honolulu
CHEF: MARTIN WYSS

Roast Duckling Waialae

2 4-pound (2-kilogram) ducklings
1 cup red wine
1 medium onion
2 stalks celery
1 medium carrot
Pepper
Rosemary
Thyme
1 quart chicken stock
3 tablespoons flour
3 tablespoons butter
2 tablespoons sugar
¼ cup vinegar
1 cup orange juice
Peel of orange
1 tablespoon butter
1 tablespoon cognac
16 tangerine segments
2 bananas, sliced
8 lychee nuts (or bing cherries)
1 tablespoon Grand Marnier

Roast the ducklings for 1 hour at
400° F. Remove breast and leg and
debone. Remove fat. Glaze pan with
½ cup red wine. Add bones, onion,
celery, carrot, pepper, rosemary,
thyme and chicken stock. Blend
flour and butter to make a roux
and use to thicken. Simmer for 1
hour.
Melt sugar to caramel. Add vinegar,
½ cup orange juice and the sauce.
Simmer. The sauce should be brown
and quite thick.
Cut peel of orange in julienne strips.
Boil the rest of the red wine for 5
minutes. Strain sauce and add orange
julienne and red wine. Heat butter
in a flat pan. Put in the boned
ducklings and flame with cognac.

serves: 4

(Continued at foot of facing page

La Boucan Specialty Restaurant, Trinidad Hilton Hotel, Port of Spain, Trinidad
CHEF: HANS ZACH

Duckling with Guava

serves: 4

wine:
Pommard
1967

1 4-pound (2-kilogram) duckling
Salt
Pepper
¼ cup guava jelly
2 tablespoons oil
6 whole fresh guavas
2 tablespoons butter
½ cup guava nectar
Soy sauce
1 teaspoon cornstarch

Clean duckling and season with salt and pepper to taste. Rub 2 tablespoons of guava jelly inside of duckling and then roast in a pan with 2 tablespoons of hot oil for about 60 to 80 minutes at 400° F. Remove duckling from the pan and skim most of the fat from the pan juices. Cut fresh guavas in half, take out the insides, then heat the shells in the oven. Melt the butter in the roasting pan and add the insides of the guavas for flavoring. Add guava nectar and leave to simmer for 10 minutes. Season with soy sauce, salt and pepper to taste. Strain the gravy and add cornstarch mixed with 1 teaspoon water to thicken gravy. To serve, cut the duckling into portions, place on platter and spread the gravy over the duckling before serving. Fill the warm guava shells with some warm guava jelly and place them around the duckling as garnish.

Roast Duckling Waialae (continued)

Remove ducklings to a plate. Add to the pan tangerine segments, sliced bananas, lychee nuts or bing cherries, the sauce and the Grand Marnier. Pour mixture over the ducklings and serve with buttered wild rice.

The Nine Muses, Hollywood, California
CHEF: HARLEY WHITE

Burmese Duck à la Nine Muses

2 2½-pound (1250-gram) ducks, split
   in half, or 1 5-pound (2.2-kilogram)
   duck, disjointed
  Salt
  Pepper
2 cucumbers
1 onion, diced
3 minced garlic cloves
2 tablespoons rendered duck or
   chicken fat
1½ cups chicken stock
½ cup dry sherry
½ teaspoon grated nutmeg
¼ teaspoon ground mace
1 cup coconut cream*

Wash and dry the ducks. Remove as much fat as possible. Place pieces, skin side up, on shallow roasting pan. Sprinkle with salt and pepper. Roast in slow oven, 325 to 350° F. After 30 minutes remove duck and puncture the skin all over, being careful not to puncture the meat. Continue this process every 30 minutes, pouring off excess fat until skin is very crisp and a deep golden brown. (Total roasting time is about 3½ hours, depending on the size of the pieces.) Remove duck to a heated platter.

Peel the cucumbers and cut lengthwise into finger-size pieces. Soak in ice water.

Brown onions and garlic in rendered fat in a large skillet. Remove excess fat. Add the chicken stock, sherry, nutmeg, and mace. Simmer about 20 minutes, stirring occasionally, until alcohol is cooked out and liquid is reduced by about one-third. Mix in the coconut cream. Heat but do not boil. Add salt and pepper to taste.

Place drained cucumbers on platter with ducks. Pour the hot sauce over all. Serve immediately.

Coconut Cream: * Add 1 cup hot (not boiling) heavy cream to 1 cup packed flaked coconut. Let stand 30 minutes. Squeeze through cheesecloth or very fine sieve to extract cream.

serves: 4

*wine:
Burgundy*

Tulip Room, Rand International Hotel, Johannesburg
CHEF: RICHARD PATZEN

Mousse de Foie de Canard

(Duck Liver Mousse)

serves: 25

wine:
Nederburg
Selected
Riesling

5 pounds (2.5 kilograms) bacon
1 medium onion
2 cloves garlic, minced
2 apples, pared and chopped fine
2 tablespoons butter
5 pounds (2.5 kilograms) duck livers
1 tablespoon salt
1 teaspoon poultry seasoning
½ cup brandy
¼ cup Madeira

Line a porcelain terrine with thin slices of uncooked bacon and set aside. Sauté onion, garlic and apple in butter; add the duck livers, salt, poultry seasoning and the rest of the bacon, finely chopped. Flame with the brandy and Madeira and pass through a very fine sieve. Fill the terrine with liver mousse and cover tightly with foil. Poach in a hot water bath in a 350° F. oven for about 70 minutes. Cool and chill. Slice directly from terrine and serve with crisp toast.

Hong Kong

Heung So Aap

(Spiced Crisp Duck)

serves: 4

1 4-pound (2-kilogram) duck
2 teaspoons salt
⅓ teaspoon black pepper
½ teaspoon monosodium glutamate
2 tablespoons chinese wine or sake
¾ teaspoon faah jui (Chinese pepper)
½ teaspoon wooi heung (five-spice powder)
1 tablespoon dark soy sauce
2 tablespoons cornstarch
  Oil for deep frying
2 tablespoons salt
6 black peppercorns, crushed
2 spring onions, chopped
2 pieces fresh ginger

Wash and dry duck. Rub with salt, black pepper, monosodium glutamate, Chinese wine, faah jui and wooi heung. Leave for 1 hour. Cover duck with greaseproof paper and steam for 2 hours. Dry thoroughly. Rub in 1 teaspoon of dark soy sauce and cornstarch. Deep fry until duck is crisp, about 15 minutes. Mix salt and crushed black peppercorns in a condiment dish. Chop onions and ginger and put in separate condiment dishes. Serve duck while very hot and crisp. Dip pieces of duck in condiments before eating.

Gourmet Room, Princess Hotel, Pembroke, Bermuda
CHEF: GUNTHER SANHOWSKI

Guinea Chick des Bermudes avec Avocado

4 guinea chicks
1 cup vinegar
1 cup salt
2 avocados
½ onion, chopped fine
2 tomatoes, peeled, seeded, and diced
1 tablespoon chopped parsley
    Juice of 4 lemons
½ cup olive oil
    Salt
    White pepper
4 drops Tabasco sauce
1 tablespoon Worcestershire sauce

Boil guinea chicks in a gallon of water with the vinegar and salt for 8 minutes. Allow to cool. Cut the cold guinea chicks in half. Take out the meat and cut into half-inch pieces. Scoop avocado meat from halved shells and cut into half-inch pieces. Reserve shells.
Mix onion, tomatoes, parsley, lemon juice, olive oil, salt, white pepper, Tabasco, and Worcestershire. Stir guinea and avocado pieces into the mixture. Serve in the avocado shells with toast and butter.

serves: 4

*wine:
Pouilly-
Fuissé
1969*

Man Wah Restaurant, Mandarin Hotel, Hong Kong

Minced Quail Sauté with Lettuce

6 quail
4 ounces (125 grams) lean pork
1½ tablespoons soy sauce
2 teaspoons salt
1 egg yolk
3 teaspoons cornstarch
½ teaspoon sugar
4 dried mushrooms
1 bamboo shoot
6 water chestnuts
5 cups peanut oil
4 ounces (125 grams) rice noodles
1 small onion, chopped
1 tablespoon chicken stock
1 teaspoon sesame oil
¼ teaspoon black pepper
24 lettuce leaves

Remove all bones from the quail; chop quail and pork in small cubes. Marinate in ½ tablespoon soy sauce, 1 teaspoon salt, egg yolk, 2 teaspoons cornstarch, and sugar for 10 minutes. Chop the mushrooms, bamboo shoots, and water chestnuts into small pieces and set aside. Heat oil very hot and deep fry the rice noodles until puffed and golden; put on a serving platter. Use 3 tablespoons heated oil to fry the drained quail and pork mixture until well done. Set aside and keep warm. Heat another 3 tablespoons oil in frying pan, add chopped onion, and sauté 1 minute. Add mushrooms, bamboo shoot, and water chestnuts and sauté another

serves: 6

(Continued at foot of facing page

*Chicken
Badam
Pasanda*

PEACOCK ROOM,
ASHOKA HOTEL,
NEW DELHI
(Chef: Roshan Lal)

Chicken Shashlik

OBEROI
INTERCONTINENTAL
HOTEL, NEW DELHI

Roast Duckling Waialae

KAHALA HILTON, HONOLULU
(Chef: Martin Wyse)

Hawaiian Hors d'oeuvres Table

Ratatouille Mexicaine

COMMANDARIA GRILL,
CYPRUS HILTON,
NICOSIA

Moschari Stifado

Filet de Boeuf au Château

LE CHÂTEAU, MELBOURNE
(Chef: Peter DeVilee)

The Forum of the XII Caesars, New York City

Pheasant Scipio

serves: 4

2 2½-pound (1250-gram) pheasants
3 cups red wine
1 tablespoon vinegar
½ carrot, diced
½ onion, diced
1 bay leaf
1 clove garlic
4 tablespoons butter
2 tablespoons flour
1 cup chicken broth
  Salt
  Pepper
1 tablespoon pasteurized blood
  (or kitchen bouquet plus 1 teaspoon
  flour)
1 cluster grapes
2 tablespoons blanched sliced almonds

Bone the pheasants but leave skin on; save the bones to marinate 4 hours with 2 cups wine, vinegar, diced carrot and onion, bay leaf, and crushed garlic clove.

The next day strain the marinade and sauté the bones and vegetables in 2 tablespoons of butter until golden brown. Add flour and cook 5 minutes, stirring well; add the strained marinade, the chicken broth, salt, and pepper and cook ½ hour. Take away from fire and strain the sauce; add the blood. Set aside and keep warm.

Sauté the pieces of pheasant on both sides in the remaining butter; finish cooking in a preheated oven at 350° F. for about 15 minutes, or until meat is tender.

Skin the grapes and warm them briefly in 1 cup wine.

On a service platter lay the pheasant pieces and surround them with the grapes. Cover the meat with the sauce and sprinkle the sliced almonds on top.

Serve with maize (pollenta), Roman gnocchi, or wild rice.

Minced Quail Sauté (continued)

minute over high heat. Return meat mixture to pan and add 1 tablespoon soy sauce, 1 teaspoon salt, chicken stock, sesame oil, and black pepper. Stir until mixed thoroughly and pour over the fried rice noodles. Serve with lettuce leaves, which may be used to wrap around the meat and noodles mixture.

Georges Rey Restaurant Français, New York City
CHEF: JEAN LE ROUZIC

Côtes d'Agneau Champvalon

8 very thick lamb chops
12 medium potatoes sliced ¼ inch thick
2 onions, sliced
  Salt
  Pepper
1 clove of garlic
1 bouquet garni (2 stalks celery and
    parsley tied in a small bunch)
  Beef stock
  Oil
  Parsley for garnish

Brown the lamb chops in a frying pan. Mix the potatoes and onions with salt and pepper. Place half the potatoes and onions on the bottom of a roasting tray and arrange the lamb on top. Add garlic and bouquet garni and the rest of the potatoes and onions and cover with the beef stock. Place tray in a 450° F. oven for about 1 hour. Serve hot with chopped parsley.

serves: 8

The Four Seasons, New York City

Beef Bourguignonne

⅓ cup oil
4 pounds (2 kilograms) top round, cut into
    1½-inch cubes
¼ pound (125 grams) pork belly, cut into
    small cubes
⅓ cup chopped onion
1 teaspoon minced garlic
2 teaspoons tomato purée
⅓ cup flour
2⅔ cups red wine
2⅔ cups beef stock
1 bay leaf
1 3-inch stalk fresh thyme (¼ teaspoon if
    dried)
1 tablespoon salt
1 teaspoon freshly ground white pepper
1½ pounds (750 grams) carrots

Heat oil in large pot and brown the beef and pork belly in it. Add onion and garlic. Stir until brown.
Add tomato purée and mix well. Add remaining ingredients except carrots and stir well. Cover and cook over low heat for 3 hours, stirring occasionally.
In the meantime, peel carrots and quarter lengthwise. Halve these pieces and place in boiling water to cover. Cook for 15 minutes and drain.
Remove meat to a serving casserole and strain sauce over it. Add carrots and heat together for 5 minutes.

serves: 6

Restaurant Napoleon, Paris
CHEF: GUY BAUMANN

Steak Tartare Maréchal Duroc

serves: 4 as hors d'oeuvres or 1 as a main course

⅔ cup first-quality beef, finely ground
1 egg yolk
1 tablespoon minced parsley
1 teaspoon minced chives
1 teaspoon minced chervil
1 teaspoon minced tarragon
1 pickled gerkin, chopped
1 tablespoon capers
¼ pared tart apple, chopped
   Fine salt
   Freshly ground pepper
½ teaspoon steak sauce (A-1 or
   Worcestershire)
½ teaspoon ketchup (optional)

Mix all ingredients thoroughly but gently. Shape in the form of a steak on serving plate. Chill very thoroughly before serving.

Mon Cher Ton Ton, Tokyo
CHEF: NORIAKI FUJITA

Sirloin Steak

serves: 4

wine: Burgundy or beer

4 prime sirloin steaks 2 inches thick
   (Kobe beef if available)
   Sauce

Marinate steaks in the refrigerator overnight in sauce. Broil over charcoal. Pass extra sauce, served very cold, at table.

Sauce

½ cup Spanish pimento
2 medium onions
½ teaspoon sugar
   Pepper
1 cup catsup
7 tablespoons freshly grated horseradish
1 tablespoon dry mustard
½ teaspoon salt
1 tablespoon minced garlic
½ cup orange juice

Slice pimento and onions and set aside. Mix all other ingredients well and stir in sliced pimento and onion. Use as marinade for steaks and as sauce.

Royal Garden Hotel, London
CHEF: GUY DE LAURENT

Saddle of Lamb Bouquetière Royal

1 saddle of spring lamb 6-7 pounds
1 large onion cut into quarters
1 bay leaf
2 medium carrots, sliced
  Pinch rosemary
2-3 ounces cooking fat
  Salt & pepper
⅓ pint stock

Suggested Garnish

1 cauliflower (divided into sprigs)
2 pounds of prepared carrots
2 pounds turnips
1 pound garden peas
1 pound fresh broccoli
6 artichoke hearts
1 pound small French beans

(Cooking time 15 to 20 minutes per pound.) Season the meat well, brush saddle with melted fat, add other ingredients, except stock, to pan and cook for one hour basting at regular intervals. Add the stock and cook for remaining time, basting as before. When cooked, place on a serving dish and strain gravy into a sauceboat.

All vegetables are cooked in salted water. When cooked, toss in butter in a shallow pan. Fill artichoke hearts with the peas and arrange tastefully in groups around the joint.

serves: 6-8

wine:
Chateau
Haut Brion

Charlie Brown's, New York City

Steak and Kidney Pie

1¾ pounds (875 grams) beef steak, cubed
1 veal kidney, thickly sliced
8 mushrooms, sliced
1 large onion, finely chopped
1 teaspoon finely chopped parsley
1½ cups brown sauce or gravy
½ cup Madeira
½ teaspoon Worcestershire sauce
  Rich pastry dough

In a 2½ quart casserole, mix together steak, kidney, mushrooms, onion and parsley. Combine brown sauce, Madeira and Worcestershire; pour into casserole. Cover with pastry dough; cut slits in dough to allow steam to escape. Bake at 350° F. 50 to 60 minutes or until crust is well browned and meat is tender.

serves: 6

Suehiro, Tokyo
CHEF: YUTAHA KUCHINA

Suehiro Steak

serves: 4

4 **Kobe beef boneless sirloin steaks 1¾ inches thick. Or ask for prime grade beef**
2 **cups cold-pressed sesame oil**
1 **carrot, chopped**
2 **stalks celery with leaves, chopped**
2 **onions, chopped**

Marinate steaks in vegetables and oil for 12 hours in summer or 20 hours in winter, turning several times. When ready to cook, broil over charcoal or in a very hot oven to desired degree of doneness. (About 7 minutes on each side will give a rare steak.) Baste with marinade oil while broiling.

Greece

Moussaka

serves: 10

2 **eggplants**
　Salt
4 **tablespoons butter**
2 **pounds (1 kilogram) minced beef**
3 **onions, chopped**
2 **tablespoons tomato purée**
¼ **cup chopped parsley**
½ **cup red wine**
½ **cup water**
　Pepper
　Dash cinnamon
3 **eggs, beaten**
1 **cup grated cheese**
½ **cup bread crumbs**
　Cooking oil

Sauce

6 **tablespoons butter**
6 **tablespoons flour**
3 **cups hot milk**
　Salt
　Pepper
　Dash nutmeg
4 **egg yolks, lightly beaten**

Wash eggplants; cut in thick slices, sprinkle with salt and let stand. Melt butter in frying pan and sauté meat and onions until meat is brown. Add tomato purée, parsley, wine, water, salt and pepper. Simmer until liquid is absorbed. Cool, stir in cinnamon, eggs, ½ cup cheese and half the bread crumbs. *Conclusion:* Quickly brown slices of eggplant in hot oil. Grease an oven-proof casserole; sprinkle bottom with remaining bread crumbs. Fill casserole with alternate layers eggplant and meat, beginning and finishing with eggplant. Cover with sauce; sprinkle with remaining grated cheese. Bake in oven for one hour at 350°F. Serve hot.
Melt butter over low heat, stirring in flour until well blended. Remove from heat, slowly stir in milk; return to heat and cook until sauce is smooth and thick. Add salt, pepper and nutmeg. Mix egg yolks with small quantity of sauce, then return mixture to bulk of sauce, stirring continuously. Cook for 2 or 3 more minutes.

Player's Grill, Johannesburg
CHEF: MICKY JOSEPH

Pepper Steak

6 tablespoons butter
1 tablespoon crushed peppercorns
1 teaspoon Worcestershire sauce
2 tablespoons brown sauce
2 tablespoons red wine
1 steak (fillet or sirloin are often used)

Mix 4 tablespoons butter, pepper- *serves: 1*
corns, Worcestershire sauce,
brown sauce and wine together and
heat for 5 minutes, stirring
occasionally. Then fry the steak in
2 tablespoons butter. When steak is
ready, let it simmer in the sauce
for 2 minutes.
Serve with sliced tomato, French
fried potatoes and peas.

India

Beef Korma

½ pint yogurt
1 cup unsweetened coconut
2 teaspoons salt
2 pounds (1 kilogram) beef, boned and diced
¼ pound (125 grams) butter
2 medium onions, sliced
2 medium onions, minced
6 tablespoons poppy seeds, ground
2 tablespoons coriander, ground
2 cloves garlic, minced
1 teaspoon dried hot red chili, crushed
Juice of 2 limes

Blend yogurt with coconut and salt *serves: 6*
and let meat marinate in the
mixture for an hour or more. Then
cook slowly in a shallow pan until
meat is tender. In a large pan, melt
butter and sauté the sliced onions
until brown. Blend the minced
onions with the next 4 ingredients
and fry for 2 minutes. Add meat
and simmer for about 5 minutes.
Before serving add lime juice.

Keema Curry

1 small onion, finely minced
2 cloves of garlic, finely minced
4 tablespoons cooking fat
1 tablespoon curry powder
3 large tomatoes, sliced fine, or 1 teaspoon tomato purée
1 pound (500 grams) minced beef or mutton
1 tablespoon yogurt
Salt to taste

Fry onion and garlic in cooking fat *serves: 4*
for 2 minutes until golden. Add
curry powder and tomatoes. Mix
thoroughly. Cook on high flame for
3 to 5 minutes. Add meat and
yogurt and mix well. Cook slowly
until done. Do not let curry get
dry; it should be fairly moist.

Le Coq d'Or, London
CHEF: JEAN C. BESNIER

La Côte de Boeuf Bordelaise

serves: 4-6

1 2-pound (1-kilogram) rib of beef
   with bone
4 shallots, parboiled 5 minutes
¾ cup dry red wine
2 tablespoons flour
6 tablespoons butter
  Salt
  Pepper
3 tablespoons bread crumbs
½ teaspoon thyme
2 tablespoons chopped parsley
6 slices poached beef marrow

Roast rib of beef for 30 minutes in a 375° F. oven.

In the same pan place 3 chopped parboiled shallots, wine and ¾ cup meat juices (or beef bouillon). Simmer for 10 minutes to reduce the sauce. Thicken with flour and 3 tablespoons butter blended well. Taste for salt and pepper. Set aside and keep warm.

Fry the other chopped shallot in a small pan with the rest of the butter until golden. Take away from the flame and add bread crumbs, thyme and chopped parsley. Season with salt and pepper. Cover rib of beef with this mixture and place under the broiler until golden. Decorate with slices of marrow. Serve sauce separately.

Hungary

Gulyas Soup

(Goulash)

serves: 6

1 pound (500 grams) brisket or
   forequarter of beef
3 medium onions
2 tablespoons sweet paprika
  Salt
4 large potatoes
1 tomato

Cut the meat in cubes, wash and put it into a saucepan together with the chopped onions, paprika, salt and a little water.

Let it simmer. When the meat is almost tender, add the potatoes, cut in cubes, and sufficient water to make thick gravy. Simmer again until the meat is quite tender. Before it is quite done, add the sliced tomato.

Csipetke

¾ cup flour
1 egg
  Pinch salt
  About ¼ cup water

Sift flour and salt. Make a depression in flour and add egg and water. Mix well. Add a little more water or flour as needed to make manageable dough. Roll out very thin, cut into small squares and boil in the soup for a minute or two before serving.

Pakistan

Kima Mutter

1 onion, chopped
¼ cup cooking fat
½ teaspoon turmeric
½ teaspoon red pepper
¼ teaspoon red pepper, ground
¼ teaspoon garlic powder
½ teaspoon ground ginger
1 tomato, chopped
1 pound (500 grams) beef, minced
¼ pound green peas

Sauté onion in cooking fat until brown. Add spices and cook for 5 minutes. Add tomato and cook for 3 more minutes. Add minced beef and cook for 15 minutes, stirring frequently until almost dry. Serve hot with rice or chapatties.

serves: 4

Old Swiss Inn, Winnipeg, Manitoba
CHEF: RENÉ AMMANN

Beef Tenderloin Wellington

Salt
Pepper
1 1½-pound (750-gram) beef tenderloin, well trimmed
Vegetable oil for frying
3 ounces (95 grams) cubed veal
2 ounces (65 grams) cubed unsmoked pork
4 ounces (125 grams) fresh whole mushrooms
6 ounces (185 grams) chopped chicken liver
1 tablespoon chopped onions
3 tablespoons brandy
2 tablespoons bread crumbs
3 egg yolks
½ cup Marsala
¼ cup fresh parsley, chopped
1 pound (500 grams) puff-pastry dough
2 ounces (65 grams) thinly sliced fat bacon

Salt and pepper tenderloin, brown quickly on both sides in a very hot pan with vegetable oil and set aside to cool.
Fry cubed veal, cubed pork, mushrooms, chicken liver, and onions in a medium hot pan and flame with brandy. While still hot, force through a meat grinder. To thicken, add bread crumbs and 2 egg yolks; season with salt and pepper. Add Marsala and parsley. Roll out pastry dough to ¼ inch thick.
Spread the meat filling on the tenderloin and cover with sliced bacon. Wrap the covered tenderloin in the dough and seal completely. Beat the other egg yolk with a tablespoon of water and brush over the dough. Decorate the top with remaining dough cut in fancy shapes. Brush again with egg wash. Bake at 350° F. 40 to 50 minutes. Let rest 10 minutes before serving.

serves: 4

wine: Dôle, Swiss red wine

Le Chaland Hotel, Plaine Magnien, Mauritius

Steak à la Creole

serves: 1

1 fillet steak
1 tablespoon butter
1 tablespoon oil
½ onion, sliced
1 tomato, peeled, seeded and chopped
1 sprig thyme
1 tablespoon chopped parsley
   Chili powder to taste

Sauté steak in butter and oil for 15 minutes. Remove from the frying pan and keep warm. Place onion, tomato, thyme and parsley and chili powder (to taste) in steak pan. Allow to cook for 10 minutes. Place the steak in the prepared sauce and allow to simmer for another 10 minutes. Serve with boiled rice and roast potatoes.

The Aristocrat Restaurant, Manila

Kare-Kare

serves: 12

2 pounds (1 kilogram) tripe
2 pounds (1 kilogram) ox tail
2 quarts water
   Anatto seeds for coloring
1 piece banana blossom (Butuan variety)*
1 pound (500 grams) string beans
4 eggplants
1 pound (500 grams) radishes
½ cup ground peanuts (toasted until
   coffee brown)
½ cup toasted ground rice
1 teaspoon monosodium glutamate
   Salt to taste

Boil tripe and ox tail in water. Skim often to remove scum. Add more water if necessary as meats cook. There should always be stock to cover. When meat is tender, about 3½ hours, set aside stock. Cut tripe and ox tail into serving pieces.
Soak and rub anatto seeds in water to cover. Cut vegetables in serving pieces and drop into boiling reserved stock to parboil, about 5 minutes. Remove and set aside. Add water in which anatto seeds have been soaked to the stock; do not include seeds. Let boil for 5 minutes. Blend in ground peanuts and ground rice. Bring to a boil. Return meats to pot and add monosodium glutamate. Just before removing from fire, add the parboiled vegetables and salt to taste.

(*Dried banana blossoms are available in oriental food stores, or fresh or frozen small artichoke hearts may be substituted.)

Restaurant des Ambassadeurs, George Hotel, Edinburgh
CHEF: G. PRANDSTATTER

Beef Olives with Rice Pilaf

8 ounces (250 grams) finely minced pork
4 medium onions
1 egg
¼ cup chopped parsley
2 tablespoons cream
4 pounds (2 kilograms) top-round beef
  Salt
  Pepper
1 tablespoon English mustard
  Flour for dredging
  Clarified butter for sautéing
1 bottle red wine
6 tablespoons beef drippings
½ cup flour
2 stalks celery
6 peeled carrots
¼ cup tomato purée
4 cups brown stock
  Bouquet garni (thyme, bay leaves,
    rosemary, crushed peppercorns tied
    together in cheesecloth bag)

For stuffing combine pork, 1 finely chopped onion, egg, chopped parsley and cream; mix well. Cut the meat into 16 thin slices across the grain and pound out thinly. Trim slices evenly to make cutlets 4″×3″ (chop up trimmings and add to the stuffing). Season each slice of meat with salt and pepper and spread with English mustard and the stuffing. Roll up neatly and secure with string or skewer. Roll the "beef olives" in flour and sauté in clarified butter until golden; remove and place in a thick-bottomed casserole. Pour red wine over the beef and let casserole simmer gently until the wine is reduced by half. In the beef skillet mix drippings and flour and cook until browned (brown roux); stir constantly to prevent burning. Set aside and let cool. Cut remaining onions, celery and 2 carrots into 1-inch slices. Brown vegetables in clarified butter; drain and add the butter and the tomato purée to the cool roux. Add the hot stock to the roux and bring it to a boil, stirring constantly, then add the bouquet garni, salt and pepper. Pour the sauce into the beef and red wine casserole. Cover tightly and allow to simmer, preferably in a very slow oven, for 1½ hours. When ready to serve, remove the string from the beef slices and place in an entrée dish on top of rice pilaf. Skim and correct seasonings

(Continued at foot of facing page

serves: 8

wine:
Mouton
Cadet

Chile

Tongue in Walnut Sauce

serves: 6

1 large tongue
2 cloves garlic
1 onion
1 carrot (quartered)
  Salt
  Pepper
2 cups soft bread crumbs
3 cups milk
  Oil
4 tablespoons chopped walnuts
2 hard-boiled eggs
2 tablespoons parsley

Clean tongue and soak in salted water for 2 hours. Score tongue across surface; cover with boiling water; add garlic, onion, carrot, salt and pepper. Cook until tender, about 2 hours. Let cool. Remove tongue from stock; peel and cut into ½-inch strips. Soak bread crumbs in milk and put through a sieve. Fry tongue lightly in oil; add bread crumbs. Add nuts just before serving; decorate with sliced or sieved egg and chopped parsley.

Beef Olives (continued)

in the sauce and strain through a fine sieve over the meat. Garnish with remaining carrots cut into strips and boiled.

Rice pilaf

½ cup butter
¼ cup chopped onions
½ pound (250 grams) Patna rice
1 thread saffron
2 cups white stock
  Salt
  Pepper
1 teaspoon fines herbes

Place half the butter in a frying pan. Add the onions. Cook gently without browning for 3 minutes. Add the rice and saffron. Cook without browning for 2 minutes, stirring to coat rice with butter. Add the stock, season with salt, pepper, and fines herbes, cover with buttered paper (or a very tight lid) and bring to a boil. Place in a hot oven for approximately 15 minutes, until rice is cooked and stock has been absorbed. Remove into a cool dish. Carefully mix in the remaining butter and correct seasonings.

That Steak Joynt, Chicago
CHEF: RILEY SIMMONS

Steak Joynt Pioneer Beef Tenderloin

8 steaks, cut from a 4-pound (2-kilogram) beef tenderloin, well trimmed
¾ cup corn oil
1 clove garlic, chopped
½ cup chopped fresh parsley
1 tablespoon freshly ground pepper
1 tablespoon salt
1 cup red dinner wine
8 spinach pancakes

Butterfly each steak with a sharp knife. Place steaks in an ovenproof glass pie dish. Top with enough oil to moisten each steak. Sprinkle with garlic, parsley, pepper and salt. Let stand in the refrigerator 24 hours.

Heat a heavy skillet very hot. Sear steaks quickly on both sides. Dribble in wine a little at a time so that the steaks will go on cooking but not drown in wine. Remove steaks when done to desired degree of doneness and place each one on a spinach pancake. Serve with sauce from skillet.

serves: 8

wine: Inglenook Napa Valley Cabernet Sauvignon, 1965

Spinach pancakes

2 large onions, chopped
4 ounces (125 grams) chopped bacon
1 cup bacon drippings
1 teaspoon nutmeg
1 pound (500 grams) chopped fresh spinach
2 teaspoons salt
2 teaspoons pepper

Sauté onion and bacon to well done but do not brown. Add bacon drippings, nutmeg and the spinach. Add salt, pepper, and eggs. Mix well. Make 8 individual pancakes in small pan. Keep warm until ready to serve.

Hotel Inter-Continental Manila, Rizal, Philippines

Tenderloin Steak Patricia

2 4-ounce (125-gram) tenderloin steaks, flattened
1 tablespoon clarified butter
½ chopped shallot
3 fresh mushrooms, sliced
1 tomato, peeled and chopped
1 teaspoon chopped parsley
Salt
Freshly ground pepper
¼ crushed garlic clove
¼ cup Irish whisky
2 tablespoons brown meat sauce

Sauté steaks in clarified butter until medium rare. Place steaks in serving dish and keep warm. Add shallots and mushrooms to the butter, half cook them. Add tomatoes, herbs, garlic. Let simmer for 2 minutes; return steaks into pan, pour whisky over, flame and finish the sauce with brown sauce.

serves: 1

The President Hotel, Johannesburg
CHEF: ERIC GASSER

Fillet of Beef "Miss Janette Goddard"

serves: 4

4 8-ounce (250-gram) fillets of beef
Salt
Pepper
4 tablespoons butter
1 onion
2 cloves garlic
1 pound (500 grams) fresh button
   mushrooms
Paprika
4 tablespoons flour
¾ cup red wine
¼ cup tomato sauce
4 tablespoons brandy
1 cup cream
4 tomatoes
1 can asparagus tips (or 16 spears fresh
   asparagus, cooked)

Season the meat with salt and pepper and sauté in butter to desired degree of doneness. Chop the onions and garlic and slice the mushrooms. Sprinkle onions and mushrooms with salt, pepper and paprika and fry in butter with the garlic. Stir in the flour, then add the wine, tomato sauce and brandy. Reduce the sauce until thick, then add cream. Do not boil after adding cream. Pour the sauce over the steaks and garnish with tomatoes and asparagus.

Beach Luxury Hotel, Karachi

Samosa

serves: 2

½ teaspoon ground ginger
½ teaspoon minced garlic
1 teaspoon salt
½ pound (250 grams) finely ground beef
½ teaspoon turmeric
½ teaspoon chili powder
½ teaspoon zeera (caraway seeds)
1 medium onion, chopped
10 fresh coriander leaves
Fresh green chilis to taste
3 tablespoons flour
1 teaspoon clarified butter
Butter for frying

Add ground ginger, garlic, and ½ teaspoon salt to the ground meat and put it to cook. After all liquid has evaporated add turmeric, chili powder, and zeera and keep stirring until cooked. Cool and add chopped onion, coriander leaves, meat, and green chilis.
With 3 tablespoons flour and ½ teaspoon salt make a dough with water. Add 1 teaspoon butter. Roll dough out and cut into strips; make a cone of each. Fill with meat mixture, crimp the edges, and fry in hot clarified butter.

Le Relais, Café Royal, London
CHEF: G. MOUILLERON

Tournedos Madame Saint Ange

½ cup puff-pastry dough
¼ cup celeriac, peeled and chopped
2 tablespoons very heavy cream
  Salt
  Freshly ground pepper
1 6-ounce (185-gram) center cut tenderloin
    steak
2 tablespoons butter
1 tablespoon chopped shallots
¼ cup sliced white button mushrooms
1 small tomato, peeled and chopped
2 tablespoons dry white wine
¼ cup brown stock
2 pinches tarragon

With the puff-pastry dough make a flan case large enough to hold steak. Bake. If pastry is baked ahead of time, reheat when ready to serve. Make a purée of the celeriac by boiling, sieving, and enriching with the heavy cream; season with salt and pepper.

Cook the tenderloin in butter in a small sauté pan; when cooked to taste remove and keep warm. Then fry the shallots in the butter until light brown. Now mix in the mushrooms, tomato, white wine, and stock.

Allow to reduce by two-thirds, taste for seasoning, add a pinch of tarragon and a little butter, and the sauce is ready. Place the celeriac purée in the flan case, cover with the steak, and pour the sauce over this. Another pinch of tarragon finishes the dish. Serve very hot.

serves: 1

wine:
Mouton
Cadet 1966

The Savoy, London
CHEF: SILVINO S. TROMPETTO

Fillet of Beef Stroganoff

1½ pounds (750 grams) of fillet of beef cut
    in pieces 1″ × ¼″
6 tablespoons butter
¼ pound (125 grams) sliced white
    mushrooms
1 tablespoon wine vinegar
1 cup of sour cream
1 teaspoon paprika
  Salt

Sauté the beef in a very hot thick saucepan with the butter for 6 to 8 minutes; when cooked remove and place in a serving dish and keep warm. Cook the mushrooms in the same saucepan for 4 to 5 minutes, then add the vinegar and cream, stirring vigorously. Do not allow sauce to boil after cream is added. Season with paprika and salt and pour over the beef. Serve hot.

serves: 4

Bush Inn Hotel, Christchurch, New Zealand
CHEF: J. DIEUDONNE

Ragout of Beef Waitaingi

serves: 6

1½ pounds (750 grams) lean beef cubes
1 cup dry red wine
4 tablespoons cider vinegar
1 teaspoon ground cloves
1 tablespoon tomato paste
2 tablespoons brown sugar
1 pound (500 grams) sliced onions
2 tablespoons oil
2 tablespoons flour
1 cup hot water
Salt
Pepper
½ pound (250 grams) mushrooms
3 tablespoons butter

Steep the beef overnight in wine, vinegar, cloves, tomato paste and brown sugar. Fry the onions in the oil. Remove onions and fry drained marinated meat and stir until well browned; sprinkle in the flour and brown. Add the hot water, marinade and mix well. Stir the mixture until it boils. Cover pan and place in a 300° F. oven until the meat is tender, about 1 hour. Correct seasoning and serve hot with sliced mushrooms fried in butter and arranged on top. Also serve boiled new potatoes, roast pumpkin and green beans or peas.

Biggs Restaurant, Chicago
CHEF: BRIAN KUZMAN

Beef Tips Basquaise

serves: 6

4 pounds (2 kilograms) tenderloin or
    sirloin tips
Salt
Pepper
½ cup butter
⅓ cup finely chopped shallots
½ cup diced green pepper
¼ pound (125 grams) mushrooms, sliced
1 cup red wine
1 can condensed beef broth
2 teaspoons Worcestershire sauce
1 can condensed bisque of tomato soup
Watercress

If tips are tenderloin they can be cut into thin slices, sprinkled with salt and pepper, and broiled until medium rare. If the tips are from a tougher cut of beef they can be roasted or braised until tender, then thinly sliced.
In a skillet melt butter, add shallots, green pepper, and mushrooms. Sauté until tender but not brown. Pour off fat. Add red wine, beef broth, and Worcestershire sauce. Bring to a boil and boil gently until liquid is reduced to half its original volume. Add bisque of tomato and simmer until sauce thickens slightly. Spoon sauce over beef tips. Garnish with watercress.

The Savoy, London
CHEF: SILVINO S. TROMPETTO

La Petite Marmite Churchill

4 quarts chicken broth or water
  Salt
1½ pounds (750 grams) lean beef (round
    roast or brisket)
3 carrots, sliced
2 turnips, diced
4 leeks, sliced
1 3-pound (1.5-kilogram) chicken
½ medium head cabbage
20 pieces marrow bone 1½ inches wide
6 celery stalks in 3-inch pieces
½ cup melted butter
20 thin slices French bread
½ pound (250 grams) Parmesan cheese

In mild broth or salted water, bring beef (in one piece), carrots, turnips and leeks to a boil. When beef is half done, add chicken, cleaned and trussed, cabbage (in one piece) and marrow bones; simmer until chicken is tender. Add celery for last 10 minutes of cooking time. Carefully remove meats and vegetables from pot and drain thoroughly. Arrange beef, chicken, cabbage and celery on an ovenproof platter, brush with butter and keep warm in a 300° F. oven. Remove fat from marrow bones and set aside. Strain consommé through a fine sieve lined with several layers of dampened cheesecloth. Measure; reduce by boiling or dilute to make about 8 cups. Reheat consommé and add to it carrot slices, turnip dice and leeks. Serve in ovenproof flat soup plates. Garnish each plate with French bread spread with marrow fat and sprinkled with grated Parmesan cheese; run under the broiler just long enough to toast cheese lightly. Pass sliced meats, cabbage and celery with soups.

serves: 10

La Taverna, Hong Kong

Costata alla Fiorentina

1 2-pound (1-kilogram) porterhouse
    steak, 2 inches thick
¾ cup olive oil
1 teaspoon salt
½ teaspoon ground black pepper
2 firm tomatoes, cut in half
2 tablespoons parsley, minced
2 tablespoons butter
  Juice of ½ lemon

Marinate steak in olive oil, salt, and pepper for 24 hours. When ready to cook, broil in a preheated oven or over charcoal coals about 7 minutes on each side. While steak is broiling, grill tomatoes sprinkled with parsley, salt, and pepper and dotted with butter. Serve on a hot plate; squeeze lemon juice on steak.

serves: 2

wine:
Chianti
Ricasoli

Pantoufle Perigourdine

KENSINGTON PALACE HOTEL, LONDON
(Chef: Larry Stove)

Chicken Swan Valley   HOTEL PARMELIA, PERTH, W. AUSTRALIA
                                              (Chef: D. R. Williams)

Auberge de France, Lythe Hill Hotel, Haslemere, Surrey, England
CHEF: CORREGER

Tournedos St. Genevieve

serves: 4

4 tournedos of beef
¼ cup pâté de foie gras
¼ cup fine white bread crumbs
6 tablespoons butter
¼ cup onion, finely sliced
¼ cup julienne strips of ham
8 large mushrooms, sliced
3 tablespoons marsala
½ cup veal stock
½ cup very heavy cream
Salt
Pepper

Make a pocket in each tournedos. Mix pâté de foie gras and bread crumbs and stuff tournedos. Gently sauté in butter to desired degree of doneness. Remove from pan and keep warm.

In the same pan brown onion, ham and mushrooms. Add more butter as needed. Deglaze pan with marsala and add veal stock. Reduce by half and add cream. Cook gently until sauce is thick. Place tournedos on a serving platter and spoon sauce over them. Serve extra sauce separately.

Le Château, Melbourne, Australia
CHEF: PETER DEVILEE

Filet de Boeuf au Château

serves: 6

wine:
*Seaview
Cabernet
Sauvignon
'64*

1 3-pound (1.5-kilogram) trimmed whole beef fillet
Salt
Pepper
4 tablespoons butter
1 small onion, chopped fine
4 ounces (125 grams) bacon
4 ounces (125 grams) chicken livers, chopped fine
¾ pound (375 grams) mushrooms, chopped fine
Pinch ground allspice
1 pound (500 grams) puff pastry
1 egg yolk

Let beef come to room temperature. Season fillet and sauté in butter until medium rare. Remove from pan and brown onions in remaining butter. Add bacon, chicken livers, mushrooms and allspice. Stir until cooked. Cool fillet and filling. Roll out pastry large enough to cover the whole fillet. Spread half the filling in the middle of the pastry and place fillet on top. Spread the rest of the filling on top of the fillet and fold pastry all around fillet and filling. Brush beaten egg yolk on pastry and seal sides and ends. Place fillet on a baking sheet with long pastry seam down. Brush pastry with egg yolk to glaze. Put in a 450° F. oven for 30 minutes. (If pastry browns before cooking is done, cover with foil.) Let rest 5 minutes before serving.

W.—E

Repulse Bay Hotel, Hong Kong
CHEF: ROLF SCHNEIDER

Pepper Steak

1 8-ounce (250-gram) fillet steak
1 tablespoon butter
2 tablespoons chopped onion
1 teaspoon crushed peppercorns
  Brandy for flaming
½ cup brown sauce
1 heaping teaspoon chopped parsley
½ clove garlic, minced
  Pinch salt
2 tablespoons Hollandaise sauce
  Watercress

Broil or pan fry steak to degree of doneness desired. Melt butter in chafing dish, add onion, and sauté until golden brown. Add crushed (not ground) peppercorns, put the steak in the pan, and flame with brandy. Remove steak from pan and add brown sauce, parsley, garlic, and salt to taste. Stir this mixture over low heat for a minute and then add the Hollandaise sauce. Pour over the steak, garnish with watercress, and serve.

serves: 1

wine: Burgundy or Bordeaux

Bahamaian Club, Britannia Beach Hotel, Nassau, Bahamas
CHEF: HENRI BUANNIC

Tournedos Chasseur

4 ounces (125 grams) butter
4 small fillets lean meat
  Salt
  Pepper
4 large fresh mushrooms, sliced
2 shallots, chopped finely
¾ cup dry white wine
½ cup beef consommé
1 teaspoon tomato purée
1 teaspoon flour
1 teaspoon melted butter
  Dash Kitchen Bouquet
4 slices toasted French bread
  Chopped parsley for garnish

Melt the butter in a skillet. Season the meat with salt and pepper and cook over a moderate flame as required: rare, medium or well done. Remove the meat and keep warm. Add the mushrooms and shallots to the skillet and sauté without coloring. Add the wine and reduce to about one-third the original volume. Add the consommé and tomato purée and bring to a boil. Thicken with the flour blended with 1 teaspoon butter; add seasoning to taste and a dash of Kitchen Bouquet for coloring.
Add the tournedos and heat for a few minutes without allowing the sauce to boil. Serve on toast; sprinkle with chopped parsley. Pass sauce.

serves: 4

Lazar Restaurant, Melbourne, Australia
CHEF: MARIA BUCSKO

Cigany Rostelyos

(Gipsy Beef)

serves: 5

wine:
dry red
wine

5 1-pound (500-gram) slices rump roast
Salt
Pepper.
½ cup flour
4 ounces (125 grams) lard
1 pound (500 grams) fresh mixed
vegetables, chopped
½ cup peeled tomatoes or tomato purée
1 bay leaf
1 cup dry red wine
½ pound (250 grams) smoked bacon,
fried crisp and drained

Flatten the meat and make small incisions in it with a sharp knife. Rub in salt and freshly ground black pepper; sprinkle meat with flour and fry quickly in hot lard for about 30 seconds on each side. Remove meat from pan and lightly fry onion and chopped vegetables in the same pan (you may have to add more lard). Add tomatoes or purée, bay leaf and red wine. Simmer for 5 minutes. Layer meat and vegetables in a casserole and pour sauce from pan over them. Cover with bacon slices. Place in oven at 350° F. for approximately half an hour or simmer tightly covered on top of stove.
Serve with boiled potatoes and fried parsley.

Fried parsley

1 large bunch parsley
Oil for deep frying

Wash parsley and dry thoroughly. Tie small bundles of 4 or 5 stalks together with cooking twine. Heat oil to 360° F. and drop a few bunches of parsley at a time into it. Let cook 3 minutes. Parsley will be bright green and crisp. Drain thoroughly and remove twine.

Don Roth's Blackhawk Restaurant, Chicago

serves: 5

Roast Prime Ribs of Beef

1 4-pound (2-kilogram) prime rib roast,
backbone removed and well trimmed
1 pound (500 grams) rock salt

Completely cover the beef with slightly dampened rock salt. Put ribs in a 500° F. oven for 1 hour, then reduce heat to 300° F. Roast for another 1¾ hours. Let meat rest out of the oven for 20 minutes; roast will be easier to carve and retain more juices.

Colony Restaurant, Windsor Hotel, Salisbury, England
CHEF: J. R. SIEVI

Fillet Steak Maison Flambé

1 8-ounce (250-gram) fillet steak
2 tablespoons butter
1 pineapple ring marinated in red wine
¼ cup dark sweet cherries, pitted
¼ cup small button mushrooms, sautéed
¼ cup asparagus tips, parboiled
3 tablespoons Scotch whisky
1 tomato, halved and grilled
1 slice pâté de foie gras

In the kitchen pan fry steak just short of desired degree of doneness. At the table in a chafing dish heat butter, pineapple ring, cherries, mushrooms, and asparagus tips. Add steak and flame with whisky. Serve on a hot plate with grilled tomato. Top steak with a slice of pâté de foie gras and pour pan juices over all.

serves: 1

wine: Château Palmer Margaux 1965

The George Hotel, Haddington, Scotland

Steak and Kidney Pot Pie

1 pound (500 grams) shoulder steak
¼ pound (125 grams) beef kidney
2 medium onions, chopped
1 tablespoon lard
  Salt
  Pepper
2 tablespoons tomato purée
1 tablespoon plain flour
  Water as needed

Cut steak and kidney into ½-inch cubes. Braise meats and onion in a stew pot with lard until all are browned. Add salt, pepper and tomato purée and mix thoroughly. Blend in flour. Cook for another 5 minutes, or until flour is well browned. Add ¼ cup water, stirring constantly. Reduce heat and cook very slowly for 1½ hours adding water, ¼ cup at a time, to keep gravy in the pan. When the cooking is finished, the meats should be well sauced but not afloat.

serves: 4

Pastry

1 pound (500 grams) self-rising flour
½ pound (250 grams) shredded suet
  About ½ cup water

Cut flour and suet together until mixture resembles coarse oatmeal. Add cold water, a tablespoon at a time, until a stiff dough is formed. Roll the dough out on a floured board to make a crust to fit the stew pot. Place crust carefully over pot and put a close-fitting lid over on the crust. Cook in a 350° F. oven for 1 hour.

Commandaria Grill, Cyprus Hilton, Nicosia, Cyprus

Ratatouille Mexicaine

serves: 4

wine:
Keo Hock

4 veal fillets
4 fillets amberjack (or sole)
  Worcestershire sauce
  Juice of 1 lemon
  Salt
  Pepper
  Cayenne
1 cup flour
1 cup milk
2 eggs
2 teaspoons chutney
2 teaspoons curry
  Oil for frying
6 slices ham
4 fresh green peppers
6 mushrooms
4 servings curry rice
8 candied cherries
1 cup bottled barbecue sauce

Cut veal fillets and fish into thin strips. Marinate the fish in Worcestershire sauce and lemon juice. Sprinkle the veal with salt, pepper and cayenne.

Prepare a batter with flour, milk, eggs, chutney (sieved), curry powder, salt, pepper and cayenne. Dredge veal and fish pieces in flour before dipping them into the batter. Deep fry to a golden brown.

Cut ham and peppers into fine julienne strips. Slice the mushrooms. Place the veal and fish fingers in the middle of a serving dish and surround them with 8 molds of curry rice. Sauté the ham, peppers and mushrooms and pour over the fingers. Put one cherry on top of each mound of rice. Warm barbecue sauce and serve separately.

Brasserie, New York City

Le Pfannkuchen

serves: 6

1½ pounds (750 grams) freshly chopped
    beef
½ pound (250 grams) freshly chopped pork
1 clove garlic
½ cup tomato paste or purée
  Pinch marjoram
  Pinch thyme
  Pinch sage
  Pinch rosemary
18 crêpes (see Index)
1 cup Hollandaise sauce (see Index)
½ cup grated Parmesan cheese

Sauté pork, beef, and garlic until brown. Discard excess fat and add tomato paste or purée. Simmer 30 minutes. Add herbs and simmer 10 minutes; set aside. Discard garlic. Fill the center of each crêpe with the meat mixture. Roll the crêpes and arrange on an ovenproof serving dish. Garnish with Hollandaise sauce and Parmesan cheese; run under broiler until sauce is bubbly and cheese slightly brown.

Commandaria Grill, Cyprus Hilton, Nicosia, Cyprus

Moschari Stifado
(Young Veal Stew with Pearl Onions)

**2 pounds (1 kilogram) lean veal, cut
   in cubes**
1 cup dry red wine
¼ cup vinegar
1 bouquet garni
1 medium onion studded with cloves
1 cup olive oil
2 bay leaves
2 or 3 sprigs rosemary
  Salt
  Pepper
2 cloves garlic
½ cup tomato purée
1 cup white stock
**2 pounds (1 kilogram) pearl onions,
   peeled**

Marinate veal cubes overnight in red wine, vinegar, bouquet garni and onion studded with cloves. Strain and dry the veal cubes; reserve bouquet garni. Heat ¾ cup oil in a frying pan and cook the veal briskly until brown. Pour meat and oil into a large stewpot; add bay leaf, rosemary, bouquet garni, salt and pepper, garlic cloves, and tomato purée. Cover meat to a depth of 1 inch with half stock, half marinade. Let simmer until reduced three-quarters. Remove bouquet garni. In a separate frying pan, brown the pearl onions in remaining oil until golden.
Place the meat cubes in half of a low pan and pour the onions in the other half. Strain sauce and pour over meat and onions. If there is not enough liquid, add a little extra broth. Top with butter paper. Cook until meat is tender. Taste for salt and pepper. Serve hot with boiled potatoes.

*serves:
4-6*

*wine:
Domaine
D'Ahera*

Brasserie, New York City
CHEF: ROBERT SPEZIA

Veal Cordon Bleu

2 slices veal tenderloin
2 slices Swiss cheese
1 slice boiled ham
¼ cup white bread crumbs
1 egg
2 tablespoons butter
  Salt
  Pepper
  Lemon wedges

Cut veal slices almost in two. Place between two sheets wax paper. Flatten with cleaver; pieces should be about 7 inches in diameter.
On one piece of the veal place one slice of cheese, then the ham, then the other slice of cheese, and finally top with the other slice of veal.
Press edges of meat together to seal. Beat egg in a deep dish; dip meat in
(Continued at foot of facing page

serves: 1

Le Chaland Hotel, Plaine Magnien, Mauritius

Paupiettes de Veau Mascotte

serves: 1

1 thin slice veal
1 banana
2 tablespoons flour
1 tablespoon cooking oil
1 tablespoon butter
½ onion, sliced
1 sprig thyme or 1 teaspoon dried thyme
1 tablespoon chopped parsley
1 tablespoon tomato paste

Place peeled banana in the middle of the slice of veal. Roll and tie up with string. Dust with flour and sauté in oil and butter for 15 minutes. Set aside and keep warm. Place onion, thyme, parsley and tomato paste in the pan used for the veal and allow to simmer for 10 minutes. Remove string from rolled veal and place meat in the onion-herb sauce to cook for 10 minutes more. Serve with deep-fried potatoes.

Buena Vista, Nassau, Bahamas
CHEF: J. P. FAURE

Veal Buena Vista

serves: 4

wine:
Piesporter
Gold-
tropfchen

4-pound (2-kilogram) rack of veal
⅓ cup chopped parsley
1 teaspoon tarragon, chopped
½ cup white wine
2 onions, sliced
Few drops Kitchen Bouquet
Salt
Pepper
2 tablespoons butter

Cut out meat on either side of backbone of rack of veal. Cut these in 1-inch slices after removing any sinews. Flatten out to very thin leaves. Pepper and salt and brown them very quickly in foaming butter in a heavy iron skillet. Add some drops of Kitchen Bouquet, chopped parsley, tarragon and dry white wine. Sauté onions until soft and barely golden in butter. Do not allow to brown or scorch. Spread onions on a heatproof serving dish and arrange veal leaves over them. Pour pan juices over meat and keep warm for 10 minutes before serving. Serve with egg noodles, barley or mashed potatoes.

Veal Cordon Bleu (continued)

egg; season with salt and pepper. Turn meat in bread crumbs and place in a preheated skillet with butter. Cook 10 to 15 minutes on a low flame until golden brown. Serve with lemon wedges.

Harlequin Restaurant, Merlin Hotel, Kuala Lumpur, Malaysia
CHEF: YVES VRAINE

Piccata Harlequin

8 thin slices veal cutlet
  Salt
  Pepper
3 tablespoons butter
½ medium onion, chopped
1½ tablespoons port
1 cup light cream
2 thin slices ham
2 slices tongue
2 medium gherkins
4 fresh mushrooms
1 teaspoon chopped parsley
2 teaspoons capers

Pound veal until slices are very thin. Sprinkle with salt and pepper and flour on both sides. Sauté in butter over high heat for 1 minute on each side; remove veal and set aside. Reduce heat and cook the onion slowly in the same butter. Add the port and cream and bring to a boil for 1 minute. Cut ham, tongue, gherkins and mushrooms in julienne strips and add to onion. Bring to a boil and cook until thickened.
Place the veal on a serving dish and pour sauce over it. Sprinkle with chopped parsley and capers.

serves: 4

wine:
dry white
wine

Biggs Restaurant, Chicago
CHEF: BRIAN KUZMAN

Veal Scaloppine with Sauce Toscane

1 pair sweetbreads
  Boiling salted water
¼ cup butter
2 ripe tomatoes, chopped
2 tablespoons onion, minced
1 can condensed chicken broth
1 can condensed cream of mushroom
  soup
1 split champagne
2 tablespoons flour
¼ cup light cream
2 pounds (1 kilogram) veal scaloppine
  (Italian style or cut in 8 pieces and
  pounded very thin)
  Salt
  Pepper
  Garlic powder
  Flour for dredging
½ cup butter
4 cups cooked rice
  Parsley, chopped

Cover sweetbreads with boiling salted water and cook at a simmer until firm and white. Drain and cool. Remove membranes and gristle and cut sweetbreads into small cubes. Melt ¼ cup butter in a skillet and sauté tomatoes and onions until tomatoes are mushy. Stir in chicken broth, mushroom soup, and champagne. Mix flour and cream. When smooth stir into sauce. Cook until sauce bubbles and thickens, stirring constantly. Fold in sweetbreads.
Sprinkle veal with salt, pepper, and garlic powder. Dip slices in flour. Heat butter and in it brown veal quickly on both sides. Spoon sauce over veal. Serve on rice garnished with parsley.

serves: 8

Restaurante Horcher, Madrid
CHEF: PACO

Veal Escaloppe Don Quijote

serves: 2

4 thin veal scallops
1 egg beaten
2 bananas
4 tablespoons butter

Pound veal very thin. Dip veal in egg and sauté 1 minute on each side in butter. Remove from pan and keep warm. Slice bananas lengthwise; dip in egg and sauté until golden brown. Arrange veal and bananas on serving plates and spoon fruit sauce over them. Serve with saffron rice.

Fruit sauce

¾ cup currant jelly
½ cup orange juice
1 tablespoon butter
1 tablespoon cornstarch
¼ cup pitted sweet cherries
¼ cup crushed pineapple
Sugar to taste

Heat jelly, orange juice and butter in saucepan until jelly melts. Mix cornstarch with enough cold water to make a smooth paste and add to jelly mixture. Cook until sauce is thickened, then add fruits. Taste for sugar. Serve hot or cold

La Taverna, Hong Kong

Tuna Veal

serves: 6

wine:
Soave Bolla

2 pounds (1 kilogram) veal, cut from
    upper part of leg
6 anchovy fillets
¼ cup tiny (cocktail) pickled onions
12 sour gherkins
2 bay leaves
  Juice of ½ lemon
  Grated peel of 1 lemon
¾ cup olive oil
½ pound (250 grams) Italian-style
    canned tuna fish in olive oil
½ bottle Soave Bolla wine
2 tablespoons capers
3 cups mayonnaise
1 lemon, sliced

Place the veal in a casserole; add anchovies, onions, gherkins, bay leaves, lemon juice and grated peel, olive oil, tuna fish, white wine, and half of the capers.
Put casserole on low heat and cook until veal is tender (add one cup chicken broth if pan becomes too dry). Remove veal, cut into slices, and place on a large flat dish. Drain off the sauce remaining in the pan and blend in mayonnaise. Pour on the veal and garnish with capers and slices of fresh lemon. Serve cool.

Gourmet Room, Princess Hotel, Pembroke, Bermuda
CHEF: GUNTHER SANHOWSKI

Poitrine de Veau Farcie Printanière
(Stuffed Breast of Veal with Garden Vegetables)

4 pounds (2 kilograms) boneless
  breast of veal
  Salt
6 tablespoons oil

Mix together all stuffing ingredients. Put stuffing on flat breast of veal and roll up, securing with string; sprinkle with salt. Heat oil in a large roasting pan on top of stove. Brown meat in oil about 5 minutes, turning to cook evenly.

serves: 5

wine:
Château de Selle (rosé)

Stuffing:

1½ pounds (750 grams) finely ground veal
  6 ounces (185 grams) streaked bacon
  1 cup heavy cream
  2 egg yolks
  1 tablespoon chopped parsley
  2 teaspoons salt
  ½ teaspoon white pepper
  ½ teaspoon nutmeg

Sauce

1 pound (500 grams) veal bones
2 large onions
1 large carrot
1 small leek
½ clove garlic
2 bay leaves
1 tablespoon pepper
2 tablespoons tomato paste
2 cups bouillon
1 tablespoon cornstarch

Put sauce ingredients along either side of meat in roasting pan (cut veal bones into pieces and chop vegetables) and bake in oven at 380° F. 2 hours. Twenty minutes before meat has finished cooking, pour bouillon over veal.

Conclusion: Remove meat from roasting pan and slice 1 inch thick; arrange on platter. Garnish with fresh carrots, turnips, green peas, mushrooms, and boiled potatoes. To thicken sauce, return roasting pan to top of stove, add cornstarch, and bring to boil. Pour thickened sauce through a strainer. Serve over the meat or on the side.

Villa d'Este, Britannia Beach Hotel, Nassau, Bahamas
CHEF: HENRI BUANNIC

Saltimbocca, Genoa Style

serves: 6

3 pounds (1.5 kilograms) thinly sliced veal cutlets
⅓ teaspoon sage
¼ pound (125 grams) thinly sliced prosciutto ham
¾ pound (375 grams) butter
¼ teaspoon salt
2 tablespoons water

Slice cutlets into pieces 5 inches square; sprinkle a little sage on each slice and cover with a slice of prosciutto the same size. Fasten with a toothpick. Melt half of the butter in a skillet, add the meat and sprinkle with salt. Cook over a high flame until the veal is well browned on both sides. Place cooked veal on a warmed serving dish with the ham on top. Add the water to the skillet and scrape the bottom well; add the rest of the butter and mix well over a low flame. Pour the gravy over the meat and serve hot.

Jamaica

Wet Grill of Mutton

serves: 4

8 thin slices cold roast mutton
Salt
Pepper
Butter
Mustard
Nutmeg
Worcestershire sauce

Score mutton slices lightly on both sides. Press into score marks on both sides a little salt, pepper, butter, mustard, nutmeg, and Worcestershire sauce.

Sauce

1 tablespoon flour
1 tablespoon butter
3 tablespoons mustard
Cayenne
Nutmeg
1 teaspoon salt
1 tablespoon Worcestershire sauce
1 cup water

Mix flour with butter, mustard, cayenne, nutmeg, salt and Worcestershire sauce; make the sauce as smooth as possible by adding water slowly. Place in frying pan over a medium flame and stir well until sauce begins to thicken. Add mutton slices and turn occasionally. Cook for 15 minutes.

Meikles Hotel, Salisbury, Rhodesia
CHEF: FRANÇOIS LASALLE

Pintades de Rhodesie en Pâté

½ pound (250 grams) calf's liver
1½ pounds (750 grams) fresh fat bacon
1 pound (500 grams) lean pork
   Salt
2 teaspoons poultry seasoning
½ teaspoon saltpeter
3 eggs
2 tablespoons brandy
2 guinea fowl
1 pound (500 grams) sliced bacon
3 tablespoons butter
2 carrots
2 onions
2 stalks celery
   Bay leaf
   Pepper
3 pounds (1.5 kilograms) puff pastry
   Fresh watercress

serves: 6

Mince all the meat finely. Season and add two of the eggs one at a time; finally stir in the brandy. Thorough mixing is essential. Remove the breastbones from the birds and stuff with the forcemeat. Wrap the birds in the bacon and brown in butter in a roasting pan. Add the diced carrots, onions, celery, and bay leaf. Sprinkle with salt and pepper and roast for 40 minutes at 400° F.
Remove from the oven and allow to cool. Roll out the puff pastry and completely encase the birds in it. You may mold the pastry to the shape of the bird to enhance the effect. Pierce the top of the pastry at several points with neat round holes and put into each a small funnel of greaseproof paper or foil, to allow steam to escape from the interior during the final cooking. Brush the pastry case with the remaining egg, beaten.
Return to the oven and roast for 30 to 35 minutes at 350° F. If the oven is top heated, use greaseproof paper to cover the birds.
Remove from the oven and place the birds on the serving dish. Remove the paper funnels. Garnish with small bunches of watercress. The sauce should be served separately.

Sauce

¾ cup Madeira
3 cups brown sauce
3 tablespoons butter

Add the Madeira to the roasting pan in which the birds were cooked and reduce for 5 to 8 minutes. Add

(Continued at foot of facing page

Peking Restaurant, Hong Kong
CHEF: CHUNG KEE PEH

Mongolian Hot Pot

serves: 6

wine:
Chinese rice
wine or
beer

2 quarts rich stock*
¼ pound mutton or lamb
½ pound beef
½ pound sole or other firm white fish
2 dozen shucked oysters
2 dozen shelled raw shrimp
¼ pound pork loin or shoulder
  Soy sauce
  Mustard
  Duck sauce
  Sour cream

Heat stock to simmering in a Mongolian fondue pot (usually made of brass, very decorative and available at stores carrying oriental wares) or any pot that can be put over a warming flame at the table. A chafing dish or a fondue pot would work successfully.

Cut meats and sole into ½-inch to 1-inch cubes. Arrange meats, fish, and whole shellfish on 6 plates. Put stock pot over warmer in the middle of the table. Provide each guest with 2 pairs of chopsticks (1 for cooking, 1 for eating) or 2 long forks. Each person dips a bite of meat or fish into the stock, cooks it to his taste, and dips it in sauce. When all the food has been cooked and eaten, serve the soup — now much richer and reduced — with hot French bread.

*This dish is only as good as the stock used in it. If you do not have a favorite recipe, try simmering together for 4 hours 4 quarts water, 1 pound stewing beef, 2 pounds beef or veal bones, 2 onions, 4 stalks celery, 6 sprigs parsley, 2 carrots, 2 parsnips, 1 bay leaf, 2 whole cloves, 6 peppercorns, 2 cloves garlic, 1 tablespoon oregano, and salt to taste. Strain (eat meat and vegetables) to 2 quarts. Check seasonings.

Pintades de Rhodesie (continued)

brown sauce and simmer, stirring gently, for 15 minutes. Remove any fat which rises to the surface, strain and stir in butter before serving.

Bush Inn Hotel, Christchurch, New Zealand
CHEF: J. DIEUDONNE

Canterbury Spiced Lamb

4 tablespoons oil
1 teaspoon anchovy paste
4 small onions
3 cloves garlic
2 tablespoons coriander
1½ pounds (750 grams) lamb, diced
1 teaspoon salt
  Pinch chili powder
½ teaspoon fenugreek
1 teaspoon chopped ginger
1 teaspoon cardamon
1 tablespoon sugar
½ teaspoon cinnamon
2 tablespoons flour
2 cups hot water
4 tablespoons vinegar
4 large tomatoes, diced
3 large carrots, diced
1 cup diced celery stalks
¼ cup heavy cream

Heat oil in a pan or casserole, add the anchovy paste and stir well until the fish odor has become aromatic. Add the onions, crushed garlic, freshly ground coriander and fry for 4 minutes. Add the lamb, salt, chili powder, fenugreek, ginger, cardamon, sugar and cinnamon. Continue to fry until the meat is browned. Add flour and brown; then add the hot water and vinegar, stir well until it boils, reduce heat and simmer until the meat is tender. Meanwhile submerge the diced vegetables in salted boiling water separately until just cooked but still crunchy. Drain and rinse in cold water. Fold cream and blanched vegetables into the meat mixture. Serve hot with steamed rice, corn on the cob, and spinach.

serves: 6

Turkey

Chopped Meat with Poached Eggs

1 pound (500 grams) lamb or beef
2 tablespoons butter
1 large onion, chopped
2 large tomatoes, peeled, seeded and
  chopped
1 teaspoon chopped parsley
  Salt
½ teaspoon black pepper
6 eggs

Put the meat through a mincer and sauté it in a pan with butter. Stir continuously. When moisture has evaporated and the meat is crumbly, add onion and stir until onion is light brown. Add tomatoes and parsley and season with salt and pepper. Thoroughly mix, cover pan and simmer for about 15 minutes. Flatten top of meat mixture and make in it 6 round indentations with the bottom of a cup. Into each of these drop an egg. Season with salt. Cover the pan once more and cook over a low heat for about 5 minutes.

serves: 6

Hotel Taprobane, Colombo, Ceylon
CHEF: C. H. CONMARÍN

Buriyani

serves: 8

3 cloves garlic, chopped
2 medium onions
3 teaspoons salt
1½ pounds (750 grams) mutton or
    chicken
5 cups water
3 cardamon seeds, crushed
½ cup yogurt
½ cup oil for frying
1 small piece ginger
  2-inch piece cinnamon
8 whole cloves
25 to 30 peppercorns
3 cups long grain rice
½ teaspoon saffron

Prepare mutton or chicken stock by cooking 1 clove garlic, chopped, 1 chopped onion, salt, meat and water in a pan. Remove meat or chicken, onion and garlic from prepared stock. Soak cardamon seeds in a tablespoon of warm water. Beat yogurt and soaked cardamons in a bowl and set aside. Heat oil and fry 1 sliced onion until brown. Add 1 clove garlic, chopped, a piece of ginger, chopped, yogurt, cinnamon, cloves, peppercorns and mutton or chicken. Add onion and garlic from stock. Keep stirring constantly until sticky. Add chicken stock and rice. Cook until water is absorbed and rice is tender. Pour saffron into center of rice, cover the rice tightly and cook over very low heat until rice is tender, dry, and fluffy.

Turkey

Gardener's Kebab

serves: 6

2 pounds (1 kilogram) lamb
6 tablespoons butter
2 large carrots
4 tomatoes peeled
1 pound (500 grams) pearl onions
1 cup shelled green peas
  Cayenne
  Salt
1 teaspoon fresh dill

Cut meat into small cubes and sauté in melted butter to seal juices. Cut carrots into round slices ⅜ of an inch thick. Add these to meat. Cover pan and cook over low heat for about an hour, or until meat appears dry. After removing seeds and membranes from tomatoes add them to meat, together with onions, peas, cayenne and salt. Replace cover and cook for 30 more minutes. Add a little water from time to time to avoid burning. When meat is cooked, add chopped dill and stir before serving.

Starco Snack Bar and Restaurant, Beirut
CHEF: ABDO AKIKI

Yakhni Truffles with Meat and Rice

¼ cup sliced brown truffles
½ pound (250 grams) mutton
2 onions
4 tablespoons butter
6 cups water
2 tablespoons flour
1 tablespoon salt
2 cloves garlic, crushed
2 sprigs fresh coriander
   White pepper
   Poultry spices
   Juice of 1 lemon

Peel, cut to pieces, wash and rinse the truffles well. Cut meat into cubes 1″ × 1½″; chop onions. Brown meat and onions in butter. Let cool and add water, flour, salt, crushed garlic, coriander and spices to taste. Allow to cook briskly for 15 minutes and to simmer 45 minutes. One hour before serving add truffles and lemon juice to the pot and allow to simmer until serving time. Serve with rice pilaf (see Index) sprinkled with black pepper.

serves: 6

Turkey

Vegetable Meat Pot

1 pound (500 grams) lamb
2 medium onions, chopped
¼ cup butter
1½ cups water
3 medium tomatoes
2 small zucchini
1 medium eggplant
¼ pound (125 grams) okra, fresh or canned
2 large green peppers
   Salt
   Pepper
½ pound (250 grams) green beans

Cut meat into small cubes. Sauté onions in butter in a pan until lightly browned. Add ½ cup water and meat, simmering until nearly tender.
Peel and slice tomatoes and zucchini. Peel eggplant and dice. Remove pointed portions from top of okra. Remove seeds from green peppers and dice.
When meat is nearly tender, add 1 cup hot water, salt and pepper. Add beans, zucchini, eggplant, tomatoes, peppers and okra in that order. Cover the pan tightly and cook until vegetables are done.

serves: 6

Turkey

Dolmades
(Stuffed Vegetables)

serves: 4

1 pound (500 grams) fatty lamb or beef
1 chopped onion
¼ cup uncooked rice
1 teaspoon chopped mint
1 teaspoon chopped dill
   Salt
   Pepper
1 tablespoon tomato sauce
2 eggplants or
4 green peppers or
4 tomatoes or
4 zucchini

Chop meat well. Make the stuffing by adding all the ingredients to the minced meat and kneading thoroughly. The quantities listed make enough stuffing for vegetables given. For an eggplant dolma, choose a short, round eggplant. Cut off stem end. Peel eggplant lengthwise in strips. Scoop out inside, leaving a shell about an inch thick. Fill this with stuffing and replace stem end.

For a green pepper dolma, slice through top of pepper but don't sever it completely. Remove seeds and membranes, fill with stuffing and close cover.

A tomato dolma is made the same way.

For a zucchini dolma, clean the outside of the vegetables and cut off one end to use as a cover. Scoop out the inside, leaving a ½-inch shell. Stuff the shell, replace cover.

To cook, the dolmades are placed in a pan containing 2 tablespoons butter and a cup of water. Cover pan and cook over a medium heat for about 35 minutes, until vegetables are soft. If different dolmades are being cooked at the same time, the eggplant should be placed upright in the pan and followed with a layer of green peppers on a rack and finally with tomatoes on a higher rack. Left-over stuffing can be formed into meatballs and cooked with the dolmades.

Speedbird House, Karachi Airport

Stuffed Lamb Pakistan

1 4½-pound (2-kilogram) boned loin or boned leg of lamb
Salt
Pepper
5 tablespoons cooking oil
1 teaspoon dry mustard
Juice of 1 lemon or 2 limes
2 tablespoons chopped onion
2 tablespoons raisins
2 tablespoons currants
¼ cup rice
½ teaspoon curry powder (very yellow)
Juice of ½ lemon or 1 lime
½ cup bouillon
1 egg
4 tablespoons vegetable shortening if necessary to supplement lamb fat

Marinate lamb in salt, pepper, 3 tablespoons of the oil, mustard and lemon juice for 2 hours. Meanwhile, sauté the chopped onion in 2 tablespoons oil; cook the onion only to a golden yellow; do not let it burn. Add the raisins, currants and rice. Fry gently and sprinkle in the curry powder. Add the lemon juice and bouillon and cook very slowly covered as for rizotto, until rice is slightly softened but not fully cooked, about 10 minutes.

Cool the rice mixture and beat in the egg to bind it.

Remove lamb from marinade and dry it off completely. Place the stuffing in the center pocket of the meat and spread evenly over entire inside of cut. Roll the meat carefully around the stuffing and tie securely in several places with string. If lamb is very lean, rub with vegetable shortening. Wrap tightly in foil, fat side up, and roast in a 400° F. oven for about 1½ hours. Carve in ⅛-inch slices so that each slice has both meat and stuffing (take care that the stuffing stays intact—a broad spatula for serving the pieces is helpful).

serves: 8

Sauce

Purée of 3 canned apricot halves or 2 peach halves
4 tablespoons chutney
Juice of ½ lemon or 1 lime
1 cup brown sauce
Salt
Pepper

Sieve apricots and chutney. Mix purée with lemon juice and brown sauce. Season lightly with salt and pepper. Serve the sauce separately. This dish can be served hot or cold. Also, the sauce is equally good served cold.

Starco Snack Bar and Restaurant, Beirut
CHEF: ABDO AKIKI

Kafta with Parsley and Onion

serves: 6

**2 pounds (1 kilogram) mutton neck
  meat**
3 ounces (185 grams) mutton fat
3 tablespoons lard
1 cup red onions, finely chopped
1 cup parsley, chopped
  Salt
  Poultry spices

Chop meat, fat and lard very fine. Mince onions and parsley; add salt and spices to taste. Mix all ingredients thoroughly with hands (the mixture will be pastelike). Form elongated meatballs from ⅓ cups of the mixture; barbecue on skewers. Let meat juices drip onto bread as meatballs cook. Serve hot with bread and green salad.

Turkey

Kofta Curry

serves: 6

1 pound (500 grams) lamb
4 cloves garlic
2 onions
2 green chilis
  Potatoes
1 egg
  Black pepper
  Ground cinnamon
  Ground cloves
  Ground cardamon
  Salt
  Clarified butter for frying
  Flour
3 tomatoes
1 teaspoon ground coriander
½ teaspoon ground turmeric
½ teaspoon chili powder
½ teaspoon ground cumin seed
½ teaspoon ground ginger
½ cup dried coconut

Mince meat, garlic and 1 onion well. Chop green chilis fine. Boil and mash potatoes. Blend these ingredients together with the egg and a pinch each of black pepper, cinnamon, cloves, cardamon and salt. Flour hands lightly and shape the meat mixture into little balls. Fry these until golden brown in clarified butter and drain. Chop remaining onion and tomatoes. Fry these together in clarified butter in a separate pan. Add coriander, turmeric, chili powder, cumin and ginger. Cook these ingredients slowly for 5 minutes. Make coconut milk from dried coconut by soaking in ½ cup water and squeezing. Add it to the pan with lemon juice to taste.
Put balls of meat into this mixture and simmer gently for 30 minutes. Do not stir the mixture, but shake pan now and again to prevent burning.
Serve with rice, chutney, peppers, onion rings, lemons and cucumber.

Midland Hotel, Manchester, England
CHEF: GILBERT LEFEVRE

Selle d'Agneau Poeke Fleurie

(Saddle of Lamb Fleurie)

1 7-pound (3.5-kilogram) saddle of
    spring lamb
½ cup brandy
½ cup white wine
  Mirapoix:
      ½ cup carrot, chopped
      ½ cup onion
1 truffle
1½ pounds (750 grams) loin of lamb
4 cups veal stock
5 cups cream
4 eggs, separated
1 pound (500 grams) chicken meat
½ pound (250 grams) spinach purée
½ pound (250 grams) carrot purée
8 tablespoons butter
6 mushrooms
2 pounds (1 kilogram) potatoes
  Salt
  Pepper

Trim and tie saddle. Roast 10 minutes at 425° F. Cool, and remove upper meat and slice thinly. Macerate in the brandy, white wine and mirapoix of vegetables. Cut 6 slices from truffle, dice remainder and marinate in brandy.

Bone loin of lamb. Fry bones lightly, cover with stock and simmer gently. Grind meat from the loin of lamb 3 times through the finest blade of a meat chopper. Mix with 2 cups cream, 2 egg whites and diced truffle. Set aside. Grind chicken and mix with 2 cups cream and 2 egg whites. Mix half with spinach purée and half with carrot purée. Turn into 12 buttered individual fancy molds.

Prepare mushrooms by making deep gashes on the tops and sautéing in butter. Peel and boil potatoes and mash with 3 tablespoons butter, salt, pepper and 4 egg yolks to make duchesse potatoes. Using a pastry bag, make 12 medallions on a greased baking sheet.

Put a layer of lamb mousse on the saddle bone. Re-form the saddle with slices of lamb and mousse alternately; cover outside entirely with mousse. Put the "frosted" saddle in a buttered pan and place in a 450° F. oven for 30 minutes.

Poach chicken-vegetable mousse dishes in a larger pan containing hot water halfway up sides of the molds for the last 15 minutes the lamb cooks. Glaze potatoes the last

(*Continued at foot of facing page*

serves: 6

wine:
Château Cos d'Estournel, St. Estephe 1957

Beach Luxury Hotel, Karachi

Biryani

serves: 4

1½ pounds (750 grams) mutton
2 pieces stick cinnamon
6 large cardamon seeds
6 whole peppercorns
1 teaspoon black cumin seeds
1 large piece ginger
6 green chilis
6 cloves garlic
1 bunch coriander leaves
1 large bunch mint leaves
½ pound cottage cheese, sieved
1 cup clarified butter
6 large onions
5 large potatoes
1 tablespoon salt
½ teaspoon saffron
2 cups boiled rice (reserve cooking water)

Boil meat; set aside.
Pound coarsely together cinnamon, cardamon seeds, peppercorns, cloves, cumin seeds, ginger, green chilis, and garlic. Cut coarsely coriander and mint leaves; mix in cottage cheese. Heat clarified butter and fry onions dark brown; remove and set aside. Put mutton and potatoes, sliced and seasoned with salt, in a large dekchi (or any heavy, tightly covered pot), then on top of mutton and potatoes put the spice mixture. Place greens, cheese, and saffron on top of meat and spices. Then add the onions and spread boiled rice over all the other ingredients. Sprinkle clarified butter and rice water over the rice. Cook all on hot fire. When water has evaporated remove and put on low fire. Spread hot charcoal on lid and lower heat.

Selle d'Agneau Poeke Fleurie
(continued)

10 minutes (check often — do not over-brown).
Remove saddle from pan and add marinade and stock and reduce. Finish with remaining cream and reduce until thick. Add 4 tablespoons of butter and strain. Put saddle on a serving dish and place potato medallions and mousses alternately around it. Put mushrooms on the spinach mousses and truffle slices on the carrot. Coat saddle with sauce. Serve remaining sauce separately.

Café de Paris, Beirut, Lebanon
CHEF: TANIOS HAJ

Stuffed Marrows and Vine Leaves

2 pounds (1 kilogram) vegetable marrows
    4 inches long
½ pound (250 grams) rice
1 pound (500 grams) mutton meat,
    minced
    Salt
    Black pepper
½ pound (250 grams) fresh vine leaves
    Soup bones
2 medium onions, sliced
¼ pound (125 grams) prunes
¼ cup lemon juice

Hollow out marrows leaving ⅛-inch shells. Clean and wash rice and mix with minced mutton; salt and pepper to taste. Fill marrows and vine leaves with rice mixture. Brown soup bones with sliced onions in a large pot. Arrange prunes over bones; place stuffed vine leaves over prunes and marrows on top of all. Fill pot with water and lemon juice to cover marrows. Close cover tightly and allow to cook for 1 hour. Remove cover and cook 10 more minutes. Arrange marrows and vine leaves on serving plates. Press gravy through a sieve and serve separately.

serves: 6

Gaylord Restaurant, Port of Spain, Trinidad
CHEF: TILAK RAJ

Rogan Josh

½ cup clarified butter
½ cup finely chopped onion
1 cup chopped tomato
    Salt
2 teaspoons finely ground coriander
2 teaspoons chili powder
2 tablespoons chopped fresh ginger
2 cloves garlic
2 teaspoons turmeric powder
2 pounds (1 kilogram) lean lamb, cut into
    1-inch cubes
2 tablespoons cream

Heat clarified butter and brown onion. Add tomato, salt, coriander, chili powder, ginger, garlic and turmeric powder. Blend and simmer for 15 minutes; add lamb. Continue cooking on low heat and stirring for another 15 minutes. Add cream and 2 cups of water and cook for 30 minutes or until meat is tender, still stirring. When meat is done add more water if extra gravy is required. Serve over boiled rice.

serves: 4-6

wine:
Mateus Rosé

Bistro Bourgogne, Esso Motor Hotel, Amsterdam
CHEF: S. TOLSMA

Saddle of Venison "Nieuw Amsterdam"

serves: 6

wine: Auxey-Duresses 1967

1 4-pound (2-kilogram) saddle of venison, larded
4 cups red wine
1 onion, sliced
1 small carrot, sliced
1 parsley sprig, chopped
1 bay leaf
1 clove
¼ teaspoon rosemary
6 peppercorns, cracked
¼ teaspoon thyme
2 teaspoons salt
2 teaspoons black peppercorns, finely ground
⅓ cup flour
½ cup butter
8 whole apples, peeled and cored
2 cups sugar-syrup
Lemon peel
2 cups white wine
¾ cup fresh cranberries
3 tablespoons Calvados
½ cup cream

Combine wine, onion, carrot, parsley, bay leaf, clove, rosemary, peppercorns and thyme. Pour over the venison and marinate for 24 hours. Remove saddle from the marinade and dry thoroughly. Reserve marinade. Rub in salt and peppercorns. Sprinkle with flour. Brown the meat on all sides in butter and roast in a 350° F. oven for about 2 hours.

Boil apples quickly in 1 cup sugar-syrup, lemon peel and white wine until slightly soft. Remove from syrup and chill. In another saucepan, boil together the remaining sugar-syrup and ½ cup cranberries until sauce is thick. Chill.

In a saucepan, bring the reserved marinade to a boil and simmer for about 15 minutes, until vegetables are soft. Add Calvados and simmer another 5 minutes. Stir in the remaining cranberries and simmer until the skins begin to break. Stir in the cream and simmer another 2 or 3 minutes until sauce begins to thicken. Put through a fine sieve and keep warm in a double boiler. When venison is ready to be served, remove to serving platter. Quickly reheat marinade sauce and pour over meat. Fill apples with cranberry sauce and arrange them around the venison.

Restaurant Ab Sofus, Göteborg, Sweden
CHEF: FRIEDRICH SCHWAKE

Roast Marinated Rack of Lamb

2 pounds (1 kilogram) rack of lamb
  Marinade
  Butter for browning
4 artichoke bottoms
½ pound (250 grams) leaf spinach
1 tablespoon finely chopped onion
  Salt
  Freshly ground white pepper
  Marinade:
1 cup dry white wine
4 tablespoons olive oil
3 tablespoons soy sauce
1 teaspoon basil
1 teaspoon rosemary
1 teaspoon thyme
1 teaspoon mint
1 teaspoon ground black pepper
1 clove garlic, crushed
  Juice of ½ lemon

Marinate the lamb for 1 hour, turning it now and then. Brown it in butter and put in oven at 425° F. for about 25 minutes. Baste with the marinade the last 10 minutes. In the meantime warm the artichoke bottoms in butter. Set aside and keep warm. Wash the spinach and cook with the onions in pan with a tight lid with just the water clinging to leaves from washing. Add salt and pepper to taste and keep warm. Slice the lamb and pour the meat juice over it. Garnish with the artichoke bottoms topped with spinach.

serves: 4

wine:
Red
Bordeaux

Michael's Caprice Restaurant, Auckland, New Zealand
CHEF: HERLUF ANDERSEN

New Zealand Lamb and Honey

2 pounds (1 kilogram) boneless leg of lamb
  Clove garlic
¼ cup clarified butter
  Salt
  Pepper
¼ cup honey
2 tablespoons flour
2 cups water or stock
½ pound (250 grams) tomatoes, chopped
½ pound (250 grams) carrots, chopped
2 tablespoons new onions, chopped
¼ pound (125 grams) ginger, minced

Rub lamb with cut clove of garlic and cut into 2-inch cubes. Melt the butter in a large saucepan. Brown the lamb cubes and season with salt, pepper, and honey. (The honey settles on the bottom of the saucepan where it turns to caramel.)
When meat is well browned, sprinkle with flour and cook for a few minutes. Add the water or stock, tomatoes, carrots, onions, ginger, and salt and pepper to taste. Cover and cook for 45 to 60 minutes in 350° F. oven. Serve on plain boiled rice.

serves: 6

Charley O's, New York City

Irish Lamb Stew

serves: 8

5 pounds (2.5 kilograms) lamb shoulder
  or chuck
1 gallon (5 litres) lamb stock
2 pounds (1 kilogram) onions, diced
3 pounds (1.5 kilograms) carrots, diced
1 stalk celery, diced
8 bay leaves
4 whole cloves
2½ pounds (1.2 kilograms) small whole
   potatoes
   Worcestershire sauce
   Salt
   Pepper

Cut the lamb into 1-inch cubes. Place in large saucepan and cover with unsalted cold water. Bring to a boil and simmer 2 to 3 minutes. Pour off all the water and thoroughly wash meat in cold water. Combine the lamb stock, onions, carrots, celery, bay leaves, and cloves. Bring to a boil and simmer 5 minutes. Add the lamb and the potatoes. Bring to a boil and simmer 25 to 30 minutes, or until vegetables are soft and meat is tender. Add a dash of Worcestershire and salt and pepper to taste.

Dumplings

½ pound (250 kilograms) matzo meal
1 tablespoon chopped parsley
1 teaspoon baking powder
3 eggs
¾ cup milk
4 tablespoons melted butter

Mix matzo meal, parsley, and baking powder together, then add eggs. Pour over milk and melted butter and mix well until thick. Let stand 20 minutes.
Shape into small ovals 1½" and poach in lamb stew until tender, or about 12 to 15 minutes. Garnish each bowl of stew with a dumpling.

The George Hotel, Haddington, Scotland

Fried Sweetbreads

serves: 1

6 ounces (185 grams) lamb sweetbreads
1 teaspoon salt
1 teaspoon lemon juice
2 tablespoons flour for dredging
   Salt
   Pepper
1 egg, beaten
½ cup white bread crumbs
2 tablespoons clarified butter
   Sprig parsley
   Lemon wedge
   Crisply fried bacon

Wash sweetbreads thoroughly in cold water and cook in boiling salted water to which lemon juice has been added for 25 minutes. Cool sweetbreads in the cooking liquid. Drain and cut diagonally into ¼-inch slices.
Dip sweetbread slices in flour seasoned with salt and pepper, then in the egg beaten with 2 tablespoons of water, then in bread crumbs. Fry briskly in butter for 2 or 3 minutes. Serve garnished with parsley, lemon wedge, and bacon.

Promenade Café, New York City

Moussaka

1 lean lamb shoulder, ground
1 medium onion
2 cloves garlic
3 tomatoes, peeled and cut in chunks
¼ cup tomato purée
   Dash Worcestershire sauce
   White pepper
   Dried oregano
   Salt
1 1-pound (500-gram) eggplant, diced
   and steamed
½ pound (250 grams) rice, cooked
1 large whole eggplant

Glaçage
1 pint white sauce (see Index)
4 egg yolks, beaten until thick
2 tablespoons cottage cheese
   Salt
   Pepper

serves: 6

Sauté lamb but do not brown. Pour off all the fat. Add the onions and sauté until they are soft. Add the rest of the ingredients except eggplants and rice. Cover and braise in a slow oven for 1½ hours. Then add diced eggplant and rice to lamb mixture; mix well and braise for 30 minutes more. Thinly slice and steam the other eggplant and reserve.

Beat all ingredients together until well mixed.
Line out baking dish with sliced steamed eggplant. Fill in moussaka 1½ inches high. Spread glaçage on top and bake for 20 minutes in medium oven (350° F.) or until golden brown.

Turkey

Shish Kebab

2 pounds (1 kilogram) leg of lamb
1 tablespoon olive oil
   Juice of ½ lemon
   Salt
   Pepper
1 medium onion, sliced
3 medium tomatoes, sliced
2 bay leaves
2 green peppers cut in 1-inch squares
1 large eggplant, cubed

Cut meat into 1-inch cubes. Blend olive oil and lemon juice and rub into meat. Put meat in a glass or porcelain dish, season with salt and pepper and cover with onions, tomatoes and bay leaves. Put dish in refrigerator for 5 hours. Slide meat on spits, alternating with slices of tomatoes, onions, green peppers and eggplant, and bay leaves. The shish kebabs may be cooked over a barbecue, an open wood fire or under a kitchen broiler. For best results, charcoal should be used.

Tulip Room, Rand International Hotel, Johannesburg
CHEF: RICHARD PATZEN

Saddle of Lamb Provençale

serves: 10

wine:
Nederburg
Selected
Cabernet

1 14-pound (6.5-kilogram) saddle of lamb
2 onions, chopped
1 clove garlic, minced
¼ cup parsley
½ cup bread crumbs
½ pound (250 grams) butter

Roast saddle for about 1½ hours at 425° F. It should be very rare. Set aside to cool somewhat. In frying pan sauté onions and garlic with butter; add chopped parsley and bread crumbs and cook until crumbs are golden. Cover the entire saddle with this mixture and brown it under the broiler. Serve with potatoes Lyonnaise.

Pommes Lyonnaise

6 large onions, diced
½ pound (250 grams) butter
6 large potatoes, peeled
Salt
Pepper

Sauté onions in 3 tablespoons butter. Remove and reserve. Cut raw potatoes into ¼-inch slices and sauté them slightly in the same pan with the rest of the butter. Add salt and pepper. Add sautéed onions, mix together and bake in a 350°F. oven for about 25 minutes.

Turkey

Tas Kebab

serves: 6

2 pounds (1 kilogram) shoulder of lamb
4 tablespoons butter
Olive oil, if necessary
2 onions, chopped
1 medium can tomatoes, juice and all
½ teaspoon salt
¼ teaspoon pepper

Remove meat from bone and cut into 1-inch cubes. Cook meat in butter, using a frying pan with a heavy bottom to prevent butter burning. If a heavy pan is not available, add a little olive oil to the butter. When meat is browned add onions and brown them. Add tomatoes and seasoning. Bring to boil, then simmer for about 45 minutes. Serve with rice pilaf (see Index).

The Four Seasons, New York City

Boned Rack of Lamb en Croûte

1 3-pound (1.5-kilogram) rack of lamb,
  boned
Salt
Pepper
6 tablespoons oil

Sprinkle lamb with salt and pepper on both sides. Heat the oil in a skillet. Place lamb in the skillet and cook over high heat for 15 minutes, turning once to brown both sides. Remove meat from skillet and allow to cool.

serves: 6

Stuffing à la Matignon

6 tablespoons clarified butter
3 tablespoons minced shallots
1 small bay leaf
¾ cup finely chopped carrots
¾ cup finely chopped celery
2 cups finely chopped mushrooms
1 teaspoon salt
¼ teaspoon white pepper
3 tablespoons lemon juice
¾ cup dry white wine

Pour the butter into a skillet and add shallots, bay leaf, carrots, and celery. Cook over medium heat for 10 minutes. Add mushrooms, salt, pepper, and lemon juice. Cook 15 minutes longer over high heat, stirring occasionally. Add wine and continue cooking and stirring until carrots are soft. Discard bay leaf. Set aside.

Conclusion

Rich yeast pastry based on 3 cups flour*
12 thin slices prosciutto
2 egg yolks

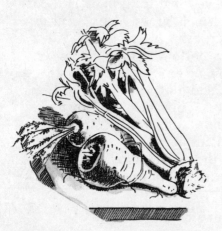

Sprinkle pastry lightly with flour. Roll out large enough to completely cover the cooked lamb. Place 7 slices of prosciutto in center of pastry. Spread about ½ the stuffing over the prosciutto. Place the cooked lamb on it and spread the remaining stuffing over the top and sides of the meat. Pat remaining slices of prosciutto over stuffing. Dilute egg yolks with 4 tablespoons water and brush on the pastry around the lamb. Fold up the pastry to completely cover the meat. Cut off and save excess dough. Pinch ends of pastry together and tuck them in so that the meat is completely sealed in—it should look like a loaf of bread. Brush the

(Continued at foot of facing page

Miramar Theatre Restaurant, Hong Kong

Sweet and Sour Pork

serves: 6

wine:
*Champagne
Rosé*

½ **pork shoulder cut in 1-inch cubes**
1 **teaspoon salt**
1 **teaspoon dark soy sauce**
1 **egg yolk**
½ **teaspoon allspice**
1 **cup cornstarch**
¼ **cup oil**
1 **clove garlic, minced**
1 **red pepper, seeded and diced**
1 **green pepper, seeded and diced**
2 **spring onions**
1 **tomato, peeled, seeded, and diced**
5 **tablespoons vinegar**
5 **tablespoons sugar**
5 **tablespoons tomato sauce**
2 **slices pineapple cut in thirds**
3 **cups cooked rice**

Parboil pork for 10 minutes. Drain. Add salt, dark soy sauce, egg yolk and allspice and let stand for 20 minutes. Coat pork with cornstarch, reserving 1 teaspoon. Heat oil and fry pork until golden brown. Remove pork and set aside. Fry garlic and red and green peppers, then add spring onions, tomatoes, vinegar, sugar, tomato sauce and 1 teaspoon cornstarch mixed with 1 teaspoon water. Return pork to pan and simmer 10 minutes. Add pineapple pieces and just heat through. Serve at once over rice.

Boned Rack of Lamb en Croûte
(continued)

pastry again with egg yolk.
Knead the dough and roll it out to about 3″ × 6″. Make 2 parallel slits about three-quarters of the way down the strip. You will have 3 strips, uncut at one end. Braid the strips and place on top of the brioche for decoration. Brush with egg yolk. Set aside in a warm place for 30 minutes while dough rises.
Bake in 375° F. oven 12 minutes, or until brown.

* Commercial brioche dough can often be bought from a bakery and would be ideal for this recipe.

Top of the Town, Hotel Inter-Continental, Auckland, New Zealand

Wild Pork Rangitoto

2 loins wild pork divided into cutlets
1 cup olive oil
1 cup dry white wine
1 pound (500 grams) stoned fresh
  cherries
½ cup red wine
½ teaspoon ground cinnamon
1 tablespoon cornstarch
½ cup butter
1 cup sauce Fine Champagne
1 pound (500 grams) potato croquette balls
  sautéed in butter
3 green apples cut in half, braised in
  white wine, sugar and butter
2 pounds (1 kilogram) mushrooms, sliced
  and sautéed in butter
3 tomatoes, grilled

Marinate cutlets in oil and wine for 24 hours. Poach the cherries in red wine with cinnamon. Drain and reduce the liquid. Thicken with cornstarch and add the cherries. Season the cutlets and fry in butter until well cooked. Place on a large serving dish along with cherries. Serve the sauce Fine Champagne and the hot potato croquettes in separate dishes. Garnish meat with apples, mushrooms, and tomatoes, halved. Serve with Cabbage Hikurangi.

serves: 6

Cabbage Hikurangi

3 pounds (1.5 kilograms) red cabbage
¾ cup chopped onions
½ pound (250 grams) lean bacon
2 tablespoons lard
¼ cup flour
¼ cup walnut halves
  Salt
  Pepper
2 cups red wine

Shred cabbage leaves very finely. Cook the chopped onions and diced bacon very slowly in the lard until all the onion moisture has evaporated; sprinkle with flour and fry until light brown. Add walnuts, then shredded cabbage. Stir thoroughly, season with salt and pepper, cover and braise in the oven for 30 minutes at 325° F. Boil up wine and add it to the cabbage. Cover and cook in oven for another 30 minutes.

Sauce Fine Champagne

3 tablespoons butter
3 tablespoons flour
½ teaspoon salt
  Scant pinch ground ginger
½ teaspoon sugar
1 teaspoon lemon juice
¼ cup cream
½ cup dry champagne

Melt butter in the top of a double boiler. Stir in flour and cook for 5 minutes. Add salt, ginger, sugar and lemon juice; mix well. Add cream and champagne and cook, stirring constantly, until sauce is thick and smooth. If sauce thickens too much, add a few more tablespoons champagne; it should be thick but not like mayonnaise.

Les Filles du Roy, Vieux Montreal, Quebec
CHEF: ROLLAND BROUILLARD

Ragoût de Boulettes et Pattes de Cochon

serves: 6

2 to 3 pounds (1 to 1.5 kilograms) ground
    pork
1 onion
  Salt
  Pepper
2 teaspoons fines herbes
  Flour for dredging
6 tablespoons fat
1 quart hot water

Mix the ground pork and onions, finely chopped, salt, pepper and fines herbes. Shape into balls and roll in flour. Heat fat and brown meatballs on all sides; add hot water and let simmer until well done. Remove the meatballs.

Ragoût

2 pork hocks
3 pints boiling water
2 onions, minced
¼ cup parsley, chopped
  Salt
  Pepper
2 teaspoons fines herbes
5 tablespoons browned flour
¼ teaspoon cinnamon
¼ teaspoon ground cloves
¼ teaspoon poultry seasoning

Scrape the pork hocks, wash, and remove hairs and toenails (if not already done). Cut in pieces and place in a pot. Add boiling water, onions, parsley, salt, pepper, and fines herbes. Boil until well cooked; add browned flour diluted with ½ cup cold water an hour before serving. Season with cinnamon, cloves, and poultry seasoning to taste. Add the pork meatballs and serve.

Speedbird House, Karachi

Sor Potal
(A Goan Specialty)

serves: 6

1 pound (500 grams) pork
½ pound (250 grams) sheep liver
¼ cup chopped onions
4 tablespoons cooking oil
4 cloves garlic
½ teaspoon freshly ground black pepper
½ teaspoon zeera (caraway seeds)
¼ teaspoon cinnamon
1 teaspoon chili powder
¼ cup vinegar
  Salt

Boil the pork and liver in water to cover for 15 minutes; and reserve the cooking water. Cut meat into ½-inch cubes.
Fry the chopped onions in the oil until they are slightly brown; then add the pork and liver cubes and fry for 10 minutes. Add the garlic, black pepper, zeera, cinnamon, chili and vinegar and also add the reserved stock. Salt to taste and cook for a further 20 minutes or until only a little gravy is left.

Royal Hotel, Copenhagen

Tenderloin of Porc de Luxe

**1 large or 2 small pork tenderloins, total
  weight about 2 pounds (1 kilogram)
  Clarified butter for frying
½ pound (250 grams) fresh asparagus
½ pound (250 grams) fresh mushrooms
 2 tablespoons butter
½ cup tomato purée
½ cup very heavy cream
  Salt
  Pepper**

serves: 6

Clean the tenderloin and cut it into small steaks; brown in butter in a frying pan, then transfer to an ovenware dish. Break tough ends off asparagus stalks and wash heads thoroughly. Cook in boiling water until half done, about 5 minutes. Drain well and reserve cooking liquid. Clean and slice the mushrooms. Sauté them lightly in the butter from the steaks and spread them, together with the asparagus, in the baking dish. Melt butter in the frying pan; add ½ cup of asparagus water, tomato purée, and cream; season with salt and pepper. Pour the sauce over the meat and vegetables. Heat approximately 15 minutes in a 425° F. oven. Serve with potatoes boiled in asparagus water and French bread.

The Forum of the XII Caesars, New York City

Rack of Pork Glazed in Amber Sugar
with Ginger Apple Slices

**4 4-ounce (125-gram) pork chops, well
   trimmed
  Salt
  Brown sugar
¾ cup grenadine syrup
 4 apple rings
 4 pieces candied ginger root, drained**

serves: 2

Sprinkle pork chops with salt and brown sugar. Cook them in the oven for about 10 minutes at 500° F., or until the sugar starts to melt. Drain excessive fat.
Place chops in pan, pour grenadine syrup over them and cook for about 5 minutes, or until brown sugar starts to caramelize. Serve on fresh apple rings. Garnish with ginger root.

*Tenderloin of Porc de Luxe*ROYAL HOTEL, COPENHAGEN

Saddle of Venison
"Nieuw Amsterdam"

BISTRO BOURGOGNE, ESSO MOTOR HOTEL, AMSTERDAM
(Chef: S. Tolsma)

Hilton Hotel, Hong Kong

Koh Lok Yok
(Sweet and Sour Pork)

serves: 4

1 pound (500 grams) lean pork
1 tablespoon dry white wine
1 tablespoon soy sauce
1 egg, beaten
1 tablespoon cornstarch
3 tablespoons flour
Oil for deep frying
1 small onion, quartered
3 green peppers, seeded and quartered
1 clove garlic, minced
3 slices pineapple, drained and quartered

Cut pork in ½-inch cubes. Mix wine, sauce, egg, cornstarch, and flour. Heat oil for deep frying to 170° F. Dip pork cubes in wine mixture and deep fry until well done and crisp on edges. Remove to an ovenproof platter covered with absorbent paper and place in 300° F. oven to keep warm. Use 3 tablespoons oil to sauté onions, green peppers, and garlic over high heat for 2 minutes, mixing well. Add sauce and bring to a boil. Thicken with wine mixture, stirring constantly. Add fried pork and pineapple, mix well, and serve hot.

Sauce

⅓ cup sugar
4 tablespoons catsup
1 tablespoon dry white wine
2 tablespoons vinegar
4 tablespoons soy sauce
1 tablespoon cornstarch
⅓ cup cold water

Mix first 5 ingredients well and add cornstarch mixed to a smooth paste with water.

The Aristocrat Restaurant, Manila

Pork and Chicken Adobo

serves: 12

1 cup vinegar
½ cup soy sauce
½ teaspoon black pepper
½ cup minced garlic
2 pounds (1 kilogram) pork, cut into cubes
1 2-pound (1-kilogram) chicken, cut in serving pieces
Oil for browning
2 ½ teaspoons monosodium glutamate

In a saucepan, combine vinegar, soy sauce, pepper, and garlic. Marinate pork and chicken for about 30 minutes. Simmer uncovered until tender. Strain sauce and set aside. Brown pork and chicken in cooking oil. Return everything to saucepan, add monosodium glutamate and simmer until sauce thickens.

R.W.–F

Charlie Brown's, New York City

Pork and Apple Pie

1½ pounds (750 grams) lean, boneless
    pork, diced
¾ cup chopped onion
1½ teaspoon sage
2 teaspoons salt
¼ teaspoon pepper
¼ cup cracker meal
2 tart cooking apples, pared, cored and
    thinly sliced
2 tablespoons lemon juice
2 tablespoons flour

  Topping:
½ package instant mashed potatoes
1 teaspoon salt
2 tablespoons butter or margarine
½ cup milk
1 tablespoon butter or margarine, melted

serves: 4

Preheat oven to 325° F. In a large bowl, combine pork with onion, sage, salt, pepper, and cracker meal. Toss with a fork to mix well. In a medium bowl, toss apples with lemon juice and flour, mixing well. In a 1½-quart round, shallow baking dish, layer apple slices (in 3 layers) alternately with pork (in 2 layers). Cover top of baking dish with foil. Bake 1½ to 2 hours, or just until pork is tender. About 10 minutes before end of cooking time, make topping: prepare mashed potatoes as package label directs, using 1½ cups water, the salt, butter and milk. Swirl potatoes decoratively over top of the pie, spreading to the edge of dish. Brush with melted butter. Run under broiler, 6 inches from heat, for 5 to 7 minutes, or until nicely browned. Let stand 5 minutes before cutting into wedges.

Hong Kong

Pax King Tan Un T'at
(Steamed Shoulder of Pork)

4 tablespoons cooking oil
1 ¼-inch-thick piece raw ginger
1 leek
4 tablespoons dark soy sauce
2 tablespoons light soy sauce
1 teaspoon Chinese cooking wine
1 teaspoon salt
2 tablespoons sugar
3½ pounds (1.75 kilograms) pork shoulder
    with bone
1 cup boiling water
1 pound Chinese cabbage

serves: 6

Heat oil, ginger, leek, soy sauce, wine, salt and sugar for 2 minutes in stewing pot. Put in shoulder of pork and brown both sides. Add boiling water and bring pot to boil. Lower flame, put on lid and simmer for 4 hours. Prick skin of meat to see if it is tender. If not, continue to simmer on low flame for another hour or longer until skin is very tender. Place cabbage in pot and cook uncovered. Allow sauce to simmer down to approximately ½ cup. Place pork on serving dish and cut into ¼-inch slices. Serve pork with sauce on a layer of cabbage.

The Four Seasons, New York City

Mousse of Ham in Whole Peaches

serves: 6

1 pound (500 grams) cooked ham
⅓ cup mayonnaise
   Cayenne pepper
   Salt
⅓ cup butter, softened
2 teaspoons port
6 large ripe peaches

Cut ham into very small pieces and put through the finest blade of a meat grinder. Place in a mixing bowl. Very slowly, beat mayonnaise, cayenne, salt, butter, and port into the ham to make a fine mousse. Cool 1 hour in the refrigerator. Remove pits from the peaches by placing a knife in the stem of the peach and cutting around the pit. This will leave about a ¾″ center opening.

Stuff peaches with mousse and serve.

Bush Inn Hotel, Christchurch, New Zealand
CHEF: J. DIEUDONNE

Honey Glazed Ham

serves: 8

3 pounds (1.5 kilograms) ham hock
½ teaspoon mixed spices
¼ teaspoon cardamon
2 tablespoons honey
12 whole cloves
½ cup pineapple juice
½ cup sweet sherry
¼ cup tomato paste

Soak ham in cold water to cover for 24 hours or more depending on the saltiness. Remove rind or skin. Leave a ¼-inch layer of fat on the meat. Rub in the mixed spices, cardamon and honey; stud with cloves. Add a little pineapple juice and sherry to the baking pan and bake for 35 to 40 minutes per pound in a 350° F. oven. Baste frequently with melted fat as it drips from ham and honey. When the honey is sufficiently caramelized, add remainder juice and sherry and tomato paste. Continue basting and reduce liquid by three-quarters. When the meat is cooked and the glaze is thick enough to coat the back of a spoon, carve the meat into thin slices and arrange overlapping on a serving platter. Spoon the glaze over the ham and serve with boiled potatoes and tossed lettuce salad.

Charlie Brown's, New York City

Brawn and Vinaigrette

Brawn

½ pound (500 grams) pork tongue
½ pound (500 grams) pigs knuckles
2 teaspoons finely chopped parsley
¼ teaspoon powdered sage
¼ teaspoon mixed herbs
½ teaspoon grated lemon rind
¼ teaspoon grated nutmeg
  Salt
  Pepper
1 cup clear gravy or beef stock

serves: 6

Cut tongue and meat from knuckles into medium dice. Add 1 teaspoon of the parsley, sage, herbs, lemon rind, nutmeg and a liberal seasoning of salt and pepper and mix well. Press tightly into a mold, fill with gravy or stock, and bake in preheated 350° F. oven for one hour and fifteen minutes. Remove from oven, cool and refrigerate. When jellied, turn out of the mold and garnish with the remaining teaspoon of chopped parsley. Serve with vinaigrette sauce.

Vinaigrette sauce

¾ cup olive oil
¼ cup lemon juice
½ teaspoon dry mustard
1 tablespoon finely chopped capers
1 teaspoon finely chopped pickles
½ teaspoon chopped parsley
½ teaspoon chopped chervil
½ teaspoon chopped chives
  Salt and freshly ground black pepper
    to taste

Combine all ingredients and mix well. Chill and serve with Brawn.

The Forum of the XII Caesars, New York City

Leek Pie with Hot Sausages

serves: 6
wine:
Champagne
Rosé

2 cups pastry (see Index)
6 leeks
2 tablespoons butter
2 tablespoons flour
¾ cup leek liquid
¾ cup heavy cream
¾ teaspoon salt
Dash pepper
1 tablespoon prepared horseradish
12 small pork sausages

Prepare pastry, your own or a mix, and line 6 small (about 4½ inches in diameter) pie pans. Save enough pastry to cover tops of pies later on. Chill.

Trim roots and green leaves from leeks. Slit leeks in half lengthwise. Wash carefully to remove all sand and cut leeks in crosswise slices about 2 inches in length. Cook in a little boiling water until tender but still slightly crisp. Drain but save leek liquid. Melt butter, stir in flour smoothly, then add leek liquid and cream gradually. Cook, stirring constantly, until sauce bubbles. Season with salt, pepper and horseradish and stir in leeks.

Start oven at 450° F. Fry sausages until nicely browned and partly cooked. Fill pastry shells with a scant ½ cup of leek mixture and lay 2 drained sausages on top. Cover top with a circle of pastry and seal edges. Bake about 20 minutes or until golden brown. Serve hot.

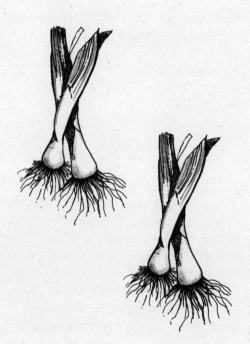

The Four Seasons, New York City

Artichokes Stuffed with Foie Gras and Choron Sauce

12 artichoke bottoms
5 tablespoons clarified butter
2 tablespoons oil
12 ½-inch-thick slices foie gras
¾ cup Choron sauce

Sauté the artichoke bottoms in butter and oil to heat but not brown. Remove to a flameproof dish. Place a slice of foie gras on each. Place a tablespoon of Choron sauce on top of foie gras. Run under broiler to brown.

serves: 6

Choron sauce
1 cup Béarnaise sauce
½ cup rich tomato sauce

Blend sauces and heat gently—do not boil. Serve lukewarm

The Four Seasons, New York City

Marrow Soufflé in Crust

6 egg yolks
4 cups Béchamel sauce (see Index)
1 teaspoon freshly grated nutmeg
   Salt
   Pepper
5 ounces (150 grams) marrow, cut in dice
7 egg whites
6 baked individual tart crusts (see Index under Pastry)

Mix egg yolks with Béchamel. Add nutmeg, salt, and pepper. Add the marrow and blend gently.
Whip the egg whites until stiff but not dry and fold them gently into the mixture. Fill the crusts three-quarters full with the soufflé mixture. Bake in a 350° F. oven 20 minutes. Serve immediately.

serves: 6

The Forum of the XII Caesars, New York City

Mushrooms of the Sincere Claudius

serves: 12

½ pound (250 grams) ham, cut in julienne
   strips
1 tablespoon butter
1 shallot, chopped
¼ cup sherry
   Juice of 1 lemon
½ pound mushroom stems cut in strips
2 cups cream sauce (see Index)
1 truffle cut in strips
2 tablespoons brandy
   Salt
   Pepper
24 slices toasted French bread
   Hollandaise sauce (see Index)
   Fresh chives for garnish

Sauté ham in butter with chopped shallot. Reduce with sherry and lemon juice. Add mushroom stems and cream sauce. Simmer 15 to 20 minutes. Add truffle and brandy. Correct seasoning. Place mixture on top of toasted French bread and cover with Hollandaise sauce. Brown under broiler. Garnish with minced chives.

Greece

Yemistes Domates Laderes

(Stuffed Tomatoes Laderes)

serves: 6

12 tomatoes
   Salt
   Pinch sugar
3 onions, grated
1½ cups olive oil
⅓ cup chopped parsley
½ cup dill, chopped
½ cup raisins
   Pepper
½ cup pignolia nuts
1 cup rice
½ cup water

Wash tomatoes, scoop out pulp; save caps. Sprinkle insides with salt and sugar. Sauté onions in ¼ cup olive oil until transparent. Mix onions, parsley, dill, raisins, salt, pepper, nuts, rice and 1 cup olive oil. Stuff tomatoes with mixture, cover with caps and put in a casserole with remaining olive oil and water. Weigh down with plate; cover and simmer for 30 minutes or until rice is cooked. Serve cold.

Jamaica

Savoury Beetroot

1 slice onion
1 tablespoon butter
½ teaspoon salt
½ teaspoon dry mustard
½ teaspoon anchovy sauce
1 teaspoon flour
3 teaspoons cream
3 teaspoons milk
1 cooked beet, medium size

Fry onion in butter. Make sauce of salt, dry mustard, anchovy sauce, flour, cream and milk; cook 5 minutes. Pour over onion. Add beet, sliced; cook for 2 more minutes. Serve cold.

serves: 2

India

Eggplant Bhurta

2 medium eggplants
1 onion, chopped
1 hot green pepper, diced
2 tablespoons butter
1 teaspoon salt
4 tablespoons yogurt

Preferably, roast eggplants on charcoal. If this is not possible, place eggplants under a broiler until skins are charred and the flesh is tender. Sauté onion and pepper in butter. Remove eggplant skins and mash pulp; add to onion mixture with salt and yogurt. Place pan over heat once more and heat thoroughly before serving.

serves: 6

Lime Rasam

¼ cup yellow split peas
3 cups water
2 teaspoons salt
1 teaspoon mustard seeds, crushed
1 hot green pepper, diced (or more, if desired)
¼ teaspoon turmeric
1 teaspoon vegetable oil
1 tablespoon fresh coriander, chopped
Juice of 2 limes

Cook peas in water with salt until tender. Sauté mustard seeds, green pepper and turmeric in oil and add to peas. Simmer for 5 minutes, add coriander, and allow to cool slightly. Before serving add lime juice.

serves: 4

India

Moghlai Biryani

serves: 8-10

4 medium onions, chopped
1 cup butter
2 tablespoons minced ginger root
1 teaspoon dried hot red chili pepper, crushed
2 cloves garlic, minced
2 pounds (1 kilogram) lamb, cubed
3 pounds (1.5 kilograms) chicken cut in small pieces
2 tablespoons salt
2 pounds (1 kilogram) rice
8 cups water
1 pint yogurt
1 teaspoon powdered cloves
1 teaspoon powdered cardamon
1 tablespoon powdered cumin
2 hot green peppers, diced
Juice of 2 limes
1 teaspoon saffron, soaked in 1 cup water
1 cup milk
4 tablespoons fresh coriander, chopped fine
½ pound (250 grams) almonds, blanched and toasted

Fry onion in half of the butter in a large pan until it is golden brown. Add ginger, red pepper and garlic. Fry, stirring constantly, for two minutes. Add lamb, chicken and half of the salt and cook uncovered until it becomes rather dry. In a separate pan, boil rice in 8 cups water with remainder of salt until it is half cooked. Drain off water. Blend yogurt with cloves, cardamon, cumin, and green peppers. Add lime juice and stir into meat mixture. Remove about two-thirds of meat and cover remainder with a layer of rice. Repeat this process until ingredients are used up making sure that the top layer is rice. Mix saffron water and milk and pour over rice; dot with the remaining butter. Cover pan and bake gently in oven at 325° F. for an hour. Garnish with coriander and almonds.

Mixed Vegetable Dish

serves: 6-8

1 tablespoon coriander seeds
1 teaspoon cumin seeds
2 dry red cayenne peppers
½ cup vegetable oil
2 large onions
2 cloves garlic, diced
½ teaspoon turmeric powder
1 pound (500 grams) cauliflower
½ pound (250 grams) peas
2 large potatoes, peeled and chopped
Salt

Sauté coriander seeds, cumin seeds and cayenne peppers in oil. Then add onion and garlic and sauté until all are slightly brown. Add turmeric powder and vegetables and stir thoroughly. Add salt. Cover pan and cook over low heat until done. Stir vegetables occasionally during cooking.

India

Alu Keema Tikki
(Stuffed Potato Cutlet)

1 pound (500 grams) potatoes
2 tablespoons butter
8 tablespoons flour
¼ teaspoon red pepper
2½ teaspoons salt
½ teaspoon black pepper
1 egg, beaten
2 tablespoons onions, chopped fine
  Vegetable oil
2 green peppers, seeded
½ pound (250 grams) cooked meat,
  finely shredded
1 tablespoon tomato sauce

Wash and boil potatoes in salted water. When cold, mash them well, adding butter, flour, red pepper, 1½ teaspoons salt and ½ teaspoon black pepper. Blend the egg with potato mixture, making it into a paste. Dredge dough in flour and roll out. Cut into 8 pieces of equal size.

Cook onion in vegetable oil until it is lightly browned. Cut green peppers fine and add to the pan together, with meat and remaining salt. Cover pan and simmer until meat is cooked and water evaporates. Mix in black pepper and tomato sauce.

Place a spoonful of this filling on each of the potato pastries. Put milk in bowl in which egg has been beaten, then use this "ell-milk" to dampen edges of pastry. Fold pastries over and seal edges. Dust with flour and deep fry in vegetable oil until golden brown. Serve hot with tomato sauce.

serves: 4

Lentil Curry

1 pound (500 grams) lentils, cooked and
  drained
1 medium onion, finely chopped
½ teaspoon turmeric
¼ cup clarified butter
1 medium onion, sliced
2 red chilis
½ teaspoon cumin seeds, ground
4 cloves garlic, crushed
  Small piece ginger, ground
  Fresh green coriander, minced
2 tomatoes, chopped

Boil lentils with chopped onion and turmeric powder. Remove from heat when soft. In a separate pan, heat clarified butter. Fry sliced onion. When slightly brown, add spices. Continue frying for a few minutes and then mix with lentils. Allow to simmer; add tomatoes and coriander.

serves: 8

India

Kheera Raita

serves: 8

2 tablespoons vegetable oil
1 teaspoon mustard seeds
1 medium onion, minced
2 cucumbers, grated
1 pint yogurt
½ teaspoon salt
1 teaspoon cumin seeds, roasted and
crushed
½ cup green pepper, minced

Heat oil in a thick pan and add mustard seeds. Cook until they stop popping. Add onion and cook until it is transparent. Remove pan from heat and let cool. Drain liquid off cucumbers and stir in onion mixture, yogurt and salt. Place in refrigerator for an hour. Garnish with cumin seeds and sweet green pepper before serving.

Potato Raita

serves: 8

4 large boiled potatoes
1 teaspoon cumin seeds, roasted and
crushed
Salt
1 hot green pepper, diced
2 pints yogurt
2 tablespoons vegetable oil
2 teaspoons mustard seed
Fresh coriander, chopped fine

Chop boiled potatoes into small pieces. Mix them with roasted cumin seeds, salt and green pepper. Stir in yogurt and mix well. Heat vegetable oil, add mustard seeds and cook until they stop popping. Add to potato and yogurt mixture. Place in refrigerator for an hour. Before serving, garnish with coriander.

Chile

Stuffed Avocado

serves: 6

4 hard-cooked eggs
1 can tuna
1 cup mayonnaise
Salt
Pepper
3 large avocados
Capers
Lettuce
Olives

Mash eggs, drained tuna and ¾ cup mayonnaise; season with salt and pepper. Peel and halve avocados and remove pits. Fill with tuna mixture, smoothing out to edge. Decorate with remaining mayonnaise and capers. Serve on lettuce leaves and garnish with olives.

Venezuela

Zanahorias Sauté

(Fried Carrots)

8 medium carrots
2 teaspoons salt
2 well beaten eggs
2 tablespoons brown sugar
   Vegetable oil for deep frying

Peel carrots and cut in half lengthwise and then crosswise. Place in a pan, cover with water, add salt and boil until tender. Beat eggs and brown sugar together. Remove carrots from water after cooking, drain well and dip into egg mixture. Deep fry in vegetable oil until golden brown; drain on absorbent paper.

serves: 6

India

Tomato Rasam

¼ cup yellow split peas
3 cups water
2 teaspoons salt
3 large tomatoes, peeled and diced
¼ teaspoon turmeric
1 teaspoon mustard seed, crushed
1 hot green pepper, diced
1 tablespoon vegetable oil
1 tablespoon fresh coriander, chopped

Cook split peas in water with salt until tender. Sauté tomatoes, turmeric, mustard and pepper in oil for 5 minutes. Add to peas and simmer for 5 minutes. Before serving add coriander.

serves: 4

Don Roth's Blackhawk Restaurant, Chicago

Creamed Spinach

2½ ounces (80 grams) salt pork
  3 tablespoons finely chopped onion
1½ pounds (750 grams) frozen spinach,
    finely ground
  Salt
  Pepper
1 cup white sauce (see Index)

Grind salt pork fine and sauté until brown. Add onion and sauté slowly 20 to 30 minutes until brown. Do not let onion burn. Add spinach, salt and pepper and let come to a boil, stirring occasionally. Add white sauce and cook about 35 minutes more, stirring frequently.

serves: 8

Peacock Room, Ashoka Hotel, New Delhi
CHEF: ROSHAN LAL

Gajar Halwa

serves: 6

1 pound (2 kilograms) carrots
4 cups milk
1½ cups sugar
¼ cup clarified butter
½ cup almonds, sliced
½ cup pistachios
½ cup raisins
1 teaspoon cardamon seeds
1 bunch fresh coriander leaves

Wash and grate carrots. Place grated carrot and milk in cooking pot. Boil over low heat for an hour, stirring continuously. By this time the milk should have evaporated and the carrots should be tender. Add sugar, clarified butter, nuts, raisins and cardamon seeds. Cook for 10 minutes, stirring continuously. The halwa is served hot and may be garnished with fresh coriander leaves and beaten silver paper (this is optional, as this paper is not easily available outside India).

serves: 8 *The Forum of the XII Caesars, New York City*

Green Bean Mousse

2 pounds (1 kilogram) fresh green beans
2 tablespoons butter
½ cup Béchamel or cream sauce (see Index)
  Salt
  Pepper
  Nutmeg to taste
2 egg yolks
¼ cup Hollandaise sauce (see Index)

One day ahead cook the green beans in salted water until very soft (slightly overdone) and drain well. Make a purée using a blender or a potato masher or even the finest blade of a grinder, then wrap the bean purée in a cheesecloth and let drain overnight in the refrigerator. Just before serving, melt the butter in a heavy skillet, add the purée and the Béchamel (or cream) sauce, season to taste with salt, pepper, and nutmeg, and stir well. Let boil for a few minutes and while still over heat add egg yolks. Beat vigorously while bringing to a boil. Pour into 8 individual ramekins and spoon Hollandaise sauce over each one. Run under broiler to brown lightly. Serve immediately.

Hoppin John Restaurant, Hamilton, Bermuda
CHEF: FRITZ REITER

Hoppin John

1 pound (500 grams) blackeyed peas
2 pig's feet
3 quarts chicken or pork stock
1 Bermuda onion, chopped
6 ounces (185 grams) lean bacon,
   finely chopped
¼ cup oil
   Salt
   Pepper
   Monosodium glutamate
1 pound (500 grams) raw rice
¼ cup butter

Boil peas and pig's feet in the stock. Fry onions and bacon in oil until golden yellow and add to the stock. Boil the peas for about half an hour and then season to taste. Remove pig's feet and add rice. Cook on low heat for 20 minutes—all liquid should disappear. Dot with butter and serve with pig's feet on the side.

serves: 12

Brasserie, New York City

Choucroute Alsacienne

3 pounds (1.5 kilograms) sauerkraut
1 pound (500 grams) onion, minced
4 tablespoons pork or beef fat
1 tablespoon peppercorns
1 bay leaf
1 quart white wine
2 tablespoons salt
6 knockwurst
1 pound (500 grams) smoked pork
1 pound (500 grams) smoked ham
1 pound (500 grams) Toulouse sausage
   (or other spicy sausage)

Rinse sauerkraut in cold water and drain. Sauté onions in fat until tender. Add sauerkraut, spices, wine, and salt. Add meats and cook for 1½ hours. Do not overcook. Discard bay leaf. Serve very hot.

serves: 6

Biggs Restaurant, Chicago
CHEF: BRIAN KUZMAN

Creamed Vegetables

serves: 6

2 packages frozen mixed vegetables (or frozen cauliflower, asparagus, peas, broccoli, or spinach)
1 can condensed cheddar cheese soup
⅓ cup heavy cream

Cook vegetables according to package directions. Drain. Add soup and cream to vegetables. Simmer until bubbly. Serve hot.
Creamed vegetables may also be poured into a shallow 1-quart casserole and topped with ½ cup dry bread crumbs mixed with ¼ cup melted butter. Bake in a preheated 400° F. oven 15 minutes or until top is lightly browned.

Hungary

Transylvanian Boiled Cabbage

serves: 8

4 pounds (2 kilograms) cabbage
1 tablespoon salt
1 sprig savory
1 medium onion
1 clove garlic
2½ pounds (1.2 kilograms) shoulder of pork
Caraway seeds
¾ cup sour cream
½ cup flour
2 teaspoons vinegar
Pepper

Cut the cleaned cabbage into narrow strips, wash, and cook until tender in salted water with the savory, onion, garlic and caraway seeds. When it is tender, thicken its stock with a combination of smoothly mixed sour cream, flour and a little vinegar and bring to a boil. Flavor with pepper.
Remove the savory before serving, and serve the cabbage steaming hot with the sliced pork.

The Brown Derby, Hollywood, California
CHEFS: JOHANNES VAN BEBBER AND FRITZ GMEINEDER

Cobb Salad

½ head lettuce
½ bunch watercress
1 small bunch chicory
½ head romaine
2 medium tomatoes, peeled
2 breasts boiled roasting chicken
6 strips crisp bacon
1 avocado
3 hard-boiled eggs
2 tablespoons chopped chives
½ cup finely grated roquefort cheese
1 cup French dressing

Cut lettuce, watercress, chicory, and romaine in fine pieces and arrange in salad bowl. Cut tomatoes in half, remove seeds, finely dice, and arrange in strips across the salad. Dice breasts of chicken and arrange over top of chopped greens. Chop bacon fine and sprinkle over the salad. Peel avocado and cut in small pieces; arrange around the edge of the salad.
Decorate the salad by sprinkling the top with chopped eggs, chopped chives, and grated cheese. Just before serving mix the salad with French dressing.

serves: 4-6

French dressing
1 cup water
1 cup red wine vinegar
1 teaspoon sugar
Juice of ½ lemon
2½ tablespoons salt
1 tablespoon ground black pepper
1 tablespoon Worcestershire sauce
1 tablespoon English mustard
1 clove garlic, chopped
1 cup olive oil
3 cups salad oil

Blend all ingredients, except oils. Add olive oil and salad oil. Mix well. Chill and shake thoroughly before serving on salad. Store tightly covered in the refrigerator.

Le Morne Brabant Hotel, Mauritius

Pickled Palm Heart

serves: 4

1 fresh heart of palm
½ cup vinegar
1 teaspoon salt
2 tablespoons fresh ginger
1 clove garlic, crushed
1 teaspoon chili powder
½ teaspoon turmeric
Olive oil

Cut the heart of palm into serving pieces. Let the pieces soak for 8 hours in water to cover to which vinegar and salt have been added. Crush ginger, garlic and chili and cook with turmeric in olive oil. Pour this over the pieces of palm heart. If not acid enough, add more vinegar. The sauce must cover the pieces of palm heart.
Preserve in sterilized jars. Let stand at least one week before using.

Canlis', Honolulu

Canlis' Salad

serves: 4-6

2 tablespoons olive oil
Salt
1 clove garlic, peeled
2 peeled tomatoes
2 heads of romaine
¼ cup chopped green onion
½ cup freshly grated Romano cheese
½ cup rendered finely chopped bacon

Into a large bowl, preferably wooden, pour 2 tablespoons of top quality imported olive oil, sprinkle with salt and rub firmly with a clove of garlic. (The oil will act as a lubricant and the salt as an abrasive.)
Remove garlic and in the bottom of the bowl put the tomatoes, cut in eighths, and then the romaine, sliced in 1-inch strips. You may add other salad vegetables but remember to put the heavy vegetables in first, then the romaine, then the condiments.

Dressing

¾ cup olive oil
Juice of 2½ lemons
½ teaspoon freshly ground pepper
¼ teaspoon chopped fresh mint
¼ teaspoon oregano
1 coddled egg
½ cup croutons

Pour the olive oil, lemon juice and seasonings into a bowl. Add the coddled egg and whip vigorously. When ready to serve, pour dressing over salad. Add the croutons last. Toss salad generously.

Venezuela

Ensalada de Aguacate y Esoinaca Estilo Andino

(Spinach Avocado Salad)

½ pound (250 grams) fresh spinach
1 onion, cut into rings
2 hard-boiled eggs, chopped
1 clove garlic, crushed
1 large avocado, cut into cubes
1 teaspoon salt
¼ teaspoon pepper

Wash spinach and cut out coarse veins and stalks. Place in a colander, pour boiling water over it and rinse in cold water. With scissors, cut spinach and place in a large salad bowl. Top spinach with onion rings and then add egg, garlic, avocado and seasonings. Toss lightly with lemon-oil dressing.

serves: 6

Lemon-oil dressing
4 tablespoons olive oil
    Juice of ½ lemon
1 tablespoon vinegar

Combine and shake well before dressing salad.

Turkey

Green Bean Salad

1 pound (500 grams) cut French beans
5 tablespoons olive oil
2 tomatoes
1 small onion, chopped
1 green pepper, chopped
    Salt
    Pepper
1 teaspoon sugar

Put beans in pan with oil, tomatoes, onion, green pepper, seasoning and sugar. If beans are fresh, add ½ cup of water. Cover pan and cook until tender. Add water as necessary, a little at a time, to prevent burning. Serve cold.

serves: 4

The George Hotel, Haddington, Scotland

Green Bean Salad

serves: 1

1 serving frozen French-cut beans
1 teaspoon salt
½ hard-cooked egg yolk
French dressing

Cook the beans in boiling water to which the salt has been added. Drain and allow to cool completely. Toss in dressing and sprinkle with sieved hard-cooked egg yolk. Serve very cold.

Turkey

Artichoke Salad

serves: 4

4 medium artichokes
Salt
Juice of 1 lemon
2 medium onions
¼ cup olive oil
1 teaspoon sugar
½ cup peas and/or carrots, diced
½ cup water
1 tablespoon chopped dill

Remove outer leaves of artichokes, leaving only inner tender leaves, and trim off upper parts of petals. Cut away bottom of artichoke and spoon out pink heart. Put cleaned artichokes in boiling salted water to cover with a few drops of lemon juice. Cook until artichokes are half done, about 30 minutes. Cut onions into rings and sauté lightly in olive oil. On no account must onion rings be allowed to change color. Drain artichokes and add onions, salt, sugar, rest of the lemon juice, peas, diced carrots and ½ cup water. Cover pan and cook over medium heat until tender, about 25 minutes. Garnish with chopped dill. Serve cold.

India

Yogurt Salad

serves: 2

2 tomatoes
¼ cucumber
2 radishes
Spring onions
2 cups yogurt
Salt
Chili powder
Paprika

Skin and chop tomatoes, slice cucumber and radishes and chop onions. Place all ingredients except paprika in a bowl and mix together. Put in refrigerator until chilled; garnish with paprika before serving.

Charley O's, New York City

Tomato and Onion Salad

3 large tomatoes
1½ large onions
   Oil and vinegar dressing
¼ cup chopped parsley
2 teaspoons cracked black pepper
3 basil leaves

Remove stems and make a shallow cross in the top of each tomato. Plunge into boiling water for 10 seconds and peel. Cut in large chunks. Cut onions in large chunks. Prepare oil and vinegar dressing and toss gently with the tomatoes and onions. Sprinkle with parsley and cracked pepper and toss again. Place basil leaves in the center of the salad and chill in refrigerator before serving.

serves: 6

The George Hotel, Haddington, Scotland

Avocado Salad

  Lettuce (about ⅙ of a large head)
2 sprigs watercress
1 clove garlic
1 teaspoon chopped chives
  Vinegar and oil salad dressing, to taste
¼ avocado, peeled and sliced
  Lemon juice

Wash and dry lettuce and watercress. Rub a wooden salad bowl with the garlic and arrange lettuce and watercress in bowl. Sprinkle with chives and toss in dressing. Add the avocado, which has been sprinkled with lemon juice to keep it from turning brown.

serves: 1

Greece

Salata Malitzanas
(Eggplant Salad)

1 large eggplant
1 small onion, finely chopped
½ cup olive oil
1½ tablespoons vinegar
  Salt
  Pepper
  Parsley
  Chopped tomato
  Black olives

Cook eggplant in oven at 350° F. until soft, approximately 1 hour. Remove skin, chop meat. Combine eggplant meat, onion, oil, vinegar, salt and pepper and mix well. Serve garnished with parsley, tomato and black olives.

serves: 6

Hilton Hotel, Hong Kong

Ngow-Yok-Fan-Keh-Yeh-Choy
(Beef, Tomato, and Cabbage Salad)

serves: 4

¼ pound (125 grams) beef, shredded
1 tablespoon soy sauce
1 tablespoon wine
1 teaspoon cornstarch
2 tablespoons cooking oil
½ pound (250 grams) cabbage, washed, shredded, and sprinkled with 1 teaspoon salt
½ pound (250 grams) tomatoes, peeled, sliced, and shredded

Marinate beef in soy sauce, wine, and cornstarch and let stand 5 minutes. Heat oil and sauté beef until color changes. Remove to platter and cool. Squeeze water from cabbage. Arrange salad on a platter as follows: cabbage on the bottom, tomatoes next, and beef on top. Pour sauce on salad before serving very cold.

Sauce

1 teaspoon ginger root juice
1½ tablespoons sesame seed oil
1 tablespoon soy sauce

Mix all ingredients thoroughly and chill.

The President Hotel, Johannesburg

Cheese Cocktail Fantasie

serves: 4

4 pineapples
1 pound (500 grams) Swiss cheese
1 can red cherries
1 cup mayonnaise
Salt
Pepper

Remove the tops from the pineapples, scoop out the flesh and cut it into ½-inch squares. Also cut the cheese into ½-inch squares. Mix the pineapple, cheese, cherries and mayonnaise together with a pinch of salt and pepper. Put the mixture back into the pineapple shells and replace the tops.

Hala Terrace, Kahala Hilton, Honolulu
CHEF: MARTIN WYSS

Macadamia Rum Cream Dressing

3 cups sweetened whipped cream
½ cup crushed Macadamia nuts
Juice of ¼ lime
2 tablespoons dark rum

Blend whipped cream, Macadamia nuts, and lime juice. Then add rum.

Mount Soche Hotel, Blantyre, Malawi
CHEF: HERBERT FUESSEL

American Eggs

4 medium very ripe tomatoes
2 cups raw mixed vegetables, finely sliced*
  Salt
  Pepper
  Lemon juice
2 hard-cooked eggs
24 cooked shrimp
  Lettuce
  Mayonnaise
  Cocktail sauce
12 gherkins
1 large cucumber, sliced
8 radishes

Cut top off tomatoes and scoop out pulp and seeds. Fill tomato shells with mixed vegetables seasoned with salt, pepper, and lemon juice. Top each tomato with half an egg and arrange shrimp around edge of tomato. Serve on beds of lettuce garnished with gherkins, cucumber slices and radish roses. Pass both mayonnaise and cocktail sauce.

serves: 4

* Artichoke hearts, green beans, onions, carrots, cauliflower, corn, mushrooms.

Mount Lavinia Hyatt, Mount Lavinia, Ceylon

Ceylon Egg Hoppers

¼ ounce (1 tablespoon) active dry yeast
4 cups flour
2 teaspoons salt
  Water from 1 coconut
2 teaspoons sugar
  Butter or coconut oil for greasing pan
20 eggs

Dissolve the yeast in ¼ cup of water. Sift the flour and salt and mix it with the coconut water and the sugar. The mixture must be a little thick in consistency. Let stand in a warm (80 degree F.) place to ferment for 3 hours.

Grate the coconut and take the 1st and 2nd extract of coconut milk (see Index) and add to the mixture to make a smooth batter the consistency of heavy cream. Heat a frying pan with a tight cover and rub it with butter or coconut oil. Pour in half a ladle of the flour

serves: 10

(Continued at foot of facing page

Brasserie, New York City

Quiche Lorraine

Pie crust

*serves: 5
as entrée
10 as first
course*

1½ pounds (750 grams) flour
1 teaspoon salt
1¼ pounds (625 grams) butter
1 cup water

Sift flour and salt. Cut butter into flour until the mixture resembles coarse cornmeal. Add water, a few tablespoons at a time, until dough just holds together. Wrap in waxed paper and chill at least 1 hour.

Filling

1 pound (500 grams) bacon
1½ pounds (750 grams) Swiss cheese
4 or 5 eggs
4 cups milk
2 cups heavy cream
1 tablespoon salt
1 teaspoon white pepper
Pinch nutmeg

Fry bacon until crisp; drain and break into pieces. Grate cheese. Set aside. Beat eggs just until mixed and add to milk and cream. Season with salt, pepper, and nutmeg.

Conclusion: Divide chilled dough into 4 pieces. Roll out each one to line a 5-inch pan. Arrange bacon, then cheese, evenly over the bottoms of the pans. Pour the custard mixture carefully into the pie crusts. Bake in a 400° F. oven for 10 minutes, then reduce heat to 325° F. and continue baking about 35 minutes or until a knife comes out clean when inserted halfway to the center of the quiche.

Ceylon Egg Hoppers (continued)

mixture; turn the pan to coat. Break an egg onto the batter and cover the pan. Cook for a few minutes until the egg is done to taste. Serve 2 egg-and-bread pancakes to each person.

Tavern on the Green, New York City

Quiche Lorraine for 72

Pastry

18 pounds (8.6 kilograms) flour
 7 pounds (3.5 kilograms) sweet butter
 5 pounds (2.5 kilograms) vegetable shortening
 2 quarts cold water
 4 tablespoons salt

Mix all the ingredients for pastry and let stand overnight in the refrigerator. The next day roll out the dough and fill 72 6-inch pie pans.

serves: 72

Filling

 20 quarts (23 litres) heavy cream
160 eggs
 20 pounds (10 kilograms) bacon
 4 tablespoons salt
 10 pounds (5 kilograms) shredded Gruyère cheese
 1 tablespoon white pepper
 1 tablespoon paprika
 5 tablespoons chives, minced

Cut all of the bacon in ½-inch pieces, and roast them. Shred Gruyère cheese. Mix cold eggs with heavy cream, white pepper and paprika. Put shredded Gruyère on the bottom of the pie pans, then add one layer of bacon, then add another layer of cheese. Fill the pie pans half full with mixture of heavy cream and eggs. Bake 1½ hours in 300° F. oven.

La Taverna, Hong Kong

Spaghetti Alla Taverna

 ¾ cup olive oil
 1 clove garlic
 4 ounces (125 grams) cooked Italian ham, cubed
 10 artichoke hearts preserved in olive oil, sliced
 1 tablespoon capers
 4 ounces (125 grams) mushrooms preserved in olive oil, finely chopped
1½ pounds (750 grams) Italian spaghetti
 1 tablespoon fresh parsley, chopped

Heat olive oil in a pan with a clove of garlic until garlic is golden.
Add the ham, artichokes, capers, and mushrooms. Stir for 3 minutes on low heat.
Bring salted water for cooking pasta to a rolling boil in a large pot. Add spaghetti and cook for 8 to 10 minutes, until spaghetti is *al dente*. Pour two glasses of cold water in pot to prevent further cooking. Drain all water from spaghetti. Place in a large serving dish and pour sauce on top; do *not* add Parmesan cheese. Garnish with parsley.

serves: 6

wine:
Bardolino
Bolla

Mama Leone's, New York City

Fettuccine all'Alfredo

serves: 6
¼ pound (125 grams) butter
3 cups heavy cream
6 egg yolks
12 ounces (375 grams) fettuccine (egg noodles)
½ cup grated Parmesan cheese

Mix butter, heavy cream and egg yolks and allow to stand at room temperature. Do not heat. Cook fettuccine, drain well and put in a large serving bowl. Pour the butter-cream-egg-yolk mixture over the pasta (the heat from the noodles will thicken the sauce). Sprinkle with Parmesan cheese and serve immediately.

Greece

Pastichio

Cream Sauce

serves: 8
6 tablespoons butter
4 cups hot milk
2 tablespoons salt
3 eggs, lightly beaten
¾ cup flour

Melt butter, add flour; cook, stirring until mixture is golden. Gradually add hot milk, and cook until sauce is smooth and thick, stirring continuously. Stir in salt; cool; stir in eggs.

Pasta

2 onions, chopped
4 tablespoons butter
2 pounds (1 kilogram) minced meat
  Salt
  Pepper
  Dash cinnamon
½ cup water
1 cup tomato purée
1 pound (500 grams) macaroni
3 eggs
1 tablespoon salt
¼ cup grated cheese

Sauté onions in butter until golden brown; add meat and cook until meat is browned. Add salt, pepper, cinnamon, water and tomato purée and cook for 5 minutes. Cook macaroni according to instructions on package. Drain, rinse, and when warm add eggs and 1 tablespoon salt; mix well. Place half of macaroni in a buttered casserole. Sprinkle with grated cheese. Add meat mixture and sprinkle with alternating layers of cheese and the remaining macaroni. The top layer should be cheese. Bake for 10 minutes in oven at 350° F. Add cream sauce on top and sprinkle with cheese. Bake for 30 more minutes, or until well browned.

India

Fried Rice

1 cup rice
1 tablespoon butter
2 onions, chopped fine
12 cardamons
4 pieces cinnamon
6 black peppercorns
12 cloves
1 teaspoon sugar
2½ cups water
1 teaspoon salt

Wash rice thoroughly and drain well. Heat butter in a fairly large pan and sauté onions in it. Crush all spices together. Add spices and sugar to onions and fry until all are golden. Pour the water and salt into this mixture. Boil for 2 minutes before adding rice. Continue cooking until all water has evaporated. Lower heat and then place in a hot oven to dry it still further.

serves: 4

Tomato Rice

2 large onions, sliced fine
1 2-inch piece fresh ginger
2 cups water
2 pounds (1 kilogram) tomatoes, peeled and cut small
4 tablespoons butter or oil
Garlic
4 peppercorns
4 cloves
2 cups raw rice
1½ teaspoons salt

Grind 1 onion and ginger into a paste. Add 2 cups water to tomatoes and cook for 5 minutes. Strain juice and set aside. Heat butter or oil, brown the other onion, and set aside half for garnish. To the remainder of butter or oil and onion add garlic, peppercorns and cloves, and fry for 5 minutes. Add rice and fry. Afterwards, add set-aside tomato juice and enough additional water to cook rice—the proportion of rice to liquid should be 1 to 2. Add salt and cook until done. Garnish with browned onions before serving.

serves: 8-10

Turkey

Rice Pilaf

serves: 6

2 cups uncooked rice
4 tomatoes
4 tablespoons butter
3½ cups water (or meat or chicken stock)
2 teaspoons salt

Wash rice well and drain. Peel tomatoes, remove seeds and cut into small pieces. Melt butter in a pan and add tomatoes, mashing them until a paste is formed. Add water or stock and boil for 2 minutes. Add rice. Stir only once, then cover pan and cook over medium heat. Do not stir. When rice has absorbed liquid, reduce heat and simmer for 20 minutes. Remove pan from stove and leave for 30 minutes, keeping pan covered. Do not stir. When transferring pilaf to serving dish, it is important to disturb the rice as little as possible to ensure that it remains fluffy.

India

Pea Pulao

serves: 8-10

1 tablespoon cumin seeds
4 tablespoons butter or oil
½ teaspoon turmeric powder
2 cups raw rice
4 cups water
1½ teaspoons salt
1 package frozen peas
1 onion, diced fine

Sauté cumin seeds in butter or oil until slightly browned. Add turmeric powder and rice and stir well. Add water and salt and cook over low heat. When rice is half cooked, add peas. Cook until rice is done. Sauté onion in butter and use as garnish.

Georges Rey Restaurant Français, New York City
CHEF: GINO BARBUTI

Soufflé Georges Rey

Crème pâtissière
12 yolks (reserve whites)
2 cups sugar
½ cup flour
4 cups milk
1 teaspoon vanilla extract

Boil the milk with the vanilla; while the milk is boiling mix with a whip the egg yolks, sugar and flour. While the milk is still boiling, add the mixture and whip over the fire mixing it constantly to avoid sticking for 5 minutes. This recipe makes enough crème for more than a dozen individual soufflés. It can also be used for filling eclairs, etc.

Soufflé
For each person to be served, you will need:
6 tablespoons crème pâtissière
2 tablespoons candied fruit
1 tablespoon kirsch
2 egg whites
1 teaspoon sugar
1 soufflé dish, buttered and sugared

In a bowl, mix the crème pâtissière, the fruit and kirsch. Then whip the egg whites with the sugar until thick like whipped cream. Mix slowly with a spoon with the crème. Return to egg whites and mix gently. Pour in the dish and place in a 450° F. oven for 15 minutes.

Caprice Restaurant, London
CHEF: BRIAN COTTERILL

Peach and Banana Flambé

1 tablespoon sugar
Juice of ½ orange
Juice of 1 lemon
2 bananas, peeled and cut in half lengthwise
2 peaches, peeled and cut in half
1 tablespoon Grand Marnier

Place sugar and the orange and lemon juice in a small flambé pan and simmer for 2 minutes. Add the bananas and peaches and simmer for a further 2 minutes, then add the Grand Marnier, flame and serve.

serves: 4

wine:
Fonseca Royal Tawny Port

Mount Soche Hotel, Blantyre, Malawi
CHEF: HERBERT FUESSEL

Parfait Saint Tropez

serves: 4

2 layers sponge cake
1 pint chocolate ice cream
1 pint vanilla ice cream
¼ cup brandy
6 ounces (180 grams) butter chocolate
Whipped cream (optional)
Angelica (optional)

In 4 individual (2½-inch diameter) molds or a 1½-quart soufflé dish place: a thin slice of sponge cake cut to fit the mold; the chocolate ice cream slightly softened to spread; another layer of sponge cake; the vanilla ice cream; and finally a double-thick layer of cake. Sprinkle the last layer of cake with brandy, wrap well in foil and freeze very firm, overnight, if possible.

To serve, melt bitter chocolate and allow to cool to spreading consistency. Unmold frozen cake and ice cream and frost with chocolate, working quickly. Top with whipped cream and angelica if desired.

The George Hotel, Haddington, Scotland

Fruit Cocktail Meringue

serves: 8

1 large can fruit cocktail (approximately 2 pounds or 1 kilogram)
½ pound (125 grams) sponge cake
4 egg whites
¼ teaspoon lemon juice
¼ teaspoon salt
6 tablespoons sugar

Place the fruit cocktail, not drained, in a shallow ovenproof dish.

Arrange the cake evenly on top of the fruit.

Place the egg whites, lemon juice and salt in a large mixing bowl. Whisk until stiff. Fold in 4 tablespoons sugar and continue beating for 5 minutes. Fold in remaining 2 tablespoons of sugar and beat until sugar is completely dissolved.

Pipe or spread meringue over prepared fruit and cake. Bake in a very slow (250° F.) oven for 1 hour, until meringue is dry, or bake in a hot oven (400° F.) until meringue is browned.

Caprice Restaurant, London
CHEF: BRIAN COTTERILL

Lemon Sorbet

1 cup sugar
2 cups boiling water
2 cups sweet wine
Juice of 2 lemons
Juice of 1 orange
3 egg whites, beaten stiff and shiny
1 cup whipped cream

Dissolve sugar in boiling water, boil for 5 minutes, strain and cool. Add the wine, fruit juices and beaten egg whites to the syrup. Pour mixture into an ice-cream freezer packed with crushed ice. Set at medium speed, scraping the sides so that it doesn't stick or form ice particles. When almost frozen, fold in whipped cream. Turn into an airtight plastic bowl and store in the freezer. To serve, let soften a little as very hard sorbet has an unpleasant texture.

serves: 4

wine:
Champagne

Turkey

Yogurt Dessert

3 cups water
3½ cups sugar
3 eggs
1 cup flour
1 teaspoon baking powder
1 cup yogurt
1 teaspoon grated lemon or orange rind
1 teaspoon lemon juice
Whipped cream

Mix water with 2½ cups sugar. Boil until it forms a syrup. Leave to cool. Beat eggs into remainder of sugar until sugar is dissolved. Sift flour with baking powder. Add yogurt, sifted flour, grated rind and lemon juice to egg mixture and beat until smooth. Grease a 9-inch square baking pan well, pour mixture into it and bake at 400° F. for 30 minutes. After removing from oven, leave pastry in the pan and cut into diamond shapes. Pour cold syrup over pastry. Leave pan uncovered until all syrup has been absorbed by pastry. When cool, chill in refrigerator. Garnish with whipped cream before serving.

serves: 8

Hotel Russell, Dublin
CHEF: P. ROLLAND

Chocolate Cake

Sponge

serves: 10

5 eggs
¾ cup sugar
¾ cup flour
6 tablespoons cocoa
  Sugar syrup
  Garnish
  Kirsch or rum
  Powdered sugar or chocolate curls

Put the eggs in a bowl and whisk with the sugar until smooth. Add flour and cocoa and mix. Put in a buttered and floured 10-inch baking tin and bake at 350° F. until done, about 30 minutes. Take sponge out of oven and let cool. When cold cut sponge in 3 layers. Moisten sponges with syrup and a little kirsch or rum, then spread garnish over them and join together. Put garnish around sides and on top of the cake. Sprinkle either powdered sugar or chocolate curls on top.

Syrup

½ cup water
1 cup sugar

Boil water and sugar for 10 minutes. Let cool.

Garnish

½ cup cream
7 ounces (220 grams) melted chocolate

Bring cream to a boil. Add melted chocolate. Whisk cream and chocolate until thick, then cool.

Top of the Town, Hotel Inter-Continental, Auckland, New Zealand

Chocolate Mousse

serves: 4-6

½ pound chocolate
2 tablespoons milk
2 tablespoons cognac
1½ ounces sugar
2 tablespoons freshly ground almonds
4 eggs, separated

Melt chocolate with milk and cognac; add sugar and ground almonds. Cool slightly and briskly stir in egg yolks. Let stand for a few minutes, then gently fold in stiffly beaten egg whites. Pour into individual dishes and chill well before serving.

Caprice Restaurant, London
CHEF: BRIAN COTTERILL

Beignet Soufflés

½ cup water
¼ cup butter
½ cup flour
1 tablespoon sugar
Pinch of salt
3 eggs
Oil for deep frying
½ cup sugar
1 teaspoon cinnamon
½ cup heavy cream, whipped
2 tablespoons grated fresh orange peel
1 tablespoon honey
1 cup custard sauce
2 tablespoons brandy

Boil water and butter. When butter has melted add the flour, sugar and pinch of salt all at once. Remove from direct heat and stir vigorously until paste leaves the sides of pan. Add eggs, one at a time, beating hard after each addition. Pipe paste through pastry bag with a plain tube into rounds or drop by heaping teaspoonfuls into 370° F. deep frying oil. The soufflés will gradually swell to 4 or 5 times their original size and when cooked will be golden brown and hollow inside.
Remove soufflés from fat and roll them in sugar mixed with cinnamon. When completely cold, fill with whipped cream mixed with orange peel and honey. Serve with luke-warm custard sauce mixed with brandy.

serves: 4

wine:
Harvey's
Bristol
Cream
Sherry

Hotel Taprobane, Colombo, Ceylon
CHEF: C. H. CONMARÍN

Watalappan

10 eggs
1 pound (500 grams) jaggery*
2 cups thick coconut milk
Dash fresh grated nutmeg
Pinch cinnamon
½ teaspoon ground cardamon
Pinch salt

Beat the eggs, yolks and white separately. Then beat well together. Mix in the jaggery, coconut milk, spices and salt. Pour into a greased mold, cover with greased paper and steam for about 1¼ hours or until firm to the touch. Serve in the mold.

* 2½ cups honey boiled down until very stiff may be substituted.

serves: 4

The Cold Buffet

THE EMPRESS,
LONDON
(Chef: Gino Scandolo)

Cobb Salad

THE BROWN DERBY,
HOLLYWOOD, CALIFORNIA
(Chefs: Johannes Van Bebber
and Fritz Gmeineder)

The Cold Table

HOTEL INTERCONTINENTAL, AUCKLAND, NEW ZEALAND

The Sweet Table

BOAC Cabin service

Chestnut Gâteau

Génoise sponge

serves: 12

8 eggs
1 cup sugar
1 cup flour
½ cup melted butter

Whisk the eggs and sugar together with a balloon whisk in a bowl over a pan of hot water. Continue until the mixture is light, creamy, double in bulk and shows the marks of the whisk. Fold in the flour very gently, then fold in the melted butter very gently. Place batter in two 9-inch round greased and floured Génoise molds and bake in a 350° F. oven approximately 30 minutes. Let cake cool in the pan for 10 minutes. Remove to a rack to finish cooling.

Decoration

½ cup cream, whipped
3 meringues
1 cup chestnut purée
¼ cup butter
¼ cup sugar
2 tablespoons rum or kirsch
Crushed meringues or chocolate shreds
Marrons glacés

When sponge is quite cold, slice into 2 layers and fill with whipped cream and broken pieces of meringues. Re-form the gâteau and, using a pallet knife, coat the sides with a mixture of chestnut purée, butter, sugar and rum or kirsch, mixed well together until light and creamy. (Reserve 2 tablespoons of this mixture for garnish.) Decorate the sides with either crushed meringues or chocolate shreds. Using a vermicelli press or a fine sieve and a wooden spoon, cover the top of the gâteau with fine threads of chestnut purée mixture. Finish the decoration with marrons glacés placed neatly around the top edge.

Coral Lanai, Halekulani Hotel, Honolulu

Popovers

makes: 25

8 eggs
1 quart milk
1 quart flour
1 teaspoon salt
¼ cup melted butter

Beat eggs and milk together. Sift flour and salt together three times and fold into eggs and milk mixture. Add butter and spoon into hot greased muffin tins.
Bake 25 minutes at 400° F.

That Steak Joynt, Chicago
CHEF: RILEY SIMMONS

Steak Joynt Flaming Hot Fudge Sundae

3 cups hot fudge sauce
2 tablespoons butter
6 tablespoons Vandermint (liqueur)
6 tablespoons brandy
1 pint vanilla ice cream

Place hot fudge in buttered flat chafing dish over heat and cook until it sizzles. Add Vandermint and brandy. Set aflame and immediately serve over scoops of rich vanilla ice cream in champagne glasses.

serves: 6

Hot fudge sauce

3½ cups sugar
¼ cup corn syrup
1 ⅔ cups milk
4 ounces (125 grams) bitter chocolate
½ cup butter
½ teaspoon vanilla extract

Cook sugar, syrup, milk and chocolate until mixture forms a very soft ball in cold water. Remove from heat and add butter. Cool without stirring until lukewarm. (If sweet butter is used, add salt to taste.) Add vanilla and stir in well. Store in refrigerator.

Turkey

Farina Nut Pudding

1 cup sugar
1 cup milk
1 cup water
2 tablespoons butter
1 cup farina
2 tablespoons pine nuts
Cinnamon

Mix sugar, milk and water. Boil until it forms a syrup, and then leave to cool. Melt butter in heavy saucepan, add farina and pine nuts. Sauté over low heat until nuts are slightly brown. Pour cool syrup over hot farina mixture and stir well. Cover pan and cook gently until syrup has been absorbed, stirring constantly. Take pan off heat. Wrap pan lid in a towel and replace on pan to absorb excess moisture. Leave for 30 minutes. Before serving, stir well and sprinkle with cinnamon.

serves: 6-8

Maile Restaurant, Kahala Hilton, Honolulu
CHEF: MARTIN WYSS

Maile Tart

serves: 12

2¼ cups sugar
¼ cup sliced roasted almonds
1 cup candied fruits
1½ cups canned pineapple, chopped
3 tablespoons Grand Marnier
2 tablespoons kirshwasser
¾ cup water
6 egg whites
2 cups heavy cream
Salt
4 pineapple slices
Maraschino cherries for garnish

Melt half the sugar in a shallow pan until brown. Add almonds and mix. Pour the mixture on a cold stainless steel tray to cool. When hard, crush with a rolling pin until almost powdery. Marinate candied fruits and chopped pineapple in Grand Marnier and kirshwasser. Slowly boil the remaining half of the sugar and ¾ cup of water until syrupy. To prevent crystallization of the sugar, do not stir while boiling. Whip 6 egg whites until stiff peaks form. Slowly pour the syrup over the meringue and continue whipping until cold.
Whip heavy cream. Set aside some whipped cream for garnish. Fold the whipped cream, candied fruits, pineapple, crushed caramel and a pinch of salt into the meringue mixture. Pour into 2 pie plates and freeze. Garnish the tarts with slice of pineapple, whipped cream and maraschino cherries. The second tart can be kept frozen 2 to 3 weeks.

Gaddi's, Hong Kong
CHEF: ARMIN SONDEREGGER

Coupe "The Peninsula"

serves: 2

2 egg yolks
2 teaspoons granulated sugar
4 tablespoons Marsala
2 tablespoons white wine
2 scoops vanilla ice cream
2 tablespoons Jamaican rum

First make sabayon: beat the egg yolks and granulated sugar together in a copper bowl. Blend the Marsala and white wine into the mixture and heat gently over hot water. Keep beating until mixture becomes a creamy white foam. Put a scoop of vanilla ice cream into each goblet. Add a few drops of Jamaican rum. Pour on the hot sabayon and serve immediately.

Turkey

Lips of the Beauty

4¾ cups water
2½ cups sugar
1 teaspoon lemon juice
½ cup butter
1½ cups flour
1 teaspoon salt
2 eggs
1 egg yolk
1¼ cups vegetable cooking fat

Place 3 cups water in a pan. Add sugar and lemon juice and boil for 15 minutes. Allow to cool. Melt butter in another pan. As soon as it begins to change color add remainder of water and bring to boil. Reduce heat to very low, add flour and salt and stir constantly for about 8 minutes. Remove from heat and allow to cool.

Add eggs one at a time, followed by egg yolk. Beat well. Knead the dough and cut into small oval pieces about 2 inches across. Fold these in half so that edges meet, forming "lips". Over moderate heat, melt cooking fat in a pan and place dough rolls in it. Increase heat and fry rolls on both sides until brown. Remove and drain. Place in a dish and pour cold syrup over hot rolls. After 15 minutes remove rolls from syrup and serve.

serves: 6-8

Turkish Flour Pudding

1 cup sugar
6 tablespoons rice flour
4 teaspoons cornstarch
4 cups milk
5 teaspoons rose water
4 almond macaroons

Blend sugar, rice flour and cornstarch together thoroughly in a large saucepan. Add milk, mix well, and cook over medium heat, stirring constantly, for about 10 minutes. Reduce heat and cook slowly. At this stage do not stir, as the flour paste has to settle and form caramel. From time to time, dip spoon into the mixture. When spoon begins to stick to caramel at the bottom, increase heat slightly until spoon smells of caramel.

Remove from heat and add rose water. Place the macaroons in an

serves: 4

(Continued at foot of facing page

Madrid Restaurant, Rizal, Philippines

Orange Soufflé

serves: 8

¼ **cup butter**
6 **tablespoons flour**
 Dash salt
1 **cup milk**
¼ **cup orange juice concentrate**
½ **cup water**
1½ **teaspoons grated lemon peel**
6 **egg yolks**
6 **egg whites**
¼ **cup sugar**

Melt butter; blend in flour and salt. Gradually stir in milk and cook over low heat, stirring constantly until thick.
Measure ¼ cup orange juice concentrate from a 6-ounce can (reserve remainder for orange sauce); combine with water and grated lemon peel. Stir into the hot mixture. Beat 6 egg yolks until thick and lemon colored. Gradually add hot mixture; mix well and let cool somewhat. Beat 6 egg whites to soft peaks; gradually add ¼ cup sugar, beating to stiff peaks. Fold yolk mixture into egg whites.
Pour into ungreased 1½-quart casserole with a paper collar.
Set dish in shallow pan filled to a depth of 1 inch with hot water. Bake in slow oven (325° F.) about 1½ hours or until knife inserted comes out clean. Peel off paper. Serve at once, breaking apart gently with two forks. Pass orange sauce.

Orange sauce

½ **cup sugar**
1½ **tablespoons cornstarch**
 Dash salt
½ **cup orange juice concentrate**
1 **cup water**
1 **tablespoon butter**

Combine sugar, cornstarch, and a dash of salt. Stir in orange concentrate and water. Cook and stir until thick. Stir in butter. Serve warm.

Turkish Flour Pudding (continued)

ovenware dish and pour hot mixture over them. Scrape caramel from pan and add to pudding. Allow to cool for about 3 hours and serve cold.

The Brown Derby, Hollywood, California
CHEFS: JOHANNES VAN BEBBER AND FRANZ GMEINEDER

Brown Derby Grapefruit Cake

1½ cups sifted cake flour
¾ cup sugar
1½ teaspoons baking powder
½ teaspoon salt
¼ cup water
¼ cup vegetable oil
3 eggs, separated
⅜ tablespoon grapefruit juice
½ teaspoon grated lemon rind
¼ teaspoon cream of tartar

serves: 8

Sift together flour, sugar, baking powder and salt into mixing bowl. Make a well in center of dry ingredients and add water, oil, egg yolks, grapefruit juice and lemon rind. Beat until very smooth. Beat egg whites and cream of tartar separately until whites are stiff but not dry. Gradually pour egg yolk mixture over whites, folding gently with a rubber spatula until just blended. *Do not stir* mixture. Pour into an ungreased 9-inch cake pan. Bake in a 350° F. oven 25 to 30 minutes, or until cake springs back when lightly touched with finger. Invert pan on cake rack until cool. Run spatula around edge of cake and carefully remove from pan. With a serrated knife, gently cut layer in half.

Grapefruit cream cheese frosting
¾ pound (375 grams) cream cheese
2 teaspoons lemon juice
1 teaspoon grated lemon rind
¾ cup powdered sugar, sifted
1 1-pound (500-gram) can grapefruit
    sections, well drained
6 to 8 drops yellow food coloring

Let cream cheese soften at room temperature. Beat cheese until fluffy. Add lemon juice and rind. Gradually blend in sugar. Beat until well blended. Crush broken grapefruit sections to measure 2 teaspoons. Blend into frosting. Stir in food coloring. Spread frosting on bottom half of cake. Top with several grapefruit sections. Cover with second layer. Frost top and sides and garnish with remaining grapefruit sections.

Speedbird House, Karachi Airport

Sindhi Banana Twirls

Pastry

serves: 8
- **¾ cup flour**
- **¼ teaspoon salt**
- **¼ cup shortening**
- **2 tablespoons cold water**

Conclusion

- **4 raw bananas**
- **2 tablespoons lemon juice**
- **¼ cup butter, melted**
- **1 tablespoon cinnamon sugar**

Sift flour and salt together. Cut in shortening until mixture looks like cornmeal. Add water, a little at a time, using just enough to make dough hold together. Roll out thinly. Cut 8 6″ × 1″ strips.

Peel the bananas, cut into halves and dip into lemon juice.
Moisten the pastry strips with cold water and wrap round the bananas in twirls which will leave some parts of the bananas exposed.
Brush the pastry with melted butter and sprinkle with the cinnamon sugar.
Place on baking tray in the top of the oven and bake for 15 to 20 minutes until crisp and brown.
Serve hot or cold with a Chantilly cream or vanilla or praline ice cream.

Greece

Tiropeta

(Cheese Pie)

serves: 16
- **½ pound (250 grams) butter**
- **12 eggs**
- **1 pound (500 grams) ricotta cheese**
- **1 pound (500 grams) goat cheese**
- **1 pound Greek pastry (filo)**

Melt half of the butter and let it cool. Beat eggs until stiff. In a separate bowl mix cheeses with cooled melted butter and add eggs. Melt remainder of butter and brush both sides of pastry sheets with it. Butter a baking pan large enough for the pastry and 2 inches deep. Place half of pastry sheets in baking pan and then add cheese mixture. Cover with remaining pastry sheets. Do not cut pastry. Bake at 350° F. for about half an hour or until golden. Cut in squares and serve hot.

Normandie Grill, Oriental Hotel, Bangkok
CHEF: MICHEL GRANGE

La Flognarde

1 apple
2 tablespoons lemon juice
2 eggs
1½ tablespoons sugar
6 tablespoons flour
½ cup milk
1 tablespoon butter
  Powdered sugar

Peel and core apple and cut in thin slices; sprinkle with lemon juice and set aside.
Beat the eggs until frothy. Sift sugar and flour together, then sift into eggs; mix gently. Add milk very slowly, mixing thoroughly but gently. Grease a 4-inch springform pan thoroughly with butter. Place in a 400° F. oven until hot. Spread batter in pan and top with apple slices. Bake until crust tests done, only about 10 minutes. (If crust is browning too fast on the edges, reduce heat to 350° F. to finish baking.) Sift powdered sugar over apples and serve immediately.

serves: 1

Greece

Galatoboureko
(Egg and Pastry Dish with Cream)

4 cups sugar
1 teaspoon lemon juice
2½ cups boiling water
8 egg yolks
6 cups warm milk
6 tablespoons cornstarch
1 cup very heavy cream
1 tablespoon vanilla
1 cup sweet butter, melted
½ pound Greek pastry (filo)

Mix 3½ cups sugar and lemon juice with boiling water and stir until dissolved. Bring to a boil again and simmer for 15 minutes. Set aside to cool. Beat egg yolks and ½ cup sugar together until mixture is thick and pale in color. Stir in warm milk alternately with cornstarch until mixture nearly reaches the boiling point. Remove from heat and stir in cream and vanilla. Butter filo sheets generously on both sides and thoroughly butter a suitable baking tray. Place half of the sheets on the baking tray. Pour cream mixture over pastry and cover cream with remaining sheets of pastry. With a sharp knife, cut top

serves: 24

(Continued at foot of facing page

Caprice Restaurant, London
CHEF: BRIAN COTTERILL

Poire Caprice

serves: 4

wine:
*Verdelho
Rare Old
Reserve
Madeira*

4 large whole pears, peeled
1 cup sugar
 Egg yolks
6 tablespoons water
6 tablespoons Marsala
 Dash of brandy
½ cup whipped cream
½ cup red currant jam
4 slices sponge cake
2 or 3 crumbled macaroons

Stew the pears gently in 2 cups water and ½ cup sugar; core them and leave to cool.

Make a cold zabaglione by putting the egg yolks, the other ½ cup sugar and 6 tablespoons of water in a bowl over a pan of hot water. Whisk with a wire balloon whisk (this gives the best aeration but a rotary egg beater will do) until pale and frothy. Stir in the Marsala and the brandy and beat vigorously until the mixture is very thick and light. Remove from the heat and continue to whisk until the mixture is cold. Fold in whipped cream. Cool in the refrigerator. Fill the cored pears with the red currant jam and arrange them on sponge cake slices. Cover with the cold zabaglione and sprinkle the crumbled macaroons over them.

Galatoboureko (continued)

pastry into a number of strips. Preheat oven to 375° F. and place baking tray in it for about 45 minutes or until pastry is golden. Remove from oven and pour cool syrup over hot galatoboureko. Do not cover dish. Leave to cool and cut into squares before serving.

Charley O's, New York City

Chocolate Mousse Cake

Chocolate Sponge Cake

 3 eggs
 6 tablespoons sugar
 ½ cup sifted flour
 ¼ cup cocoa
 2 tablespoons melted butter

Preheat oven to 350° F. Beat eggs, adding sugar a little at a time. Sift in flour and cocoa. Stir in melted butter. Mix until well blended. Pour into a 6-inch round (2-inch deep) baking pan. Bake for 25 minutes at 350° F. Cool.

serves: 6

Mousse

 4 egg whites
 1 cup sugar
 2 tablespoons unflavored gelatin
    softened in ½ cup cold water
 3 squares dark sweet chocolate
 2 cups heavy cream, whipped

Beat together egg whites and 2 tablespoons of the sugar until mixture forms peaks. Using a candy thermometer cook remaining sugar with 2 tablespoons of water in a saucepan until sugar is dissolved and temperature reaches 245° F. Beat the hot syrup into the meringue, pouring the syrup in a thin stream. Dissolve the gelatin in ¼ cup of boiling water. Combine the melted gelatin with egg white mixture. Melt chocolate and add to mixture, blending thoroughly. Fold in whipped cream.

Slice the cake horizontally into 3 layers. Place 1 layer of the cake in a circular mold 6 inches in diameter. Then pour half of the mousse filling into the mold and repeat with another layer of cake and the balance of the mousse. Top with third layer of cake and chill for 30 minutes before frosting.

Chocolate icing

 5 squares dark sweet chocolate
 ¼ cup water

Melt the chocolate and blend with the water. Frost the top of the cake and chill again before serving.

The Four Seasons, New York City

Chocolate Velvet

serves: 8

1 basic sponge sheet 11″ × 16″
3 egg yolks
1 tablespoon instant coffee
¼ cup kirsch
¼ cup rum
¼ cup crème de cacao
⅓ cup (firmly packed) praline paste
  (can be bought in a can)
6 tablespoons melted butter
1½ pounds semi-sweet chocolate, melted
3 egg whites
  Pinch of salt
¼ cup confectioner's sugar
2 cups heavy cream, whipped
  (unsweetened)

Semi-sweet chocolate icing
5 squares semi-sweet chocolate
¼ cup boiling water

Completely line a rounded 1-quart mold with basic sponge cake by cutting out a circle to fit the bottom of the mold. Then, from the remaining cake cut 1 long or 2 short strips to cover the sides. Reserve any cake left over for the top.

Mix egg yolks, coffee, kirsch, rum, crème de cacao and praline paste. Beat until smooth. Add hot butter and hot melted chocolate.

Beat egg whites with salt until they form soft peaks. Add sugar, a tablespoon at a time, beating well after each addition. Continue beating 5 more minutes, or until very stiff. Fold whipped cream and beaten egg whites into original mixture. Pour into the sponge-lined mold. Cover top with remaining sponge cake, fitting together any bits and pieces if there is not a single piece big enough. Place in refrigerator for 2 hours or until filling is firm. To serve, loosen sides of mold with a sharp knife. Turn out upside-down on a plate. Frost all over with semi-sweet chocolate icing.

Melt chocolate. Mix chocolate and water, blending well. Frost cake all over and chill.

Mama Leone's, New York City

Zabaglione

6 egg yolks
2 tablespoons sugar
  Sweet sherry
  Sweet vermouth

Beat the egg yolks until they are thoroughly mixed. Measure them. Add sugar and ¾ the measure of the egg yolks of sherry and ¼ the measure of vermouth. Cook in the top of a double boiler over hot, not boiling, water, beating constantly, until the mixture thickens. Pour into dessert glasses and chill. Before serving, top with a tablespoon of whipped cream and a cherry, if desired.

serves: 4

The Four Seasons, New York City

Génoise

(French Sponge Cake)

6 eggs
6 egg yolks
1 cup sugar
1 cup sifted flour
½ cup clarified butter
1 teaspoon vanilla

Combine eggs, egg yolks and sugar in a bowl. Set the bowl over a saucepan containing 1 or 2 inches of hot water. It should not touch the bowl and should never boil. Place over low heat and beat the mixture continuously as it warms. The eggs are warm enough when, if you put your finger into them, not more than 1 drop falls from your finger, and the mixture looks like a bright yellow syrup. Remove from the heat and beat with an electric mixer at high speed for about 15 minutes or until the mixture becomes light, fluffy and cool. It will almost triple in bulk and will look very like whipped cream. Sprinkle the flour, a little at a time, over the beaten eggs. Fold in gently, by hand. Add the clarified butter and vanilla. Be very careful not to overmix or you will dissipate the air beaten in — which is what makes the Génoise light.
Pour the batter into whatever type of pan or pans required. This recipe

serves: 8

(Continued at foot of facing page

Brasserie, New York City

Swiss Chocolate Cake

Chocolate sponge

serves: 8

3 eggs
⅓ cup sugar
¼ cup flour
2 tablespoons cocoa
2 tablespoons butter, melted and cooled

Beat eggs and sugar until smooth; add flour, cocoa and butter. Mix gently but thoroughly. Turn into an 8-inch buttered cake pan and bake at 350° F. for about 18 minutes. The cake is done when it springs back from the touch and begins to pull away from the sides of the pan. Cool the sponge cake in the pan for 10 minutes. Remove and let cool thoroughly.

Filling

4 ounces (125 grams) malted chocolate
2 tablespoons rum
2 tablespoons butter
1 tablespoon dry instant coffee
½ cup heavy cream, whipped

Melt the chocolate with the butter and rum over hot, not boiling, water. Add coffee. Let mixture cool. Fold in whipped cream.

Frosting

4 ounces (125 grams) malted chocolate
2 tablespoons sugar
½ cup water

Melt chocolate over hot water. Add sugar and water. Beat over very cold water until frosting is of spreading consistency. If it hardens too much, beating over warm water will re-soften it.

Conclusion: Cut sponge cake into 3 layers. Spread the filling between the layers and reassemble the cake (a deep springform pan is convenient). Chill the filled cake thoroughly. When cold, unmold cake and spread with frosting.

Génoise (continued)

yields 2 9-inch or 3 8-inch layers. Bake in 350° F. oven for 25 or 30 minutes or until cake pulls away from pan and is golden brown and springy when touched lightly on top. Remove from pans immediately and cool on a cake rack.

Century Plaza Hotel, Los Angeles
CHEF: WALTER ROTH

"Clair de Lune" avec Sauce aux Mûres de Bois

2 tablespoons raisins
2 tablespoons kirsch
2 tablespoons soft marzipan
1 scoop French vanilla ice cream
2 egg whites
2 teaspoons sugar
1 round slice almond-flavored sponge or
  pound cake

Soak raisins in kirsch for several hours or overnight. Drain and mix raisins with marzipan. Form marzipan into a ball. Slightly soften ice cream; wrap it around marzipan to form a larger ball. Return to freezer to get *very* hard.

When ready to serve preheat oven to 500° F. Beat egg whites to form a stiff, shiny meringue. Place cake round on a wooden cutting board; place ice cream-marzipan ball on top of cake and quickly cover ice cream completely with meringue to form "la lune". Brown only a minute or two in oven. Serve immediately. Serve blackberry sauce separately.

Sauce aux mûres de bois

2 cups fresh blackberries
½ cup sugar
1 teaspoon carnstarch
2 teaspoons lemon juice
1 tablespoon blackberry liqueur
  or brandy

Mash blackberries. Bring berries and sugar to a boil over low heat. Cook 3 or 4 minutes, stirring constantly. Press berries through a sieve. Mix cornstarch with lemon juice (add a teaspoon or more of water if necessary) to form a smooth paste. Pour a little blackberry purée in starch mixture, then return to main purée pan. Heat until sauce thickens. Stir in liqueur or brandy. Serve hot or cold (store extra sauce in the refrigerator).

serves: 1

wine:
Korbel Extra
Dry Champagne

Restaurante Horcher, Madrid
CHEF: PACO

Crêpes Sir Holden

Crêpes

serves: 4

½ cup flour
½ teaspoon salt
1 egg
½ cup milk (more if needed)
Oil for cooking

Sift salt and flour together. Add egg and milk and blend to make a smooth, thin batter. (An electric blender makes excellent crêpe batter in seconds.)

Lightly oil a small skillet and put over medium heat. When pan is hot enough to make drops of water jump before evaporating, pour in about three tablespoons batter and tilt pan to coat evenly. Turn when bubbles form on top side. Set aside and keep warm when done.

Filling

1 cup fresh strawberries or raspberries
1 tablespoon framboise liqueur
1 tablespoon Cointreau
1 tablespoon Grand Marnier
2 tablespoons brandy
¼ cup sugar
2 tablespoons butter
1 pint vanilla ice cream
¼ cup crushed almonds

Wash and sort berries a few hours before using. Drain well and let dry. To finish filling, place berries in a saucepan or chafing dish. Mix liqueurs and pour over berries; flame. When flames die, lift out berries with a slotted spoon. Sprinkle crêpes with liqueur mixture and set them aside. Return berries to pan and heat gently with sugar and butter just until sugar is dissolved. Stir carefully to prevent crushing berries. Keep warm.

Place 2 scoops of ice cream on each serving plate and cover with 2 liqueur-flavored crêpes. Spoon warm berry mixture over crêpes and sprinkle with crushed almonds and serve at once.

The Tower Suite, New York City

Tower Suite Lemon and Lime Crêpes

4 tablespoons lime butter
4 dessert crêpes
4 thin lemon slices
4 thin lime slices
2 tablespoons brandy
4 tablespoons lemon whipped cream
2 teaspoons crushed almonds

Melt lime butter in a pan until it begins to bubble. Add the crêpes and cook on both sides. Refold the crêpes over the lemon and lime slices. Flame with brandy. Serve on a warm dessert plate. Spoon sauce left from flaming and lemon-whipped cream on the side of the plate. Sprinkle the crêpe and the lemon whipped cream with the crushed almonds.

serves: 2

Lime butter

4 tablespoons unsalted butter
2 teaspoons finely grated lime peel
1 teaspoon lime juice

Soften butter. Work grated peel and juice in. Store in the refrigerator.

Lemon whipped cream

½ cup heavy cream
¼ cup superfine sugar
1 tablespoon finely grated lemon peel
2 teaspoons lemon juice

Whip cream. Mix in sugar and peel. Add lemon juice just before using.

Hotel Inter-Continental Manila, Rizal, Philippines

Crêpes Veuve Joyeuse
(Lemon Soufflé Crêpes)

12 large crêpes (see Index)
1 lemon rind
1 cup water
½ cup sugar
1½ tablespoons butter
1 tablespoon flour
½ cup milk
¾ cup granulated sugar
½ teaspoon vanilla
3 egg yolks
4 egg whites
12 tablespoons granulated sugar

Prepare the crêpes and keep warm. Peel the lemon in tiny strips. Blanch for 2 minutes in boiling water and soak in 1 cup of water and ½ cup of sugar which have been boiled together for 15 minutes. Make a thick white sauce by heating the butter, flour, milk, sugar and vanilla together. Remove from the fire and beat in the egg yolks and lemon rind. Finally, fold

serves: 6

(Continued at foot of facing page

Panorama Room, Hotel Vancouver, Vancouver, British Columbia
CHEF: HUBERT SCHECK

Crêpes Hotel Vancouver

Crêpes

serves: 6

1¼ cups all-purpose flour
3 eggs
1 cup milk
¼ cup water
½ teaspoon salt
4 tablespoons clarified butter

Beat all ingredients except butter together to form a smooth batter. Let rest 1 hour. Cook thin crêpes in clarified butter. (Crêpes may be made in advance and stored in the refrigerator or frozen.)

Filling

6 tablespoons soft nougat
12 Chinese gooseberries, peeled and sliced
4 tablespoons crème patisserie
¼ cup kirsch
4 egg whites
2 tablespoons sugar
2 tablespoons crushed hazelnuts
1 cup chocolate sauce
½ cup heavy cream, whipped
2 tablespoons Grand Marnier

Spread ½ tablespoon nougat on each crêpe and place 1 sliced Chinese gooseberry on top. Cover with crème patisserie and roll up. Beat egg whites until foamy. Add sugar gradually and continue beating to form a stiff meringue. Fold in crushed hazelnuts. Place crêpes on a buttered silver tray and pipe meringue mixture on top. Bake at 350° F. 6 minutes, brown slightly under broiler, and serve with thick chocolate sauce mixed with whipped cream and Grand Marnier.

Crêpes Veuve Joyeuse (continued)

in the stiffly beaten egg whites. Place a heaping tablespoon of lemon filling on half of each crêpe, fold over and place in a 400° F. oven. As the soufflé cooks, the crêpes should swell and open. They should be done in about 15 minutes. Remove, sprinkle with sugar and brown rapidly under the broiler. Serve at once.

Mama Leone's, New York City

Pan di Spagna

(Italian Rum Cake)

1 tablespoon soft butter
½ cup warm milk
2 eggs, separated
1 cup sugar
1 teaspoon baking powder
3 pounds flour

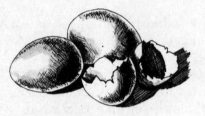

Combine soft butter and warm milk   *serves: 12*
and set aside.
In a small mixing bowl place the
egg yolks and half the sugar, in a
large mixing bowl the egg whites
and the rest of the sugar. With an
electric mixer at medium speed,
beat the egg yolks and sugar until
the mixture is pale yellow. Set aside.
Wash and dry beaters of the mixer.
Set it at highest speed and beat the
egg yolks into the egg whites.
Reduce the speed to medium and
mix for 5 minutes. Gradually add
the milk-butter mixture. Sift baking
powder and flour together. Reduce
mixer speed to low and gradually
incorporate the flour. Mix until
smooth. Pour batter into a greased
9-inch cake pan and place
immediately in a preheated 350° F.
oven. Baking should take 30
minutes, but use a cake tester to
make sure the layer is done. Place
a 24-inch sheet of aluminum foil on
a flat surface. Invert the cake pan
over it until it is completely cool.

Cream for filling
3 tablespoons sugar
2 cups milk
3 tablespoons cornstarch
1 teaspoon vanilla extract
½ cup rum
¼ cup toasted almonds

Mix sugar, milk, cornstarch and
vanilla in a saucepan and mix with
an electric beater until well blended.
Cook over a low flame, stirring
constantly. When the mixture comes
to a boil, remove from the fire. Stir
vigorously until it is cool.

Conclusion: Cut the cake horizontally
into 3 layers. Place the bottom layer
on a cake platter and spoon some
rum over it. Spread evenly about
(*Continued at foot of facing page*

International Inn, Winnipeg, Manitoba
CHEF: FERNAND KIROUAC

Hot Cheese Tartlettes

Crust

serves: 8

½ pound (250 grams) pastry flour
6 tablespoons shortening
6 tablespoons butter
1 egg
2 tablespoons water

Sift pastry flour twice. Cut in shortening and butter and mix well to fine crumbs. Add the whole egg, then the water gradually until dough can be rolled.

Cheese filling

2 eggs
1 cup sugar
1½ pounds (750 grams) cream cheese

Beat eggs and sugar until stiff; add cream cheese and whisk until smooth.

Brandy sauce

1 cup and 2 tablespoons milk
4 egg yolks
6 tablespoons sugar
1 teaspoon cornstarch
3 teaspoons brandy
1 tablespoon marzipan
3 cooked apples
  Graham-cracker crumbs

In the top of a double boiler bring all but 1 tablespoon of the milk to near boiling. Mix together egg yolks, sugar, cornstarch, and reserved tablespoon of milk. When well blended add to hot milk and cook for a few minutes, then incorporate brandy.

Roll dough to ⅛ inch thick and place in 15 tartlette shells. For each shell make a ball of marzipan and place two wedges of cooked apple beside marzipan ball in bottom of shell. Fill tartlette almost full with the cheese filling, then sprinkle with fine graham-cracker crumbs and bake at 350° F. 25 to 30 minutes. Do not overbake. Serve with brandy sauce.

Pan di Spagna (continued)

⅓-inch of custard over the cake. Cover with the second layer of cake and repeat the process until all 3 layers are used. Spread remaining custard over the top and sides of the cake and sprinkle it with chopped almonds. Refrigerate at least 1 hour before serving.

The Forum of the XII Caesars, New York City

Stuffed Chocolate Crêpes Triomphantes

¼ cup whipped cream
2 teaspoons pistachios
2 dashes of maraschino liqueur
1 teaspoon sugar
4 dessert crêpes
3 pats butter
1½ teaspoons superfine sugar
1 teaspoon grated orange rind
Juice of ½ orange
3 tablespoons cognac
1 tablespoon rum
1 tablespoon Grand Marnier
4 squares semi-sweet chocolate, melted
2 scoops chocolate ice cream
Whipped cream for garnish

Mix first 4 ingredients together. Divide among the crêpes and roll them up.
In crêpe Suzette pan melt butter and 1½ teaspoons of fine sugar. Add orange rind. When the sugar is almost brown, add juice from ½ orange. Remove pan from fire.
Add cognac, rum, and Grand Marnier, then flame. Remove crêpes to warm dessert plates.
Add melted chocolate to pan and mix well with liquid remaining there. Pour over the crêpes. Place ice cream to the left of the crêpes and whipped cream to the right and serve at once.

serves: 2

Shepheard's Hotel Restaurant, Cairo

Om Aly

Pastry

3 cups flour
2 egg yolks
4 tablespoons butter
½ teaspoon salt
¾ cup water
4 cups clarified butter

Mix flour, egg yolks, butter, salt and water. Work paste until soft. Cut into egg-size pieces. Cover with a wet napkin and let rest for 30 minutes.
Roll batter thin on an oiled marble table. Fry rolled dough piece by piece in browned butter.

serves: 12

Conclusion

8 cups milk
8 cups sugar
2½ cups Chantilly cream
1 pound (500 grams) almonds
½ pound (250 grams) pistachios
½ pound (250 grams) walnuts
1 pound (500 grams) raisins
2 teaspoons vanilla extract

Heat milk to boiling with sugar and vanilla. Lay cooked dough in a baking dish then cover with a layer of nuts and raisins. Repeat to fill the dish. Add boiling milk and let stand for 5 minutes until platter is soaked with milk. Cover with Chantilly cream. Place dish in a 400° F. oven until top is brown, about 15 minutes. Serve hot.

Sulo Restaurant and Cocktail Lounge, Rizal, Philippines

Mango Wasiwas

serves: 6

Wine: Mumm "Cordon Rouge", Brut

3 ripe mangoes
6 pieces suman sa ibos (native rice bar)

Peel fresh mangoes and cut into halves. Flatten the "suman" and shape in proportion to the mango halves to be placed on top of rice bars. Set aside.

Sauce

2 tablespoons butter
2 tablespoons sugar
1 cup mango nectar
1 cup fresh orange juice
4 pieces lemon peel
1 teaspoon vanilla extract
1 tablespoon caramelized brown sugar
3 teaspoons cornstarch
  A dash of salt
1 tablespoon kirsch
1 tablespoon Cointreau
1 tablespoon Grand Marnier
3 tablespoons brandy

Melt the butter in a pan and add sugar. Then add the mango nectar, fresh orange juice, lemon peel, vanilla extract, and caramelized sugar. Let boil for a few minutes. Thicken with cornstarch. Add salt. Add the "suman" and the mango halves. Let boil for 2 minutes, then pour in the liqueurs and set aflame with brandy. Serve with the "suman" as base and mango half on top of it.

Publick House, Sturbridge, Massachusetts

Squash Pie

serves: 8

1½ cups cooked squash
½ cup light brown sugar
½ cup granulated sugar
1 tablespoon molasses
½ teaspoon nutmeg
½ teaspoon cinnamon
½ teaspoon ginger
¼ teaspoon cloves
½ teaspoon salt
2 eggs, slightly beaten
1 cup milk

Mix ingredients in the order given. Line a 9-inch pie plate with crust. Pour mixture into lined pie plate and bake in a 350° F. oven approximately 1 hour.

Pie crust pastry

3 cups pastry flour
1½ cups shortening
1 teaspoon salt
  About 6 tablespoons milk

Mix flour, shortening and salt well. Add enough milk, a tablespoon at a time, to make pastry hold together. Roll and line pie plate.

The George Hotel, Haddington, Scotland

Syrup Tart

Flan Pastry

½ cup butter
2 tablespoons sugar
1 egg
1 cup flour
Water, if needed

Cream butter and sugar. Mix in the egg and then add flour. Add a little water, a teaspoon at a time, if necessary to make dough hold together. Do not overmix. Gather dough into a ball with a spatula and wrap in waxed paper; let rest in the refrigerator at least 30 minutes.

serves: 6

Filling

2 cups light corn syrup
½ cup fine white bread crumbs
¼ cup water
Juice of 1 lemon
Shredded yellow peel of 1 lemon

Heat the syrup and mix in bread crumbs and water. Add lemon juice and grated peel.

Conclusion: Stand a 1″ × 8″ greased flan ring on a greased cookie sheet. Roll out the pastry quite thin and arrange in the flan ring.
Pour the syrup mixture into the pastry. Decorate the top with strips of pastry. Bake in a 350° F. oven for 30 or 40 minutes. Serve hot with custard sauce or cold with plain or whipped cream.

The Tower Suite, New York City

Pear Almond Mousse

2 cups heavy cream
½ cup sugar
1 tablespoon unflavored gelatin,
    softened in ½ cup cold water
½ cup boiling water
2 egg yolks, beaten
2 tablespoons Williams Pear Brandy
2 medium fresh pears
¼ cup sliced almonds

Whip cream with ⅓ cup sugar. Dissolve gelatin in boiling water. Beat the egg yolks with the remaining sugar and the brandy for about 5 minutes. Peel 2 medium pears and slice them. Toast the sliced almonds.
Stir the dissolved gelatin into the egg-yolk mixture, add the pears and almonds and fold into the whipped

serves: 6

(Continued at foot of facing page

Caprice Restaurant, London
CHEF: BRIAN COTTERILL

Oranges Oriental

serves: 4

wine:
Fonseca
Royal Tawny
Port or
Harvey's
Bristol
Cream
Sherry

4 large or 8 small oranges
1¼ cups sugar
2 tablespoons corn syrup

Peel the skin finely from the oranges using a potato peeler or sharp knife. Cut the skin into matchstick strips and to remove bitterness soak in salt water for 24 hours. Drain and wash in cold water, then poach the peel in a light syrup made with 2 cups water and ¼ cup sugar for 15 minutes. Drain the peel and finish cooking it in a strong syrup made with 2 cups water, ½ cup sugar and 2 tablespoons corn syrup. Simmer slowly until the peel is slightly brittle and very sweet tasting.

Remove absolutely all white membrane from the oranges with a sharp knife. Place in a basin.

Make a syrup with 1 cup water, ½ cup sugar and the orange peel and boil gently until the syrup is heavy and sticky. Pour over oranges and marinate for several hours in a cool place.

Serve the oranges with the candied peel on top. Garnish with orange water ice.

Pear Almond Mousse (continued)

cream. Pour into a 1½-quart mold and chill for 2 hours.

Chocolate sauce: Melt a cup of chocolate ice cream and pour over the mousse.

Fort Charles Grill, Barbados Hilton, St. Michael, Barbados

Banana Bread

1 cup sugar
1 pound (500 grams) ripe bananas
4 eggs
½ cup corn oil
4 cups flour
1 teaspoon baking soda
1 teaspoon ground ginger
½ cup buttermilk
1 teaspoon vanilla extract

Beat sugar and the peeled bananas together. Add the eggs and mix well; stir in corn oil. Sift flour, baking soda and ginger together. Add to banana-egg mixture alternately with buttermilk. Stir in vanilla extract. Pour batter into 2 greased loaf pans and bake at 300° F. for 35 to 45 minutes or until a cake tester comes out clean. Cool on a rack, then wrap in airtight film or foil. The flavor improves if bread is allowed to age a day or two.

The Forum of the XII Caesars, New York City

Coffee Diabolius

Spiraled peel of 1 large orange—
   removed in one piece
Whole cloves
1 cinnamon stick
2 heaping teaspoons sugar
6 tablespoons dark Jamaican rum
6 tablespoons cognac
2 cups hot double-strength coffee

serves: 2

Stud orange peel with cloves at approximately 2-inch intervals. Place cinnamon stick and sugar over heat in brûlot bowl (or chafing dish) and melt sugar, but do not burn. Add rum and continue heating mixture.

Fix one end of orange peel on a long, pronged fork and dip in the mixture for a few seconds, mashing the peel slightly against side of bowl with fork. Raise the orange peel so that one end slowly touches the liquid and, very slowly, dribble cognac down the orange peel. It will ignite along the entire peel and may continue to burn for 30 seconds or longer; cloves will turn bright amber. When flame has died out, return orange peel to bowl. Add coffee and stir. Remove cinnamon. Ladle steaming coffee into brûlot or demitasse cups.

INDEX
of Recipes

INDEX
of Restaurants and Locations